EXPERT **RESUMES** for
Computer and **Web Jobs**

Wendy S. Enelow and
Louise M. Kursmark

Expert Resumes for Computer and Web Jobs

© 2001 by Wendy S. Enelow and Louise M. Kursmark

Published by JIST Works, an imprint of JIST Publishing, Inc.
8902 Otis Avenue
Indianapolis, IN 46216-1033
Phone: 1-800-648-JIST   Fax: 1-800-JIST-FAX   E-Mail: info@jist.com

Visit our Web site at **www.jist.com** for information on JIST, free job search information, book chapters, and ordering information on our many products!

See the back of this book for additional JIST titles and ordering information. Quantity discounts are available for JIST books. Please call our Sales Department at 1-800-648-5478 for a free catalog and more information.

Acquisitions and Development Editor: Lori Cates Hand
Cover Designer: Katy Bodenmiller
Interior Designer: Trudy Coler
Page Layout Technicians: Trudy Coler and Aleata Howard
Proofreaders: Gayle Johnson and David Faust
Indexer: Larry Sweazy

Printed in the United States of America
05 04 03 02 01 9 8 7 6 5 4 3 2

We have been careful to provide accurate information in this book, but it is possible that errors and omissions have been introduced. Please consider this in making any career plans or other important decisions. Trust your own judgment above all else and in all things.

Trademarks: All brand names and product names used in this book are trade names, service marks, trademarks, or registered trademarks of their respective owners.

ISBN 1-56370-798-5

CONTENTS AT A GLANCE

Resumes for Help Desk Administrators and Analysts, Technical Call Center Representatives, Technical Support Technicians, Data Library and Warehousing Specialists, Technical Training Specialists, Technical Writers, Technology Sales and Marketing Professionals, and Technology Business Development Professionals.

Resumes for Network Administrators and Analysts, Network Engineers, PC and Computer Specialists, Systems Administrators, Systems Engineers and Analysts, and Certified Professional Systems Engineers.

Resumes for Web Designers, Web Graphic Artists, Web Applications Developers, Webmasters, Internet Sales and Marketing Professionals, E-Business Managers, and E-Commerce/Internet Executives.

Resumes for Technology Project Managers; IT, IS, and MIS Project Managers; Telecommunications Technology Managers; Technology Leaders; and Technology Industry Consultants.

Resumes for IT, IS, and MIS Managers; Technology Operations Managers and Executives; CIOs, Vice Presidents, and Directors of Technology; Telecommunications Industry Executives; and Technology Industry Management Executives.

Where to go on the Web for help with your job search: general job search advice, technology career information, resume key words, company information, interviewing tips, and salary information.

How to find professional resume writers in your area.

TABLE OF
CONTENTS

ABOUT THIS BOOK

The technology revolution of the past two decades and, in particular, the past five years, has changed the complexion of the world's employment market forever. As a result, there have been three remarkable occurrences:

1. **Virtually everyone in every place is, or can be, part of the technology revolution,** from the graduate student who has just earned his Master of Science in Information Technology to the 55-year-old grandmother whose expertise in C++ programming keeps her in demand for a wide variety of temporary/contract positions.

2. **There are now thousands of new careers in technology.** Twenty years ago, who had heard of Web site designers, Java scripters, C++ programmers, database administrators, and CIOs? Now, there is a wealth of new career opportunities, and every economic projection indicates tremendous and continuous growth in the demand for technology professionals.

3. **Hundreds of new industries have emerged,** from Internet Web site hosting to the design and manufacture of advanced telecommunications and networking technologies. Most of these industries did not exist even 10 years ago. In turn, they are further adding to the number and diversity of careers that are now available within the technology industries.

It is critical to note that these new occupations and professions are not restricted to just the technology industry. In fact, they exist in virtually every industry, from old-line manufacturing to emerging health care ventures; from hundred-year-old utility companies to your local grocery chain; from major retail conglomerates to small real estate brokerages; and every other industry imaginable. Perhaps, most important to you, there are dramatically more employment opportunities than there are qualified professionals, and that's great news for you!

To take advantage of all of these opportunities, you must first develop a powerful, performance-based resume. To be a savvy and successful job seeker, you must know how to communicate your qualifications in a strong and effective written presentation. Sure, it's important to let employers know essential technical details, such as the programming languages or operating systems with which you are experienced. But a powerful resume is much more than just a list of technical competencies; it is a concise yet comprehensive document that gives you a competitive edge in the job market. Creating such a powerful document is what this book is all about.

We'll explore the changes in resume presentation that have arisen as a result of the tremendous surge in technology. In years past, resumes were almost always printed on paper and mailed. Today, e-mail has become the chosen method for resume distribution in many industries. In turn, many of the traditional methods for "typing" and presenting resumes have changed dramatically. This book will instruct you in the methods for preparing resumes for e-mail, scanning, and Web site posting, as well as the traditional printed resume.

By using *Expert Resumes for Computer and Web Jobs* as your professional guide, you will succeed in developing a powerful and effective resume that opens doors, gets interviews, and helps you land your next great opportunity!

INTRODUCTION

According to the U.S. Department of Labor, technology is the fastest-growing industry and fastest-growing segment of the employment market. What's more, it is anticipated that this trend will continue for years to come, through the year 2008. We are in the midst of a technology revolution that has clearly surpassed the Industrial Revolution in terms of the volume of change, the speed of change, and the long-term results of those changes.

In turn, this revolution has created a wealth of new career opportunities for

- **Technology professionals** (hardware and software engineers, programmers, systems analysts, database administrators, network administrators, Web site designers, field service technicians, and so on)

- **Technology support professionals** (sales and marketing professionals, e-commerce business development experts, training specialists, field support personnel, technical writers, and so on)

- **Technology management professionals** (CIOs, CKOs, and CTOs; vice presidents, directors, and managers of technology, systems, and MIS; and so on)

To take advantage of these opportunities, you must be an educated job seeker. That means you must know what you want in your career, where the hiring action is, what technical skills you need to attain your desired career goals, and how best to market your qualifications. It is no longer enough to be a talented technologist! Now, you must be a strategic marketer, able to package and promote your experience to take advantage of this wave of employment opportunity.

There's no doubt that the employment market has changed dramatically from only a few years ago. According to the U.S. Department of Labor (2000), you should expect to hold between 10 and 20 different jobs during your career. No longer is stability the status quo. Today, the norm is movement, onward and upward, in a fast-paced and intense technology market. And to stay on top of all the changes and opportunities, you must proactively control and manage your career.

Technology Job Search Questions and Answers

Whether you're currently employed in the technology industry or looking to enter the industry for the first time, here's some practical advice:

How Do You Enter the Technology Profession?

As with any other industry, education, credentials, and experience are the keys to entry and long-term success. It is difficult to obtain a position in the technology industry without some related work experience, relevant education, or technical credentials. Here are a few pointers:

- **If you're just starting to plan and build your career,** consider a four-year degree in a technology-related discipline (such as Information Systems, Information Technology, Computer Science, or Engineering) or completion of a technology certification program. For example, there is currently a huge market demand for Microsoft Certified Systems Engineers (MCSEs). Be advised, however, that you must stay current on new technical certification programs and how they are accepted in the market. Today, MCSEs are in. Tomorrow, who knows?

- **If you're a technology professional who wants to make the move to a true technology company,** sell your technology knowledge and experience in order to "connect" yourself to the industry. Perhaps you're a network administrator, database administrator, programmer, or MIS manager in a traditional, nontechnology industry. The technical skills and experiences you've acquired are real and valuable to others. Make the case that you're not an outsider, but rather an insider who understands technology and its applications.

- **If you're a successful sales and marketing professional, customer service specialist, or trainer** but have no technology experience, focus your resume on your revenue performance and the people skills you bring to an organization. "Sell" the fact that you built and managed customer relationships, improved revenues, designed innovative training programs, and the like. Place the emphasis on you and your performance, not unrelated products or services.

- **If you're an experienced business manager or executive** but have never worked in the technology industry, highlight the value you bring to an organization: your leadership skills, achievements, financial contributions, and more. Many companies seeking talented and effective leadership are more than willing to provide technical training to the "right" candidate.

What Is the Best Resume Strategy if You're Already in the Technology Industry?

If you're already employed in the technology field but are interested in moving onward and upward, remember one critical fact:

> **Your resume is a marketing tool written to sell YOU!**

If you're a C++ programmer, *sell* the fact that you've helped to manage development projects, restored nonperforming systems, and created new, user-friendly applications. If you're a technical consultant, *sell* major projects, key clients, and innovative technologies. If you're a CIO, *sell* your achievements—financial, operational, and technological.

When writing your resume, your challenge is to create a picture of knowledge, action, and results. In essence, you're stating "This is what I know, this is how I've used it, and this is how well I've performed." Success sells, so be sure to highlight yours. If you don't, no one else will.

WHERE ARE THE JOBS?

The jobs are everywhere—from the technology giants such as IBM, Cisco, and Hewlett Packard seeking well-qualified hardware, software, and network engineers to the small manufacturing company recruiting a Webmaster and an MIS director.

- The jobs are in **development** of new products, technologies, systems, and applications.

- The jobs are in the **manufacture** of these products and technologies.

- The jobs are in the **sale, marketing,** and **support** of these products and technologies.

- The jobs are in the **installation, operation, maintenance,** and **management** of these technologies in nontechnology companies—virtually *every* other company in the world.

- The jobs are in the **delivery** of technology services, as either an employee or a contractor/consultant.

The jobs are in every market sector, every industry, and every profession. Technology is everywhere.

HOW DO YOU GET THE JOBS?

To answer this question, we need to review the basic principle underlying job search:

Job search is marketing!

You have a product to sell—yourself—and the best way to sell it is to use all appropriate *marketing channels* just as you would for any other product.

Suppose you wanted to sell televisions. What would you do? You'd market your products using newspaper, magazine, and radio advertisements. You might develop a company Web site to build your e-business, and perhaps you'd hire a field sales representative to market to major retail chains. Each of these is a different *marketing channel* through which you're attempting to reach your audience.

The same is true for job search. You must use every marketing channel that's right for you. Unfortunately, there is no single formula. What's right for you depends on your specific career objectives—type of position, type of industry, geographic restrictions, salary requirements, and more.

Following are the most valuable marketing channels for a successful job search within the technology industry. These are in order from most effective to least effective.

1. **Referrals.** There is nothing better than a personal referral to a company, either in general or for a specific position. Referrals can open doors that, in most instances, would never be accessible any other way. If you know anyone who could possibly refer you to a specific company, contact that person immediately and ask for assistance.

2. **Networking.** Networking is the backbone of every successful job search. Although you may consider it a task, it is essential that you network effectively with your professional colleagues and associates, past employers, past coworkers, suppliers, neighbors, bankers, and others who may know of opportunities that are right for you. Another good strategy is to attend meetings of professional associations in your area to make new contacts and expand your professional network. And particularly in today's nomadic job market—where you're likely to change jobs every few years—the best strategy is to keep your network "alive" even when you're *not* searching for a new position.

3. **Responses to online job postings.** One of the greatest advantages of the technology revolution is an employer's ability to post job announcements and a job seeker's ability to respond immediately via e-mail. It's a wonder! In most (but not all) instances, these are bona fide opportunities, and it's well worth your while to spend time searching for and responding to appropriate postings. However, don't make the mistake of devoting *too* much time to searching the Internet. It can consume a huge amount of your time that you should spend on other job search efforts.

   To expedite your search, here are some of the largest and most widely used online job posting sites—presented alphabetically, not necessarily in order of effectiveness or value (see the appendix for a complete listing of job search Web sites):

   www.careerbuilder.com

   www.careermosaic.com

   www.careerpath.com

   www.dice.com

   www.flipdog.com

   www.hotjobs.com

   www.monster.com

   www.sixfigurejobs.com

   www.wantedtechnologies.com

4. **Responses to newspaper and magazine advertisements.** Although the opportunity to post online has reduced the overall number of print advertisements, they still abound. Do not forget about this "tried and true" marketing strategy. If they've got the job and you have the qualifications, it's a perfect fit.

5. **Targeted e-mail campaigns (resumes and cover letters) to recruiters.** Recruiters have jobs, and you want one. It's pretty straightforward. The only catch is to find the "right" recruiters that have the "right" jobs. Therefore, you must devote the time and effort to preparing the "right" list of recruiters.

There are many resources on the Internet where you can access information about recruiters (for a fee), sort that information by industry (information technology, software, communications, and so on), and then cross-reference with position specialization (programming, Web design, sales, executive management, and so on). This allows you to identify just the "right" recruiters who would be interested in a candidate with your qualifications. What's more, because these campaigns are transmitted electronically, they are easy and inexpensive to produce.

When working with recruiters, it's important to realize that they *do not* work for you! Their clients are the hiring companies that pay their fees. They are not in business to "find a job" for you, but rather to fill a specific position with a qualified candidate, either you or someone else. To maximize your chances of finding a position through a recruiter or agency, don't rely on just one or two, but distribute your resume to many that meet your specific criteria.

6. **Online resume postings.** The Net is swarming with reasonably priced (if not free) Web sites where you can post your resume. It's quick, easy, and the only *passive* thing you can do in your search. All of the other marketing channels require action on your part. With online resume postings, once you've posted, you're done. You then just wait (and hope!) for some response.

7. **Targeted e-mail and print campaigns to companies.** Just as with campaigns to recruiters (see item 5 above), you must be extremely careful to select just the right companies that would be interested in a candidate with your qualifications. The closer you stick to "where you belong" in relation to your specific experience, the better your response rate will be. You can also conduct these campaigns via e-mail, but only when you are targeting technology companies. If you are looking at companies outside the technology industries, we believe that print campaigns (paper and envelopes mailed the old-fashioned way) are a more suitable and effective presentation—particularly if you are a management or executive candidate.

8. **In-person "cold calls" to companies and recruiters.** We consider this the least effective and most time-consuming marketing strategy for technology jobs. It is extremely difficult to just walk in the door and get in front of the right person, or any person who can take hiring action. You'll be much better off focusing your time and energy on other, more productive channels.

WHAT ABOUT OPPORTUNITIES IN CONSULTING AND CONTRACTING IN THE TECHNOLOGY INDUSTRY?

Are you familiar with the term "free agent"? It's the latest buzz word for an independent contractor or consultant who moves from project to project and company to company as the work load dictates. According to a recent article in *Quality Progress* magazine (November 2000), 10 years ago less than 10 percent of the U.S. work force was employed as free agents. Currently, that number is greater than 20 percent and is expected to increase to 40 percent over the next 10 years. The demand for free agents is vast, and the market offers excellent career opportunities.

The reason for this growth is directly related to the manner in which companies are now hiring—or not hiring—their technical work force. The opportunity now exists for companies to hire on a "per project" basis and avoid the costs associated with full-time permanent employees. Companies hire the staff they need just when they need them—and when they no longer need them, they're gone.

The newest revolution in online job search has risen in response to this demand: job auction sites where employers bid on prospective employees. Individuals post their resumes and qualifications for review by prospective employers. The employers then competitively bid to hire or contract with each candidate. The two largest and most well-established job-auction Web sites are www.bid4geeks.com and www.freeagent.com. Check them out. They're quite interesting, particularly if you're pursuing a career in technical consulting or contracting.

Conclusion

Career opportunities abound within the technology industries and professions today. What's more, it has never been easier to learn about and apply for jobs. Arm yourself with a powerful resume and cover letter, identify the most appropriate marketing channels, and start your search today. You're destined to reach the next rung on your career ladder.

PART I

Resume Writing, Strategy, and Formats

CHAPTER 1

Resume Writing Strategies for Technology Professionals

If you're reading this book, chances are you've decided to make a career move. It may be because:

- You're graduating from college or technical school and are ready to launch your professional career.

- You've just earned your graduate degree and are ready to make a step upward in your career.

- You're ready to leave your current position and move up the ladder to a higher-paying and more responsible position.

- You've decided on a career change and will be looking at opportunities in new media and other emerging technology industries.

- You're unhappy with your current company or management team and have decided to pursue opportunities elsewhere.

- You've been laid off, downsized, or otherwise left your position and you must find a new one.

- You've completed a contract assignment and are looking for a new "free-agent" job or perhaps a permanent position.

- You're relocating to a new area and need to find a new job.

- You're returning to the workforce after several years of unemployment or retirement.

- You're simply ready for a change.

There may even be other reasons for your job search besides these. However, no matter the reason, a powerful resume is an essential component of your search campaign. In fact, it is virtually impossible to conduct a search without a resume. It is your calling card that briefly, yet powerfully, communicates the skills, qualifications, experience, and value you bring to a prospective employer. It is the document that will open doors and generate interviews. It is the first thing people will learn about you when you forward it in response to an advertisement, and it is the last thing they'll remember when they're reviewing your qualifications after an interview.

Your resume is a sales document, and you are the product! You must identify the *features (what you know* and *what you can do)* and *benefits (how you can help an employer)* of that product, then communicate them in a concise and hard-hitting written presentation. Remind yourself over and over as you work your way through the resume process that you are writing marketing literature designed to sell a new product—*you*—into a new position.

Your resume can have tremendous power and a phenomenal impact on your job search. So don't take it lightly. Rather, devote the time, energy, and resources that are essential to developing a resume that is well-written, visually attractive, and effective in communicating *who* you are and *how* you want to be perceived.

Resume Strategies

Following are the nine core strategies for writing effective and successful resumes.

RESUME STRATEGY #1: WHO ARE YOU AND HOW DO YOU WANT TO BE PERCEIVED?

Now that you've decided to look for a new position, the very first step is to identify your career interests, goals, and objectives. *This task is critical,* because it is the underlying foundation for *what* you include in your resume, *how* you include it, and *where* you include it. You cannot write an effective resume without knowing, at least to some degree, what type or types of positions you will be seeking.

There are two concepts to consider here:

- **Who you are:** This relates to what you have done professionally and/or academically. Are you a programmer, network administrator, systems analyst, or telecommunications engineer? Are you a technology sales professional, field support specialist, or technical training manager? Are you a recent graduate from the DeVry Institute of Technology with a certificate in computer programming? Who are you?

- **How you want to be perceived:** This relates to your current career objectives. If you're a computer analyst looking for a position in project management, don't focus just on your technical qualifications. Put an equal emphasis on projects, personnel, schedules, team leadership, and more. If you're a technical sales engineer interested in a product-management position, highlight your involvement in product development, product support, multidisciplinary teaming, and other skills related to the design, creation, commercialization, and launch of new products.

The strategy, then, is to connect these two concepts by using the *Who you are* information that ties directly to the *How you want to be perceived* message to determine what information to include in your resume. By following this strategy, you're painting a picture that allows a prospective employer to see you as you wish to be seen—as an individual with the qualifications for the type of position you are pursuing.

WARNING: If you prepare a resume without first clearly identifying what your objectives are and how you want to be perceived, your resume will have no focus and no direction. Without the underlying knowledge of "This is what I want to be," you do not know what to highlight in your resume. In turn, the document becomes an historical overview of your career and not the sales document it is designed to be.

RESUME STRATEGY #2: SELL IT TO ME... DON'T TELL IT TO ME

We've already established the fact that resume writing is sales. You are the product, and you must create a document that powerfully communicates the value of that product. One particularly effective strategy for accomplishing this is the "Sell It to Me... Don't Tell It to Me" strategy that impacts virtually every single word you write on your resume.

If you "tell it," you are simply stating facts. If you "sell it," you promote it, advertise it, and draw attention to it. Look at the difference in impact between these examples:

Tell It Strategy: Assisted in development of company Web site and e-commerce capability.

Sell It Strategy: Member of 8-person technology team credited with the design and implementation of company Web site and launch of e-commerce capability (now generating $2.1 million in annual product sales).

Tell It Strategy: Increased sales revenues within the Northeastern U.S. region.

Sell It Strategy: Delivered a 45% revenue increase and 22% gain in customer base while managing technology sales throughout the $8.4 million Chicago sales territory.

Tell It Strategy: Improved systems performance, reliability, and functionality.

Sell It Strategy: Reengineered all system hardware and software, implemented quality assurance standards, upgraded supporting business processes, and significantly improved overall IT performance, reliability, and functionality.

What's the difference between "telling it" and "selling it"? In a nutshell...

Telling It	Selling It
Describes features.	Describes benefits.
Tells what and how.	Sells why the "what" and "how" are important.
Details activities.	Includes results.
Focuses on what you did.	Details how what you did benefited the company, department, team members, customers, and so on.

RESUME STRATEGY #3: USE KEY WORDS

No matter what you read or who you talk to about job search, the concept of key words is sure to come up. Key words (or, as they were previously known, buzz words) are words and phrases specific to a particular industry or profession. For example, key words for technology include *architecture, artificial intelligence, CASE tools, C++, functionality, hardware, Internet, software, systems analysis, technical training, user support,* and many, many more.

When you use these words and phrases—in your resume, in your cover letter, or during an interview—you are communicating a very specific message. For example, when you include the words "software development" in your resume, your reader will most likely assume that you have experience in user needs analysis, software engineering, testing, prototype development, troubleshooting, hardware interface, and more. As you can see, people will make inferences about your skills based on the use of just one or two individual words.

Here are a few other examples:

- When you use the words **multimedia technology,** people will assume you have experience with videoconferencing, teleconferencing, CD-ROM, graphic interfaces, Internet broadcasting, and more.

- When you mention **e-commerce,** readers and listeners will infer that you have experience with the Internet, online technology, online advertising and promotion, secure ordering, and more.

- By referencing **systems architecture** in your resume, you convey that you have experience with hardware, software, systems configuration, systems migration, applications, functionality, systems performance, and more.

- When you use the word **network,** most people will assume you are familiar with LAN and WAN technology, network protocols, network interfaces, network administration, and the like.

Key words are also an integral component of the resume scanning process, whereby companies and recruiters electronically search resumes for specific terms to find candidates with the skills, qualifications, and technical expertise for their particular hiring needs. In many instances, electronic scanning has replaced the more traditional method of an actual person reading your resume (at least initially). Therefore, to some degree, the *only* thing that matters in this instance is that you have included the "right" key words to match the company's or the recruiter's needs. Without them, you will most certainly be passed over.

Of course, in virtually every instance your resume will be read at some point by human eyes, so it's not enough just to throw together a list of key words and leave it at that. In fact, it's not even necessary to include a separate "key word summary" on your resume. A better strategy is to incorporate key words naturally into the text within the appropriate sections of your resume.

Keep in mind, too, that key words are arbitrary; there is no defined set of key words for a Web site developer, Novell network administrator, or any other profession. Employers searching to fill these positions develop a list of terms that reflect the specifics they desire in a qualified candidate. These might be a combination of technical skills, education, length of experience, and other easily defined qualifications, along with "soft skills," such as leadership, problem-solving, and communication.

> **NOTE:** Because of the complex and arbitrary nature of key word selection, we cannot overemphasize how vital it is, especially in the technology industry, where resume scanning and other electronic tools are so frequently used, to be certain that *all* of the key words that represent your experience and knowledge are included in your resume!

How can you be sure that you are including all the key words and the right key words? Just by describing your work experience, projects, technical qualifications, and the like, you will naturally include most of the terms that are important in your field. To cross-check what you've written, review online job postings for positions that are of interest to you. Look at the precise terms used in the ads and be sure you have included them in your resume (as appropriate to your skills and qualifications).

Another great benefit of today's technology revolution is our ability to find instant information, even information as specific as technology industry key words! Refer to the appendix for a listing of Web sites that have thousands and thousands of technology key words, complete with descriptions. These are outstanding resources.

RESUME STRATEGY #4: USE THE "BIG" AND SAVE THE "LITTLE"

When deciding what you want to include in your resume, try to focus on the "big" things—new products, new technologies, system enhancements, productivity and quality gains, major projects, major customers, improvements to functionality, new applications, sales increases, profit improvements, and more. Give a good broad-based picture of what you were responsible for and how well you did it. Here's an example:

> Managed a $12 million robotics development project in cooperation with the company's largest retail customer. Orchestrated the entire project, from initial planning and design through prototype development and final customer delivery. Matrix-managed a 42-person development team.

Then, save the "little" stuff—the details—for the interview. With this strategy, you will accomplish two things: You'll keep your resume readable and of a reasonable length (while still selling your achievements), and you'll have new and interesting information to share during the interview, rather than merely repeating what is already on your resume. Using the above example, when discussing this experience during an interview you could elaborate on the design process, your involvement with marketing, the specific technologies that were involved, and the long-term benefits of the system.

RESUME STRATEGY #5: MAKE YOUR RESUME "INTERVIEWABLE"

One of your greatest challenges is to make your resume a useful interview tool. Once you've passed the key word scanning test and are contacted for a telephone or in-person interview with a real person, the resume becomes all-important in leading and prompting your interviewer during your conversation.

Your job, then, is to make sure the resume leads the reader where you want to go and presents just the right organization, content, and appearance to stimulate a productive discussion. To improve the "interviewability" of your resume, consider these tactics:

- Make good use of Resume Strategy #4 (Use the "Big" and Save the "Little") to invite further discussion about your experiences.

- Be sure your greatest "selling points" are featured prominently, not buried within the resume.

- Conversely, don't devote lots of space and attention to areas of your background that are irrelevant or about which you feel less than positive; you'll only invite questions about things you really don't want to discuss.

- Make sure your resume is highly readable—this means plenty of white space, an adequate font size, and a logical flow from start to finish.

RESUME STRATEGY #6: ELIMINATE CONFUSION WITH STRUCTURE AND CONTEXT

Keep in mind that your resume will be read *very quickly* by hiring authorities! You may agonize over every word and spend hours working on content and design, but the average reader will skim quickly through your masterpiece and expect to pick up important facts in just a few seconds. Try to make it as easy as possible for readers to grasp the essential facts:

- Be consistent: For example, put job titles, company names, and dates in the same place for each position.

- Make information easy to find by clearly defining different sections of your resume with large, highly visible headings.

- Define the context in which you worked (for example, the company, your department, the specific challenges you faced) before you start describing your activities and accomplishments.

RESUME STRATEGY #7: USE FUNCTION TO DEMONSTRATE ACHIEVEMENT

When you write a resume that focuses only on your job functions, it can be dry and uninteresting and will say very little about your unique activities and contributions. Consider the following example:

> Responsible for the development and administration of all database functions for the company.

Now, consider using that same function to demonstrate achievement and see what happens to the tone and energy of the sentence. It becomes alive and clearly communicates that you deliver results.

> Reengineered the corporation's database systems, introduced new applications, and improved user satisfaction by 18%.

Try to translate your functions into achievements and you'll create a more powerful resume presentation.

RESUME STRATEGY #8: REMAIN IN THE REALM OF REALITY

We've already established that resume writing is sales. And, as any good salesperson does, one feels somewhat inclined to stretch the truth just a bit. However, be forewarned that you must stay within the realm of reality. Do not push your skills and qualifications outside the bounds of what is truthful. You never want to be in a position where you have to defend something that you've written on your resume. If that's the case, you'll lose the opportunity before you ever get started.

RESUME STRATEGY #9: BE CONFIDENT

You are unique. There is only one individual with the specific combination of employment experience, technical qualifications, achievements, and educational credentials that you have. In turn, this positions you as a unique commodity within the competitive job search market. To succeed, you must prepare a resume that is written to sell *you*, and highlight *your* qualifications and *your* success. If you can accomplish this, you will have won the job search game by generating interest, interviews, and offers.

There Are No Resume-Writing Rules

One of the greatest challenges in resume writing is that there are no rules to the game. There are certain expectations about information that you will include: principally, your employment history and your educational qualifications. Beyond that, what you include is entirely dependent upon you and what you have done in your career. What's more, you have tremendous flexibility in determining how to include the information you have selected. In chapter 2, you'll find a complete listing of each possible category you might include in your resume, the type of information in each category, preferred formats for presentation, and sample text you can edit and use.

Although there are no rules, there are a few standards to live by as you write your resume. The following sections discuss these standards in detail.

CONTENT STANDARDS

Content is, of course, the text that goes into your resume. Content standards regard the writing style you should use, items you should be sure to include, items you should avoid including, and the order and format in which you list your qualifications.

Writing Style

Always write in the first person, dropping the word "I" from the front of each sentence. This style gives your resume a more aggressive and more professional tone than the passive third-person voice. Here are some examples:

First Person

> Lead 12-person team in the design and market commercialization of next-generation SAP technology.

Third Person

> Mr. Jones manages a team of 12 in the design and market commercialization of next-generation SAP technology.

By using the first-person voice, you are assuming "ownership" of that statement. You did such-and-such. When you use the third-person, "someone else" did it. Can you see the difference?

Stay Away From...

Try *not* to use phrases such as "responsible for" or "duties included." These words create a passive tone and style. Instead, use active verbs to describe what you did.

Compare these two ways of conveying the same information:

Duties included the development, implementation, and marketing of an innovative intranet system offering a secure portal with centralized access to records, test results, and medical information. *Responsible for* training and customer-service staff, vendor-employed network engineers, and Web developers. *Also responsible for* $1.3 million operating budget.

Managed development, implementation, and marketing of an innovative Intranet system offering a secure portal with centralized access to records, test results, and medical information. *Supervised* training and customer-service staff. *Directed* the activities of vendor-employed network engineers and Web developers. *Developed and administered* $1.3 million operating budget.

Resume Style

The traditional **chronological** resume lists work experience in reverse-chronological order (starting with your current or most recent position). The **functional** style de-emphasizes the "where" and "when" of your career and instead groups similar experience, talents, and qualifications regardless of when they occurred.

Today, however, most resumes follow neither a strictly chronological nor strictly functional format; rather, they are an effective mixture of the two styles, usually known as a "combination" or "hybrid" format.

Like the chronological format, the hybrid format includes specifics about where you worked, when you worked there, and what your job titles were. Like a functional resume, a hybrid emphasizes your most relevant qualifications—perhaps within chronological job descriptions, in an expanded summary section, in several "career highlights" bullet points at the top of your resume, or in project summaries. Most of the examples in this book are hybrids and show a wide diversity of organizational formats that you can use as inspiration for your own resume.

Resume Format

Resumes, principally career summaries and job descriptions, are most often written in a paragraph format, a bulleted format, or a combination of both. Following are three job descriptions, all very similar in content, yet presented in each of the three different formats. The advantages and disadvantages of each format are also addressed.

Paragraph Format

Team Leader—Client/Server Implementation Project   1994 to 1997

BELL ATLANTIC CORPORATION, Baltimore, Maryland

Co-led $950 million investment to develop client/server order-entry system to service operations in 50 locations throughout 6 Northeastern states and

continues

support 1,600 users processing 140,000 orders per year ($32 billion in revenue). Directed a staff of 73. Wrote and presented the business case for $7.9 million in board-approved funding.

Planned and orchestrated a successful technology development and implementation project, achieving all performance goals and objectives and delivering the project on time and within budget. Most notably, increased billing accuracy from 80% to 91% and coordinated integration of $1.2 million of capital equipment into existing data center. Delivered major cost reductions including 66% savings in development of technical specifications (through competitive RFP and subsequent negotiation of offshore development contract) and 15-person reduction in client staffing expense.

Advantages:

Requires the least amount of space on the page. Brief, succinct, and to the point.

Disadvantages:

Achievements get lost in the text of the second paragraph. They are not visually distinctive, nor do they stand alone to draw attention to them.

Bulleted Format

Team Leader—Client/Server Implementation Project   1994 to 1997

BELL ATLANTIC CORPORATION, Baltimore, Maryland

- Co-led $950 million investment to develop client/server order-entry system to service operations in 50 locations throughout 6 Northeastern states and support 1,600 users processing 140,000 orders per year ($32 billion in revenue). Directed a staff of 73.

- Wrote and presented a business case for $7.9 million in board-approved funding.

- Planned and orchestrated a successful technology development and implementation project, achieving all performance goals and objectives and delivering the project on time and within budget. Most notably, increased billing accuracy from 80% to 91%.

- Coordinated integration of $1.2 million of capital equipment into existing data center.

- Delivered major cost reductions including 66% savings in development of technical specifications (through competitive RFP and subsequent negotiation of offshore development contract) and 15-person reduction in client staffing expense.

Advantages:

Quick and easy to peruse.

Disadvantages:

Responsibilities and achievements are lumped together with everything of equal value. In turn, the achievements get lost further down the list and are not immediately recognizable.

Combination Format

> **Team Leader—Client/Server Implementation Project**   1994 to 1997
>
> **BELL ATLANTIC CORPORATION,** Baltimore, Maryland
>
> Co-led $950 million investment to develop client/server order-entry system to service operations in 50 locations throughout 6 Northeastern states and support 1,600 users processing 140,000 orders per year ($32 billion in revenue). Directed a staff of 73.
>
> - Wrote and presented a business case for $7.9 million in board-approved funding.
>
> - Planned and orchestrated a successful technology development and implementation project, achieving all performance goals and objectives and delivering project on-time and within budget. Most notably, increased billing accuracy from 80% to 91%.
>
> - Coordinated integration of $1.2 million of capital equipment into existing data center.
>
> - Delivered major cost reductions including 66% savings in development of technical specifications (through competitive RFP and subsequent negotiation of offshore development contract) and 15-person reduction in client staffing expense.

Advantages:

Our recommended format. Clearly presents overall responsibilities in the introductory paragraph and then accentuates each achievement as a separate bullet.

Disadvantages:

If you don't have clearly identifiable accomplishments, this format is not effective. It also may shine a glaring light on the positions where your accomplishments were less notable.

E-Mail Address and URL

Be sure to include your e-mail address prominently at the top of your resume. As we all know, e-mail has become one of the most preferred methods of communication in job search, particularly within the technology industry.

We advise against using your employer's e-mail address on your resume. Not only does this present a negative impression to future employers, it will become useless once you make your next career move. And since your resume may exist in cyberspace long after you've completed your current job search, you don't want to direct interested parties to an obsolete e-mail address. Instead, obtain a private e-mail address that will be yours permanently. A free e-mail address from a provider such as Yahoo!, Hotmail, or NetZero is perfectly acceptable to use on your resume.

In addition to your e-mail address, if you have a URL where you have posted your Web resume, be sure to also display that prominently at the top of your resume. For more information on Web resumes, refer to chapter 3.

To draw even more attention to your e-mail address, consider this format for the top of your resume:

JOHN L. GREEN

johngreen23938@aol.com

999 Old Mill Lane	Phone: (888) 556-1238
Smithville, VA 22890	Fax: (888) 556-1239

PRESENTATION STANDARDS

Presentation regards the way your resume looks. It regards the fonts you use, the paper you print it on, any graphics you might include, and how many pages your resume should be.

Font

Use a font (typestyle) that is clean, conservative, and easy to read. Stay away from anything that is too fancy, glitzy, curly, and the like. We've listed a few recommended fonts at the top of the next page. Other fonts that work well for resumes include Franklin Gothic, Myriad Roman, Helvetica, Univers, Palomino, Souvenir, and Fritz.

Although it is extremely popular, Times New Roman is our least preferred font simply because it is overused. More than 90 percent of the resumes we see are typed in Times New Roman. Your goal is to create a competitive-distinctive document, and, to achieve that, we recommend an alternative font.

Your choice of font should be dictated by the content, format, and length of your resume. Some fonts look better than others at smaller or larger sizes; some have "bolder" boldface type; some require more white space to make them readable.

Tahoma	Times New Roman
Arial	Bookman
Krone	Book Antiqua
Soutane	Garamond
CG Omega	Century Schoolbook
Century Gothic	Lucida Sans
Gill Sans	Verdana

Once you've written your resume, experiment with a few different fonts to see which one best enhances your document.

Type Size

Readability is everything! If the type size is too small, your resume will be difficult to read and difficult to skim for essential information. Interestingly, a too-large type size, particularly for senior-level professionals, can also give a negative impression by conveying a juvenile or unprofessional image.

As a general rule, select type from 10 to 12 points in size. However, there's no hard-and-fast rule, and a lot depends on the font you choose. Take a look at the following examples:

Very readable in 9-point Verdana:

Designed an easy-to-navigate Web page for a retail company, using a version of Netscape Composer with limited capabilities; included a home page, product page, and order form, with strong graphics and hyperlinks.

Difficult to read in too-small 9-point Gill Sans:

Designed an easy-to-navigate Web page for a retail company, using a version of Netscape Composer with limited capabilities; included a home page, product page, and order form, with strong graphics and hyperlinks.

Concise and readable in 12-point Times New Roman:

Primary focus: European rollout of SAP system, implementing new functionality into a live, productive system. Project manager and chief architect of Euro currency conversion project: Security, Systems Testing, and Training. Manage virtual, cross-functional team of 20.

A bit overwhelming in too-large 12-point Bookman Old Style:

Primary focus: European rollout of SAP system, implementing new functionality into a live, productive system. Project manager and chief architect of Euro currency conversion project: Security, Systems Testing, and Training. Manage virtual, cross-functional team of 20.

Type Enhancements

Bold, *italics,* <u>underlining,</u> and CAPITALIZATION are ideal to highlight certain words, phrases, achievements, projects, numbers, and other information you want to draw special attention to. However, do not overuse these enhancements. If your resume becomes too cluttered, nothing stands out.

> **NOTE:** Resumes intended for electronic transmission and computer scanning have specific restrictions on font, type size, and type enhancements. We discuss these details in chapter 3.

Page Length

A one- or two-page resume is preferred. Use three or more pages only in a particularly unusual circumstance. For instance, if you're an experienced CIO with a 25-year career and a host of major accomplishments in every position, don't short-change yourself by insisting on a two-page resume. If you're a free agent with many diverse projects under your belt, a longer resume that includes just about all of your projects could give you a competitive edge over other less experienced freelancers.

If you must create a resume that's longer than two pages, consider making it more reader-friendly by segmenting the information into separate components. For instance, you might summarize your project-management experience on page 1 of the resume, then create an addendum that provides more detail about each project. Or you could write an all-encompassing technical summary, then detail a long list of specific technologies on a separate page.

Paper Color

Be conservative. White, ivory, and light gray are ideal. Other "flashier" colors are inappropriate for individuals in the technology industry.

Graphics

An attractive, relevant graphic can really enhance your technical resume. When you look through the sample resumes in chapters 4 through 10, you'll see some excellent examples of the effective use of graphics to enhance the visual presentation of a resume. Just be sure not to get carried away... be tasteful and relatively conservative.

White Space

We'll say it again—readability is everything! If people have to struggle to read your resume, they simply won't make the effort. Therefore, be sure to leave plenty of white space. It really does make a difference.

ACCURACY AND PERFECTION

The very final step, and one of the most critical in resume writing, is the proof-reading stage. It is essential that your resume be well written, visually pleasing, and free of any errors, typographical mistakes, misspellings, and the like. We recommend that you carefully proofread your resume a minimum of three times, and then have two or three other people also proofread it. Consider your resume an example of the quality of work you will produce on a company's behalf. Is your work product going to have errors and inconsistencies? If your resume does, it communicates to a prospective employer that you are careless, and this is the "kiss of death" in a job search.

Take the time to make sure that your resume is perfect in all the little details that do, in fact, make a big difference to those who read it.

CHAPTER 2

Writing Your Resume

For many technology professionals, resume writing is *not* at the top of the list of fun and exciting activities! How can it compare to solving a programming bug, developing a new technology, advancing an e-commerce application, cracking a longstanding systems malfunction, or launching a global systems upgrade? In your perception, we're sure that it cannot.

However, resume writing can be an enjoyable and rewarding task. Once your resume is complete, you can look at it proudly, reminding yourself of all that you have achieved. It is a snapshot of your career and your success. When it's complete, we guarantee you'll look back with tremendous self-satisfaction as you launch and successfully manage your job search.

The very first step in finding a new position or advancing your career, resume writing can be the most daunting of all tasks in your job search. For most of you in technology, writing may not be your primary skill. In fact, writing is a right-brain skill, the exact opposite of what you do when you use your left brain to develop theory, analyze, synthesize, extrapolate, plan a process, or handle a variety of other functions related to the technology industry.

Therefore, to make the writing process easier, more finite, and more "analytical," we've consolidated it into five discrete sections:

- **Career Summary.** Think of your Career Summary as the *architecture* of your resume. It is the accumulation of everything that allows the system (you) to work. It is the backbone, the foundation of your resume.

- **Technical Qualifications.** Your Technical Qualifications are equivalent to the functionality, the underlying foundation of the system and of your career. This section is a consolidated yet comprehensive summary of your specific technical qualifications and expertise.

- **Professional Experience.** Professional Experience is much like the software and applications of your system. It shows how you put all of your capabilities to work... in ways that benefit "users" (employers).

- **Education, Credentials, and Certifications.** Think of this section as the *system specifications,* the specific qualifications of the system and of your career.

- **The "Extras"** (Professional Affiliations, Civic Affiliations, Publications, Public Speaking, Honors and Awards, Personal Information, and so on). These are the *bits and bytes* of your resume, the "extra stuff" that helps distinguish you from others with similar technical qualifications.

Step-by-Step: Writing the Perfect Resume

In the preceding section, we outlined the five core resume sections. Now, we'll detail the particulars of each section—what to include, where to include it, and how to include it.

CONTACT INFORMATION

Before we start, let's briefly address the very top section of your resume: your name and contact information.

Name

You'd think this would be the easiest part of writing your resume... writing your name! But there are several factors you may want to consider:

- Although most people choose to use their full, formal name at the top of a resume, it has become increasingly more acceptable to use the name by which you prefer to be called.

- Bear in mind that it's to your advantage to have readers feel comfortable calling you for an interview. Their comfort level may decrease if your name is gender-neutral, difficult to pronounce, or very unusual; they don't know who they're calling (a man or a woman) or how to ask for you. Here are a few ways you can make it easier for them:

> Lynn T. Cowles (Mr.)
>
> (Ms.) Michael Murray
>
> Tzirina (Irene) Kahn
>
> Ndege "Nick" Vernon

Address

You should always include your home address on your resume. If you use a post office box for mail, include both your mailing address and your physical residence address.

Telephone Number(s)

Your home telephone number should be included. If you're at work during the day, when you can expect to receive most calls, consider including a work phone number (if it's a direct line and you can receive calls discreetly). Or you can include a mobile phone number (refer to it as "mobile" rather than "cellular," to keep up with current terminology) or a pager number (however, this is less desirable because you must call back to speak to the person who called you). You can include a private home fax number (if it can be accessed automatically), but do not include your work fax number.

E-Mail Address

In chapter 1, we addressed positioning your e-mail address and URL at the top of your resume. Without question, individuals in technology professions should list a private e-mail address. Do not use your employer's e-mail address, even if you access e-mail through your work computer. Instead, obtain a free, accessible-anywhere address from a provider such as Yahoo! or Hotmail.

As you look through the samples in this book, you'll see how resume writers have arranged the many bits of contact information at the top of a resume. You can use these as models for presenting your own information. The point is to make it as easy as possible for employers to contact you!

Now, let's get into the nitty-gritty of the five core content sections of your resume.

CAREER SUMMARY

The Career Summary is the section at the top of your resume that summarizes and highlights your knowledge and expertise.

You may be thinking, "But shouldn't my resume start with an Objective?" Although many job seekers still use Objective statements, we believe that a Career Summary is a much more powerful introduction. The problem with Objectives is that they are either too specific (limiting you to a "C++ Programmer position") or too vague (doesn't everyone want a challenging opportunity with a progressive organization offering the opportunity for growth and advancement?). In addition, they can be read as self-serving, since they describe what *you* want rather than suggesting what you have to offer an employer.

In contrast, an effective Career Summary allows you to position yourself as you wish to be perceived and immediately "paint a picture" of yourself in relation to your career goal. It is critical that this section focus on the specific skills, qualifications, and achievements of your career that are related to your current objectives. Your summary is *not* an historical overview of your career. Rather, it is a concise, well-written, and sharp presentation of information designed to *sell* you into your next position.

This section can have various titles, such as:

Career Achievements	Management Profile
Career Highlights	Professional Qualifications

continues

Career Summary	Professional Summary
Career Synopsis	Profile
Executive Profile	Summary
Expertise	Summary of Achievements
Highlights of Experience	Summary of Qualifications

Or, as you will see in the first example format (Headline Format), your summary does not have to have any title at all.

Here are five sample Career Summaries. Consider using one of these as the template for developing your Career Summary, or use them as the foundation to create your own presentation. You will also find some type of Career Summary in just about every resume included in this book.

Headline Format

SENIOR INFORMATION TECHNOLOGY EXECUTIVE

Information Systems / Telecommunications / Web / Voice & Data

Harvard University MBA—Specialization in Information Systems and Technologies

Paragraph Format

PROFILE   Highly skilled and experienced **Database Developer / Technical Project Lead** with a track record of managing on-time, on-budget projects that deliver substantial business benefits. Solid business background and innate understanding of how technology systems impact business processes. Known for ability to rapidly assess business needs and quick-start technology solutions.

Core Competencies Summary Format

PROFESSIONAL SUMMARY

PRODUCT DEVELOPMENT, SALES & MARKETING PROFESSIONAL

Advanced Technology Industries

Technology Development & Commercialization   Marketing & Business Development

Technology Design, Engineering & Manufacturing	Market Planning & Competitive Positioning
Technology Transfer & Commercialization	New Product & New Technology Launch
Integrated Systems & Technology Solutions	Negotiations, Presentations & Consultations
Advanced Telecommunications & Satellite Systems	Partnerships, Alliances & Joint Ventures
Operating Management	Sales & Customer Management
Plant Operations & Profit/Loss Management	Sales Team Building & Team Leadership
Performance, Productivity & Quality Improvement	Key Account Development & Management
World Class Production & Manufacturing Practices	Multimedia Customer Communications
Reengineering & Process Improvement	Territory Development & Management

Guest Speaker, 1999 Technology Roundtable Conference

Winner, 1998 Technology Sales Council Award for Excellence

Bullet List Format

PROFESSIONAL QUALIFICATIONS

- Network Administrator / Database Administrator with 10 years of professional experience.

- Proficient in the use of TCP/IP, WAN and LAN networks, and network protocols.

- Expert in the design, integration, and management of multi-tiered databases.

- Outstanding project-management and team-building/team leadership skills.

- Project budget responsibility for up to $2.5 million annually.

- Keen problem-solving, troubleshooting, and communication skills.

Category Format

CAREER HIGHLIGHTS

Experience:	12 years in IT Systems Design, Analysis, Programming & Operations
Education:	MS—Information Technology—University of California
	BS—Computer Operations—California Institute of Technology
Publications:	"Enhancing Systems Functionality," *DPMA Annual Journal,* 1999
	"Power In Performance," *Computing Weekly,* 1998
Awards:	Technologist of the Year, Dell Corporation, 2000
	Product Design Award, Dell Corporation, 1997
	Recognition of Outstanding Project Leadership, Dell Corporation, 1997

TECHNICAL QUALIFICATIONS

The Technical Qualifications section is a vital component of just about every technology professional's resume. It is here that you will summarize all of your technical skills and qualifications to clearly demonstrate the value and knowledge you bring to an organization.

There are instances, however, for which a Technical Qualifications section may *not* be appropriate. These may include the following:

- Senior technology executives (CIO, CTO, CKO, MIS Director, VP of Information Technology)
- Technology sales and marketing professionals
- Technology support professionals

For these individuals, technical qualifications are not the *focus* of the resume, although their technical experience is vital. For senior executives, the resume should focus on organizational development and leadership, financial and operational achievements, and other "general management" functions and achievements. For sales and marketing professionals, the resume should highlight performance, numbers, and revenue/market growth. For support professionals, the emphasis is on customer relationship management, troubleshooting, and problem-solving.

Here are five samples of Technical Qualifications sections that you can use as a model. More inspiration can be found in the sample resumes in chapters 4 through 10.

Technical Skills Summary Format

COMPUTER / NETWORKING SKILLS

Operating Systems:	Windows 98/95/3.x; Novell 3.x/4.x; NT 4.0 Workstation; MS-DOS 6.22
Protocols/ Networks:	TCP/IP, NetBeui, IPX/SPX, Ethernet 10/100Base-T
Hardware:	Hard drives, printers, scanners, fax/modems, CD-ROMs, Zip drives, Cat5 cables, hubs, NIC cards
Software:	*Commercial:* Microsoft Office Modules, FileMaker Pro, PC Anywhere, MS Exchange, ARCserve, Artisoft ModemShare, Norton/McAfee Anti-Virus, Ghost
	Industry-specific: e-Credit, ICC Credit, Energizer, Midanet, Flood Link, Greatland Escrow, Allregs, Echo Connection Plus, Contour (Handler, Closer, Tracker, and LP Module)

Double-Column Bullet Format

TECHNOLOGY PROFILE:

Programmer / Systems Analyst / Project Manager with expert qualifications in

- Systems specification, design & analysis
- Voice & data communications
- Data systems engineering & integration
- Application architecture & deployment
- Multimedia & videoconferencing systems
- Internet & intranet solutions
- C++ programming & HTML coding
- Project planning & team leadership

Multiple-Column List Format

TECHNICAL SKILLS

- Oracle
- Delphi
- Enterprise Technologies 4.0
- TELNET

- PMRS
- Windows 95/NT
- MIS IIS
- ARCserve

- HP900 Database
- Novell
- Unix
- TM1

- SunSparc
- Banyan
- FTP
- ADP

- JAM
- TCP/IP

Combination Technical Qualifications/Education Format

COMMUNICATIONS EDUCATION/KNOWLEDGE

Bachelor of Science in Telecommunications, University of Missouri, Columbia, Missouri

- Graduate, ABC Technologies Career Path Program, 1999

- **Certifications:** Panduit, Mohawk, Bertek, Belden, and ABC Technologies fiber-optics; ABC Technologies Systimax certification in Installation, Sales, and Design/Engineering

- **Training:** New Bridge on basic LAN environments, Bay Networks, and AT&T Pardyne DSU/CSU

- **Installation/Repair:** System 75/G3, Merlin and Partner; Dimension PBX 100, 400 & 600 Installation and Repair of Tier 1/Tier 2 Levels

- **Call Center Applications:** UCD & DGC Groups

- **Other:** All Comkey products; all other AT&T vintage PBX switches; Unix language; basic/advanced electronics

Combination Career Summary/Technical Skills Summary Format

— TECHNOLOGY PROFILE —

Highly motivated and enthusiastic **IT professional** with proven experience in both team- and project-management capacities. Outstanding analysis, programming, and debugging capabilities. Ability to work autonomously and as a team player, with demonstrated strengths in leadership and mentoring situations. Easily adaptable to change, with an eagerness to learn and expand capabilities. Industry expertise includes

2D / 3D Graphing	Geometry Management
Speech Recognition	Taxation Software

Languages: C++, C, Visual C++, MFC, ATL, ASP, Java, COM, Windows

PROFESSIONAL EXPERIENCE

Your Professional Experience is the meat of your resume—the "software and applications," as we discussed before. It's what gives your resume substance, meaning, and depth. It is also the section that will take you the longest to write. If you've had the same position for 10 years, how can you consolidate all that you have done into one short section? If, on the opposite end of the spectrum, you have had your current position for only 11 months, how can you make it seem substantial and noteworthy? And, for all of you whose experience is in between, what do you include, how, and where?

These are not easy questions to answer. In fact, the most truthful response to each question is, "It depends." It depends on you, your experience, your achievements and successes, and your current career objectives.

Here are five samples of Professional Experience sections. Review how each individual's unique background is organized and emphasized, and consider your own background when using one of these as the template or foundation for developing your Professional Experience section.

Achievement Format

Emphasizes each position, overall scope of responsibility, and resulting achievements.

PROFESSIONAL EXPERIENCE:

ABC TECHNOLOGY INTERNATIONAL, INC., Tokyo, Japan

Board Member / Senior Consultant (1998 to Present)

President & Chief Executive Officer (1990 to 1998)

Recruited by corporate joint venture partners to launch the start-up of a new technology company to market remote radar systems technology and imagery worldwide. Given full leadership, negotiating, and decision-making responsibility for creating a strategic business plan, negotiating complex government approvals and funding, developing market vision and tactical business development plans, staffing, establishing a global distributor network, and building an operating infrastructure.

- Created and commercialized Japan's first radar satellite company (replacing less reliable optical/solar technology), requiring a massive initiative to educate the marketplace in the functionality of this

continues

---

pioneering technology. Far exceeded the financial, technological, and operational objectives of investors, the Japanese government, and the industry.

- Devoted five years to obtaining government funding ($600 million), negotiating sales and distribution rights, establishing business operations, and developing advanced technologies.

- Launched operations in 1996 and achieved profitability by end of first year. Built sales to $25 million with a staff of 150. Major clients included Georgia Pacific, BP, Lockheed Martin, Canadian Coast Guard, and Swedish and Norwegian governments. Won business in Indonesia, Singapore, and Colombia.

- Structured and negotiated a second round of government financing ($250 million) to fund the development of a second satellite system. Spurred further growth and expansion throughout new markets.

EXCEL TECHNOLOGIES, Washington, DC

Vice President—Marketing (1994 to 1998)

Recruited to provide executive marketing and business development leadership for an innovative RCA / Sony joint venture to commercialize satellite remote sensing technology from government to the private sector. Created the entire marketing organization, established a "for-profit" business culture, and recruited talented sales professionals.

- Established a worldwide sales and marketing division and built revenues to $22 million. Delivered phenomenal growth in international markets (60% of total company sales). Negotiated profitable sales in China, Germany, UK, Spain, Israel, Japan, and Brazil.

- Personally structured and negotiated marketing agreements, partnerships, and alliances with foreign governments, international sales agents, and product/technology development firms worldwide.

- Built in-house software and applications development group to eliminate reliance on third-party vendors.

- Reduced workforce from 300 to 150, recruited 70+ professional staff, introduced field sales automation, and restructured field sales teams. Rationalized and balanced technology offerings.

Challenge, Action, and Results (CAR) Format

Emphasizes the challenge of each position, the action you took, and the results you delivered.

PROFESSIONAL EXPERIENCE:

Director of Networking & Telecommunications (1998 to Present)

Telecommunications Project Manager (1997 to 1998)

Telecommunications Engineer (1994 to 1997)

PACBELL TECHNOLOGY SERVICES CORPORATION, Los Angeles, California

Challenge: To transition an antiquated organization into a state-of-the-art telecommunications organization to support PTSC's rapid market growth and services expansion. Working to position the company as one of the top 5 players in the global technology market.

Action: Built an entirely new telecommunications organization with new architecture, hardware, software, and network protocols. Restaffed with experienced telecommunications operators, engineers, and project managers. Full P&L responsibility.

Results:

- Orchestrated the selection and implementation of a T1 backbone to support the implementation of a global telecommunications network. Invested over $2.8 million to build one of the nation's most sophisticated networks in the world.

- Achieved/surpassed all corporate objectives for system performance, functionality, reliability, and quality. Earned top rankings from internal and external audit teams evaluating the corporation's technological competencies.

- Dramatically increased user/customer responsiveness and satisfaction. Closed 2000 with less than .2% customer complaints and a better than 98.7% customer retention rate.

- Partnered with HP, IBM, and Dell to integrate their systems architecture with proprietary networks and network protocols.

- Contributed to a more than 125% increase in annual gross sales and a 150%+ increase in bottom-line profitability.

Functional Format

Emphasizes the functional areas of responsibility within the job and associated achievements.

EMPLOYMENT EXPERIENCE:

Chief Information Officer (CIO) RADIO TECHNOLOGIES, INC.
1996 to Present

(High-growth, $300+ million company with 35 locations in the US & UK)

CIO, Vice President of Business Technology, and member of a 6-person Corporate Executive Board credited with transitioning this $35 million company into one of the nation's premier special-events companies. Given full strategic planning, leadership, and decision-making authority for building the corporation's entire IT organization, infrastructure, and operations. Led technology organization through $100 million public bond offering (Jamestown) and $65 million venture capital funding (XYZ Ventures).

Built the entire IT organization from concept into a state-of-the-art centralized IT/IS model with distributed services worldwide. Recruited, trained, and developed a staff of 37 technologists, including remote IT managers, a centralized network and operational team, and a matrix-managed finance/business team. Control over $100 million in annual operating and capital-expense budgets.

Infrastructure Development:

- Partnered with MIT, Cisco, and an independent software company to develop high-speed **WAN technology**, one of the most critical drivers in the company's sustained and profitable growth. Developed a 20-node T1/T3 WAN within 2 years and achieved/maintained 99.9% uptime.

- Directed technology integration for **16 acquisitions** (30 sites) over 30 months. Built IT systems where none existed, replaced obsolete technology with legacy systems, and achieved Y2K compliance for all operations. Introduced and achieved corporation-wide technology standardization.

- Built **data center** from start-up into a 24x7 operation supporting high-end SUN Unix systems and an NT platform primarily hosting Oracle databases (ERP applications).

- Designed **LAN** models and standardized voice communications using a mix of open-standard PBXs, voice mail, and voice over IP. Built MCI back-up **ISDN** network and multiple secure Internet protocols.

Solutions & Applications:

- Revitalized fledgling **Oracle implementation** and took ABC "live" in less than 10 months. Modules included AP, AR, GL, Purchasing, Inventory, Project Management, and HR.

- Designed "new" **Internet computing architecture,** migrating Oracle applications onto a 3-tier Web-based environment. Delivered 100% migration of 92 customizations within 60 days.

- Integrated 13 **e-mail systems** (Lotus Notes, Eudora) into one system (Microsoft Exchange) to facilitate collaborative participation among all ABC companies and operating sites.

- Led the selection and implementation of AT&T's VPN solution for direct access to ABC's **private network**.

Internet/Intranet Development:

- Led the design, development, and execution of five major Internet/Intranet sites. Developed business and market strategies, financial plans, Web site interfaces, and e-commerce transactional processes that supported successful launches, solid functionality, and consistently strong performance.

    intranet.abc.com (ABC Intranet deployed to 1,000 users)

    www.nightstar.com (independent LLC company)

    www.industry.com (e-commerce site)

    www.lite.poly.edu/html/milso_case.htm (sponsored research with Merrill Lynch)

    www.abc-link.com (password-protected outsourced server—"Certnet" for ABC project management)

Consulting and Project Format

Emphasizes clients and project highlights.

PROJECT HIGHLIGHTS

DEVELOPER: Maxx Data Applications

CLIENT: Value Enhancement Services, Inc., June 1999–Present

PROJECT:

- Prepare system and design requirements for the Maxx system.
- Write specifications and database definitions.
- Work with development and team and end users to complete system development.
- Continue to modify and enhance the system.

PLATFORMS:

- Microsoft Access 97 and 2000, VBA, ADO, SQL Server
- Microsoft Excel 97, UML Use Case Studies, UML Use Case Diagrams

continues

BENEFITS:

- System helps clients recover "lost" money by identifying oversights, overpayments, and missed opportunities following an expense audit conducted by Value Enhancement.

- On the first project following implementation, slashed audit time in half—from 3 months to 6 weeks—and doubled recovered funds, thereby doubling revenue to the firm.

DEVELOPER: Microsoft Access Database

CLIENT: City of Plano, Texas, May 2000–June 2000

PROJECT:

- Stepped in on short notice to identify enhancement requirements, then define, specify, and complete enhancements to the Construx project-management system.

PLATFORMS: MS Access 97, VBA, MS Excel 97

BENEFITS:

- Responded to client urgency to complete system modification on a rapid timeframe… completed using only 23 of the 40 hours allocated.

Y2K PROJECT COORDINATOR

CLIENT: CompUSA (through Rent-a-Tech consulting firm), May 1998–January 2000

PROJECT:

- Work with employees and contractors in all CompUSA business areas to define requirements for system functions and required results.
- Develop MS Access systems to analyze and compute project metrics.

PLATFORMS:

- MS Access 97, MS Excel 97, ABT

BENEFITS:

- Completed project on time, with no errors or incidents, and $3 million under budget…ranked by *Dallas Morning News* as one of the best-conducted Y2K projects in the Dallas/Fort Worth area.

Technology Skills Format
Emphasizes technological expertise and notable projects/achievements.

—PROFESSIONAL EXPERIENCE—

HONEYWELL IAC   May 1999–August 2000

Applications Engineer, Specialty Chemicals Division, Cincinnati, OH

Procter & Gamble Shampoo and Conditioner Plant Expansion,
Mariscala, Mexico—June–August 2000

- Assisted in definition of HPM and PLC logic for core control box.
- Developed software (CL, control language) to simulate batch production of shampoo and conditioner.

B.F.Goodrich Carbopol Plant Upgrade Project, Paducah, KY—
January–June 1999

- Implemented and adapted old TDC 2000 MFC database, interlocks, and complex control loops into current TPS (Total Plant System) control system.
- Implemented and adapted old GE FANUC PLC ladder logic to a series of logic points in the Honeywell system that wrote and read to the PLC through a serial interface.
- Developed installation qualification and operational qualification documentation for testing procedures.
- Assisted in startup and commissioning of new control system—loop checking, troubleshooting wiring problems, and testing complex control schemes.

Control System Engineer, North American Projects Division, Phoenix, AZ

TCO Project, Tengiz, Kazakhstan—April–December 1999,
May–June 1998

- Translated and then implemented Control Bailey control schematics into current TPS control system.
- Assisted in creating serial interface points on Honeywell system to connect to Wonderware system.
- Developed software to simulate a nitrogen-generation unit for expansion area added to Tengiz plant.
- Assisted in establishing termination drawings that entailed segregation of IS and non-IS field wires.
- Created intelligent P&IDs of the refinery using Rebis and AutoCAD software.

continues

- Came on board midstream while project was in danger of being lost due to client dissatisfaction. Met critical deadlines through intensive team efforts; contract extended for contingency phase.

Control System Engineer, CSCC, Ashland, KY

Ashland Petroleum Steam Project, Catlettsburg, KY—
July 1998–March 1999

- Established real-time steam model for Catlettsburg refinery using G2-based Visual-MESA (a steam optimization program).

- Developed real-time control schematics for G2-based ASM (Abnormal Situation Management).

- Created a search program for ASM using G2 code.

- Calculated boiler efficiency curves for all boilers in the refinery.

- Worked with interface technology between G2 and Microsoft products.

- Rapidly learned G2 programming on the job. Became primary project engineer midstream. Contract extended.

EDUCATION, CREDENTIALS, AND CERTIFICATIONS

Your Education section should include college, certifications, credentials, licenses, registrations, and continuing education. Be succinct, and be sure to bring any notable academic credentials or certifications to the forefront—either in your Education section or in your Career Summary, as demonstrated in the first Career Summary example shown previously. If you have attended numerous continuing education programs, list only the most recent, most relevant, and most distinguishing.

Here are five sample Education sections that illustrate a variety of ways to organize and format this information.

Academic Credentials Format

EDUCATION:

MBA—Information Systems & Technology—Xavier University—1994

BSEE—Electronics Engineering & Systems Design—The Ohio State University—1992

Highlights of Continuing Professional Education:

- Robotics & Systems Automation, Rensselaer Polytechnic University, 2001

- Advanced Computer Science Applications, The Ohio State University, 2001
- Executive Leadership Skills, Dale Carnegie, 2000
- Web Systems Design & Integration, University of Cincinnati, 1998

Microsoft Systems Certified Engineer (MSCE), 1998

FCC Registered Mobile Radio Operator, 1992

Executive Education Format

EDUCATION

Executive Development Program	STANFORD UNIVERSITY
Executive Development Program	UNIVERSITY OF CALIFORNIA AT IRVINE
Bachelor of Science Degree	UNIVERSITY OF CALIFORNIA AT LOS ANGELES

Certifications Format

TECHNICAL CERTIFICATIONS & EDUCATION:

Microsoft Certified Systems Engineer (MCSE), 2000

Microsoft Certified Professional (MCP), 1999

Cisco Certified Network Associate (CCNA), 1999

Computer Systems Management Major, University of Michigan, 1994

A.A.S. Degree in Computer Technology, Michigan Community College, 1991

Professional Training Format

PROFESSIONAL TRAINING & DEVELOPMENT

Computer Statistics & Methodologies, Baruch College, 1999

Computer Operations Management, Baruch College, 1999

continues

C++ Programming for Technology Professionals, University of Maryland, 1998

Voice & Data Systems Design, New York University, 1998

Network Administrator, New York University, 1996

Anne Arundel Community College, Arnold, Maryland, 1994–1996

Non-Degree Format

TECHNICAL TRAINING & EDUCATION:

UNIVERSITY OF ILLINOIS, Urbana, Illinois

BBA Candidate—Management Information Systems (Senior class status)

UNIVERSITY OF MICHIGAN, Ann Arbor, Michigan

Dual Major in Computer Systems & Programming (2 years)

Graduate, 200+ hours of continuing professional and technical education through DPMA, Chicago Technology Institute, IBM, HP, and DePaul University.

THE "EXTRAS"

The primary focus of your resume is on information that is directly related to your career goals. However, you also should include things that will distinguish you from other candidates and clearly demonstrate your value to a prospective employer. And, not too surprisingly, it is often the "extras" that get the interviews.

Following is a list of the other categories you might or might not include in your resume depending on your particular experience and your current career objectives. Review the information. If it's pertinent to you, use the samples for formatting your own data. Remember, however, that if something is truly impressive, you may want to include it in your Career Summary at the beginning of your resume in order to draw even more attention to it. If this is the case, it's not necessary to repeat the information at the end of your resume.

Affiliations—Professional

If you are a member of any professional, leadership, or technology associations, be sure to include that information on your resume. It communicates a message of professionalism, a desire to stay current with the industry, and a strong professional network. Here's an example:

PROFESSIONAL AFFILIATIONS

- Member, Data Processing Management Association (Training Program Chairperson—1999)
- Member, Institute for Technology Enterprise (Convention Chairperson—1998)
- President, Project Management Institute (New York Chapter—1997–98)

Affiliations—Civic

Civic affiliations are fine to include if they

- are with a notable organization,
- demonstrate leadership experience, or
- may be of interest to a prospective employer.

However, things such as treasurer of your local condo association and volunteer at your child's day-care center are not generally of value in marketing your qualifications. Here's an example of what to include:

- Volunteer Chairperson, United Way of America—Detroit Chapter, 1998 to Present
- President, Lambert Valley Conservation District, 1997 to Present
- Treasurer, Habitat for Humanity—Detroit Chapter, 1996 to 1997

Public Speaking

Experts are the ones who are invited to give public presentations at conferences, technical training programs, symposia, and other events. So if you have public-speaking experience, others must consider you an expert. Be sure to include this very complimentary information in your resume. Here's one way to present it:

- Keynote Speaker, 2000 Conference of Internet Executives—Las Vegas
- Presenter, 1999 International DPMA Conference—Dallas
- Presenter, 1997 IBM Technology Training Symposium—New York

Publications

If you're published, you must be an expert (or at least most people will think so). Just as with your public-speaking engagements, be sure to include your publications. They validate your knowledge, qualifications, and credibility. Publications can include books, articles, online Web site content, manuals, and other written documents. Here's an example:

- Author, "Winning Web Marketing Strategies," *TechBusiness Magazine*, January 2001
- Author, "Web Marketing 101: Compete To Win," *TechBusiness Online*, February 1999
- Co-Author, "Op-Cit Technology Training Manual," Op-Cit Corporation, December 1998

Honors and Awards

If you have won honors and awards, you can either include them in a separate section on your resume or integrate them into the Education or Professional Experience section, whichever is most appropriate. If you choose to include them in a separate section, consider this format:

- Winner, 2000 **"President's Club"** award for outstanding contributions to new product development.
- Winner, 1999 **"Innovator's Club"** award for outstanding contributions to technology innovation.
- Named **"Graduate Student of the Year,"** Hofstra University, 1991
- **Summa Cum Laude Graduate,** Washington & Lee University, 1989

Teaching and Training Experience

Many professionals in the technology industry also teach or train at institutions and organizations other than their full-time employer. If this is applicable to you, you will want to include that experience on your resume. If someone hires you (paid or unpaid) to speak to an audience, it communicates a strong message about your qualifications and credibility. Here's a format you might use to present this information:

- Adjunct Faculty—Information Technology, Contra Costa Community College, Spring 2000
- Instructor—Programming Principles, Contra Costa Community College, Fall 1999
- Instructor—Systems Architecture, Valley Mead University, Fall 1999–Spring 2000

NOTE: If teaching or training is your primary occupation, you will not include this section in your resume. Rather, your teaching and training will be in your Professional Experience section.

Personal Information

We do not recommend that you include such personal information as birth date, marital status, number of children, and related data. However, there may be instances when personal information is appropriate. If this information will give you a competitive advantage or answer unspoken questions about your background, then by all means include it. Here's an example:

- Born in Argentina. U.S. Permanent Residency Status since 1987.
- Fluent in English, Spanish, and Portuguese.
- Competitive Triathlete. Top-5 finish, 1987 Midwest Triathlon and 1992 Des Moines Triathlon.

Consolidating the Extras

Sometimes you have so many extra categories at the end of your resume that spacing becomes a problem. You certainly don't want to have to make your resume a page longer to accommodate five lines, nor do you want the "extras" to overwhelm the primary sections of your resume. Yet you believe the "extra" information is important and should be included. Or perhaps you have a few small bits of information that you think are important but don't merit an entire section for each "bit." In these situations, consider consolidating the information using one of the following formats. You'll save space, avoid over-emphasizing individual items, and present a professional, distinguished appearance.

PROFESSIONAL PROFILE

Affiliations	American Management Association
	Data Processing Management Association
	Information Technology Executives Leadership Council
Public Speaking	Keynote Speaker, AMA Leadership Conference, Dallas, 2000
	Presenter, DPMA National Conference, San Diego, 1998
	Panelist, DPMA National Conference, Chicago, 1996
Foreign Languages	Fluent in English, Spanish, and German

ADDITIONAL INFORMATION

- Founder and Program Chair, Detroit Technical Professionals Association.
- Bilingual—Spanish/English.
- Available for relocation.

Writing Tips, Techniques, and Important Lessons

At this point, you've done a lot of reading, probably taken some notes, highlighted samples that appeal to you, and are ready to plunge into writing your resume. To make this task as easy as possible, we've compiled some "insider" techniques that we've used in our professional resume writing practices. These techniques were learned the hard way through years of experience! We know they work; they will make the writing process easier, faster, and more enjoyable for you.

GET IT DOWN—THEN POLISH AND PERFECT IT

Don't be too concerned with making your resume "perfect" the first time around. It's far better to move fairly swiftly through the process, getting the basic information organized and on paper (or onscreen), rather than agonizing about the perfect phrase or ideal formatting. Once you've completed a draft, we think you'll be surprised at how close to "final" it is, and you'll be able to edit, tighten, and improve formatting fairly quickly.

WRITE YOUR RESUME FROM THE BOTTOM UP

Here's the system:

- **Start with the easy things**—Education, Professional Affiliations, Public Speaking, and any other extras you want to include. These items require little thought and can be completed in just a few minutes.

- **Write short job descriptions for your older positions, the ones you held years ago.** Be very brief and focus on highlights such as rapid promotion, project highlights, notable achievements, technology innovations, industry recognition, or employment with a well-respected, well-known company.

Once you've completed this, look at how much you've written in a short period of time! Then move on to the next step.

- **Write the job descriptions for your most recent positions.** This will take a bit longer than the other sections you have written. Remember to focus on the overall scope of your responsibility, major projects, and significant achievements. Tell your reader what you did and how well you did it. You can use any of the formats recommended earlier in this chapter, or you can create something that is unique to you and your career.

Now, see how far along you are? Your resume is 90 percent complete with only one small section left to do.

- **Write your career summary.** Before you start writing, remember your objective for this section. The summary should not simply rehash your previous experience. Rather, it is designed to highlight the skills and qualifications you have that are most closely related to your current career objective(s). The summary is intended to capture the reader's attention and "sell" your expertise.

That's it. You're done. We guarantee that the process of writing your resume will be much, much easier if you follow the "bottom-up" strategy. Now, on to the next tip.

INCLUDE NOTABLE OR PROMINENT "EXTRA" STUFF IN YOUR CAREER SUMMARY

Remember the "bits and bytes" sections that are normally at the bottom of your resume? If this information is particularly notable or prominent—you won a notable award, spoke at an international technology conference, invented a new product, or taught at a prestigious university—you may want to include it at the top in your Career Summary. Remember, the summary section is written to distinguish you from the crowd of other qualified candidates. As such, if you've accomplished anything that clearly demonstrates your knowledge, expertise, and credibility, consider moving it to your Career Summary for added attention. Refer to the sample Career Summaries (especially the third and fifth ones) earlier in the chapter for examples.

USE RESUME SAMPLES TO GET IDEAS FOR CONTENT, FORMAT, AND ORGANIZATION

This book is just one of many resources where you can review the resumes of other technology professionals to help you in formulating your strategy, writing the text, and formatting your resume. What's more, these books are published precisely for that reason. You don't have to struggle alone. Rather, use all the available resources at your disposal.

Be forewarned, however, that it's unlikely you will find a resume that fits your life and career to a "T." It's more likely that you will use "some of this sample" and "some of that sample" to create a resume that is uniquely "you."

STICK TO THE HIGHLIGHTS

If you have more information than will fit comfortably into a single category on your resume, include just the highlights. This is particularly relevant to the "extra" categories such as Professional Affiliations, Civic Affiliations, Foreign Languages, Honors and Awards, Publications, Public Speaking, and the like. Suppose you have won 10 different awards throughout your career, but you're limited in the amount of space available at the bottom of your resume. Rather than list all 10 and force your resume onto an additional page, simply title the category "Highlights of Honors & Awards" or "Notable Honors & Awards" and include just a sampling. By using the word "highlights," you are communicating to your reader that you are providing just a partial listing.

INCLUDE DATES OR NOT?

Unless you are over age 50, we recommend that you date your work experience and your education. Without dates, your resume becomes vague and difficult for the typical hiring manager or recruiter to interpret. What's more, it often communicates the message that you are trying to hide something. Maybe you haven't worked in two years, maybe you were fired from each of your last three positions, or maybe you never graduated from college. Being vague and creating a resume that is difficult to read will, inevitably, lead to uncertainty and a quick toss into the "not interested" pile of candidates. By including the dates of your education and your experience, you create a clean and concise picture that one can easily follow to track your career progression.

AN INDIVIDUAL DECISION

If you are over age 50, dating your early positions must be an individual decision. On the one hand, you do not want to "date" yourself out of consideration by including dates from the 1960s and early 1970s. On the other hand, it may be that those positions are worth including for any one of a number of reasons. Further, if you omit those early dates, you may feel as though you are misrepresenting yourself (or lying) to a prospective employer.

Here is a strategy to overcome these concerns while still including your early experience: Create a separate category titled "Previous Professional Experience" in which you summarize your earliest employment. You can tailor this statement to emphasize just what is most important about that experience.

If you want to focus on the reputation of your past employers, include a statement such as this:

> • Previous experience includes several programming, applications-development, and project-management positions with **IBM, Tandem, and Hewlett Packard.**

If you want to focus on the rapid progression of your career, consider this example:

> • Promoted rapidly through a series of increasingly responsible project-management positions with Digital Equipment Corporation, earning six promotions in eight years.

If you want to focus on your early career achievements, include a statement such as

> • Led the design, development, and market launch of X-TEL's second-generation software, now a **$2.1 million profit center** for the corporation.

By including any one of the above paragraphs, under the heading "Previous Professional Experience," you are clearly communicating to your reader that your employment history dates further back than the dates you have indicated on your resume. In turn, you are being 100 percent above-board and not misrepresenting yourself or your career. What's more, you're focusing on the success, achievement, and prominence of your earliest assignments.

Dates in the Education Section?

If you are over age 50, we generally do not recommend that you date your education or college degrees. Simply include the degree and the university with no date. Why exclude yourself from consideration by immediately presenting the fact that you earned your college degree in 1958, 1962, or 1966—about the time the hiring manager was probably born? Remember, the goal of your resume is to share the highlights of your career and open doors for interviews. It is *not* to give your entire life story. As such, it is not mandatory to date your college degree.

However, if you use this strategy, be aware that the reader is likely to assume there is *some* gap between when your education ended and your work experience started. Therefore, if you choose to begin your chronological work history with your first job out of college, omitting your graduation date could actually backfire, because the reader may assume you have experience that predates your first job. In this case, it's best either to *include your graduation date* or *omit dates of earliest experience*, using the summary strategy discussed above.

ALWAYS SEND A COVER LETTER WHEN YOU FORWARD YOUR RESUME

It is expected, and it's appropriate job search etiquette. When you prepare a resume, you are writing a document that you can use for each and every position you apply for, assuming that the requirements for all of those positions will be similar. The cover letter, then, is the tool that allows you to customize your presentation to each company or recruiter, addressing their specific hiring requirements. It is also the appropriate place to include any specific information that has been requested such as salary history or salary requirements (see the following section).

NEVER INCLUDE SALARY HISTORY OR SALARY REQUIREMENTS ON YOUR RESUME

Your resume is *not* the correct forum for a salary discussion. First of all, you should never provide salary information unless a company has requested that information and you choose to comply. (Studies show that employers will look at your resume anyway, so you may choose not to respond to this request, thereby avoiding pricing yourself out of the job or locking yourself into a lower salary than the job is worth.)

When contacting recruiters, however, we recommend that you do provide salary information, but again, only in your cover letter. With recruiters you want to "put all of your cards on the table" and help them make an appropriate placement by providing information about your current salary and salary objectives. For example, "Be advised that my current compensation is $75,000 annually and that I am interested in a position starting at a minimum of $85,000 per year." Or, if you would prefer to be a little less specific, you might write, "My annual compensation over the past three years has averaged $50,000+."

ALWAYS REMEMBER THAT YOU ARE SELLING

As we have discussed over and over throughout this book, resume writing is sales. Understand and appreciate the value you bring to a prospective employer, and then communicate that value by focusing on your achievements. Companies don't want to hire just anyone; they want to hire "the" someone who will make a difference. Show them that you are that candidate.

CHAPTER 3

Printed, Scannable, Electronic, and Web Resumes

Technology is what you do for a living. Our expertise is in writing and in guiding clients through the complex process of job search. And that's where we have one up on you! We understand technology as it relates directly to resume development, writing, and presentation, and that is the information that we will share.

The Four Types of Resumes

In today's employment market, there are four types of resume presentations:

- Printed
- Scannable
- Electronic (e-mail attachments and ASCII text files)
- Web

The following sections give details on when you would need each type, as well as how to prepare these types of resumes.

THE PRINTED RESUME

The printed resume is what we know as the "traditional resume," the one that you mail to a recruiter, take to an interview, and forward by mail or fax in response to an advertisement. When preparing a printed resume, your objective is to create a sharp, professional, and visually attractive presentation. Remember, that piece of paper conveys the very first impression of you to a potential employer, and that first impression goes a long, long way. Never be fooled into thinking that just because you have the best technical qualifications in your industry, the visual presentation of your resume does not matter. It does, a great deal.

THE SCANNABLE RESUME

The scannable resume can be referred to as the "plain-Jane" or "plain-vanilla" resume. All of the things that you would normally do to make your printed resume look attractive—bold print, italic, multiple columns, sharp-looking font, and more—are stripped away in a scannable resume. You want to present a document that can be easily read and interpreted by scanning technology.

While the technology continues to improve, and many scanning systems can in fact read a wide variety of type enhancements, it's sensible to appeal to the "lowest common denominator" when creating your scannable resume. Follow these formatting guidelines:

- Use a commonly used, easily read font such as Arial or Times New Roman.

- Don't use bold, italic, or underlined type.

- Use a minimum of 11-point type size.

- Position your name, and nothing else, on the top line of the resume.

- Keep text left-justified, with a "ragged" right margin.

- It's okay to use common abbreviations (for instance, scanning software will recognize "B.S." as a Bachelor of Science degree). But when in doubt, spell it out.

- Eliminate graphics, borders, and horizontal lines.

- Use plain round bullets or asterisks.

- Avoid columns and tables, although a simple two-column listing can be read without difficulty.

- Spell out symbols such as % and &.

- If you divide words with slashes, add a space before and after the slash to be certain the letters aren't misread. An exception to this guideline is technical terms such as AS/400, which should not include extra spaces around the slash.

- Print using a laser printer on smooth white paper.

- If your resume is longer than one page, be sure to print on only one side of the paper, put your name and telephone number on the top of page 2, and don't staple the pages together.

- For best possible results, mail your resume (don't fax it), and send it flat in a 9 × 12 envelope so that you won't have to fold it.

Of course, you can avoid scannability issues completely by sending your resume electronically, so that it will not have to pass through a scanner to enter the company's databank. Read the next section for electronic resume guidelines.

THE ELECTRONIC RESUME

Your electronic resume can take two forms: e-mail attachments and ASCII text files.

E-mail Attachments

When including your resume with an e-mail, simply attach the word-processing file of your printed resume. Because a vast majority of businesses use Microsoft Word, this is the most acceptable format and will present the fewest difficulties when attached.

However, given the tremendous variety in versions of software and operating systems, not to mention printer drivers, it's quite possible that your beautifully formatted resume will look quite different when viewed and printed at the other end. To minimize these glitches, use generous margins (at least .75 inch all around), don't use unusual fonts, and minimize fancy formatting effects.

Test your resume by e-mailing it to several friends or colleagues, then having them view and print it on their systems. If you use WordPerfect, Microsoft Works, or another word-processing program, consider saving your resume in a more universally accepted format such as RTF or PDF. Again, try it out on friends before sending it to a potential employer.

ASCII Text Files

You'll find many uses for an ASCII text version of your resume:

- To avoid formatting problems, you can paste the text into the body of an e-mail message rather than send an attachment. Many employers actually prefer this method. Pasting text into an e-mail message lets you send your resume without the possibility of also sending a virus.

- You can readily copy and paste the text version into online job application and resume bank forms, with no worries that formatting glitches will cause confusion.

- Although unattractive, the text version is 100 percent scannable.

To create a text version of your resume, follow these simple steps:

1. Create a new version of your resume using the Save As feature of your word-processing program. Select "text only" or "ASCII" in the Save As option box.

2. Close the new file.

3. Reopen the file, and you'll find that your word processor has automatically reformatted your resume into Courier font, removed all formatting, and left-justified the text.

4. To promote maximum readability when sending your resume electronically, reset the margins to 2 inches left and right, so that you have a narrow column of text rather than a full-page width. This margin setting will not be retained when you close the file, but in the meantime you can adjust the text formatting for best screen appearance. For instance, if you choose to include a horizontal line (perhaps something like this: +++++++++++++++++++++++++) to separate sections of the resume, by working with the narrow margins you won't make the mistake of creating a line that extends past the normal screen width. You also won't add hard line breaks that create odd-length lines when seen at normal screen width.

5. Review the resume and fix any "glitches" such as odd characters that may have been inserted to take the place of "curly" quotes, dashes, accents, or other nonstandard symbols.

6. If necessary, add extra blank lines to improve readability.

7. Consider adding horizontal dividers to break the resume into sections for improved skimmability. You can use any standard typewriter symbols such as *, -, (,), =, +, ^, or #.

To illustrate what you can expect when creating these versions of your resume, here's an example of the same resume (top portion only) in traditional printed format (page 49), scannable version (page 50), and electronic (text) format (page 51).

THE WEB RESUME

This newest evolution in resumes combines the visually pleasing quality of the printed resume with the technological ease of the electronic resume. You host your Web resume on your own Web site (with your own URL), to which you refer prospective employers and recruiters. Now, instead of a "plain-Jane" version of your e-mailed resume, with just one click a viewer can access, download, and print your Web resume—an attractive, nicely formatted presentation of your qualifications.

What's more, because the Web resume is such an efficient and easy-to-manage tool, you can choose to include more information than you would in a printed, scannable, or electronic resume. Consider separate pages for achievements, project highlights, technology qualifications, management skills, and more if you believe they would improve your market position. Remember, you're working to sell yourself into your next job!

For those of you in multimedia and related technology industries, you can even take it one step further and create a virtual multimedia presentation that not only tells someone how talented you are, but also visually and technologically demonstrates it. Web resumes are an outstanding tool for people seeking jobs in the computer industry.

A simplified version of the Web resume is an online version of your Microsoft Word resume. Instead of attaching a file to your e-mail, you can include a link to the online version. This format is not as graphically dynamic as a full-fledged Web resume, but can be a very useful tool for your job search. For instance, you can offer the simplicity of text in your e-mail, plus the instant availability of a word-processing document for the recruiter or hiring manager who is interested. For a demonstration of this format, go to www.e-resume-central.com and click on "See a Sample."

Tricia Standish

3725 Oaklawn Drive

Cincinnati, Ohio 45242
(513) 555-0202

tstandish@netscape.net

Expertise **SYSTEMS INTEGRATION ENGINEERING AND TECHNICAL SUPPORT INDUSTRIAL CONTROLS INDUSTRY**

Experience **SENIOR APPLICATIONS ENGINEER,** *1995-August 2000*

APPLICATIONS ENGINEER, *1980-1995*

- Honeywell Measurex Corporation, Cincinnati, OH
- Measurex Corporation, Cincinnati, OH (Headquarters: Cupertino, California) (acquired by Honeywell, 2/1997)
- The Ohmart Corporation, Cincinnati, OH (acquired by Measurex, 2/1995)

Provided multifaceted programming, integration, and technical support services for manufacturer of industrial controls. Position encompassed three distinct areas:

☑ **Technical support of the sales effort:** Tested samples submitted by the customer; conducted product demonstrations both in our factory and at the customer site; assisted with consultative selling based on my in-depth product knowledge.

☑ **Technical support of the product itself:** Managed installation, startup, and upgrading of systems sold; provided emergency troubleshooting at especially troublesome sites; provided full project management for larger installations.

☑ **Systems integration:** Enhanced the basic product line by adding SCADA capabilities, allowing the system to communicate with and perform supervisory control of the customer's existing control devices, including PLCs and temperature controllers.

The print version of the resume.

Tricia Standish

3725 Oaklawn Drive

Cincinnati, OH 45242
(513) 555-0202
tstandish@netscape.net

EXPERTISE   Systems Integration Engineering and Technical Support
Industrial Controls Industry

EXPERIENCE   Senior Applications Engineer, 1995-August 2000

Applications Engineer, 1980-1995

HONEYWELL MEASUREX CORPORATION, Cincinnati, OH
MEASUREX CORPORATION, Cincinnati, OH (Headquarters: Cupertino, California) (acquired by Honeywell, 2/1997)

THE OHMART CORPORATION, Cincinnati, OH (acquired by Honeywell, February 1995)

Provided multifaceted programming, integration, and technical support services for manufacturer of industrial controls. Position encompassed three distinct areas:

• Technical support of the sales effort: Tested samples submitted by the customer; conducted product demonstrations both in our factory and at the customer site; assisted with consultative selling based on my in-depth product knowledge.

• Technical support of the product itself: Managed installation, startup, and upgrading of systems sold; provided emergency troubleshooting at especially troublesome sites; provided full project management for larger installations.

• Systems integration: Enhanced the basic product line by adding SCADA capabilities, allowing the system to communicate with and perform supervisory control of the customer's existing control devices, including PLCs and temperature controllers.

The scannable version of the resume.

```
TRICIA STANDISH

-----------------------------------------------------

3725 Oaklawn Drive

Cincinnati, OH 45242

(513) 555-0202

tstandish@netscape.net


-----------------------------------------------------

EXPERTISE

Systems Integration Engineering and Technical Support

Industrial Controls Industry


-----------------------------------------------------

EXPERIENCE

Senior Applications Engineer, 1995-August 2000

Applications Engineer, 1980-1995


---HONEYWELL MEASUREX CORPORATION, Cincinnati, OH

---MEASUREX CORPORATION, Cincinnati, OH (Headquarters: Cupertino,
California) (acquired by Honeywell, 2/1997)

---THE OHMART CORPORATION, Cincinnati, OH (acquired by Honeywell,
February 1995)


Provided multifaceted programming, integration, and technical support
services for manufacturer of industrial controls. Position encompassed
three distinct areas:


* TECHNICAL SUPPORT OF THE SALES EFFORT: Tested samples submitted by
the customer; conducted product demonstrations both in our factory and
at the customer site; assisted with consultative selling based on my
in-depth product knowledge.


* TECHNICAL SUPPORT OF THE PRODUCT ITSELF: Managed installation,
startup, and upgrading of systems sold; provided emergency
troubleshooting at especially troublesome sites; provided full project
management for larger installations.


* SYSTEMS INTEGRATION: Enhanced the basic product line by adding SCADA
capabilities, allowing the system to communicate with and perform
supervisory control of the customer's existing control devices,
including PLCs and temperature controllers.
```

The electronic/text version of the resume.

The Four Resume Types Compared

This chart quickly compares the similarities and differences between the four types of resumes we've discussed in this chapter.

	PRINTED RESUMES	SCANNABLE RESUMES
TYPESTYLE/ FONT	Sharp, conservative, and distinctive (see our recommendations in chapter 1).	Clean, concise, and machine-readable: Times New Roman, Arial, Helvetica.
TYPESTYLE ENHANCEMENTS	**Bold,** *italics,* and underlining for emphasis.	CAPITALIZATION is the only type enhancement you can be certain will transmit.
TYPE SIZE	10-, 11-, or 12-point preferred... larger type sizes (14, 18, 20, 22, and even larger, depending on typestyle) will effectively enhance your name and section headers.	11, 12-point, or larger.
TEXT FORMAT	Use centering and indentations to optimize the visual presentation.	Type all information flush left.
PREFERRED LENGTH	1 to 2 pages; 3 if essential.	1 to 2 pages preferred, although length is not as much of a concern as with printed resumes.
PREFERRED PAPER COLOR	White, Ivory, Light Gray, Light Blue, or other conservative background.	White or very light with no prints, flecks, or other shading that might affect scannability.
WHITE SPACE	Use appropriately for best readability.	Use generously to maximize scannability.

ELECTRONIC RESUMES	WEB RESUMES
Courier.	Sharp, conservative and distinctive... attractive onscreen and when printed from an online document.
CAPITALIZATION is the only enhancement available to you.	**Bold,** *italics,* and underlining, and color for emphasis.
12-point.	10-, 11-, or 12-point preferred... larger type sizes (14, 18, 20, 22, even larger, depending on typestyle) will effectively enhance your name and section headers.
Type all information flush left.	Use centering and indentations to optimize the visual presentation.
Length is immaterial; almost definitely, converting your resume to text will make it longer.	Length is immaterial; just be sure your site is well organized so viewers can quickly find the material of greatest interest to them.
N/A.	Paper is not used, but do select your background carefully to maximize readability.
Use white space to break up dense text sections.	Use appropriately for best readability both onscreen and when printed.

Are You Ready to Write Your Resume?

To be sure that you're ready to write your resume, go through the following checklist. Each item is a critical step that you must take in the process of writing and designing your own winning resume.

- ❑ Clearly define "who you are" and how you want to be perceived.

- ❑ Document your key skills, qualifications, and knowledge.

- ❑ Document your notable career achievements and successes.

- ❑ Identify one or more specific job targets or positions.

- ❑ Identify one or more industries that you are targeting.

- ❑ Research and compile key words for your profession, industry, and specific job targets.

- ❑ Determine which resume format is best for you and your career.

- ❑ Select an attractive font.

- ❑ Determine whether you need a print resume, an electronic resume, a Web resume, or all three.

- ❑ Secure a private e-mail address (not your employer's).

- ❑ Review resume samples for up-to-date ideas on resume styles, formats, organization, and language.

PART II

Sample Resumes for Computer and Web Jobs

CHAPTER 4

Resumes for Computer Operators and Technicians

- Computer Operators

- Computer Analysts

- Computer Systems and PC Technicians

- Hardware Technicians

- Electronics Technicians

- Systems Installation and Configuration Technicians

- Field Service Technicians

- Field Engineers

- Systems Technicians

John B. Lankford

2020 West Main Street, Apt. 231 — Hendersonville, Tennessee 37075

Home: (615) 555-5466 — E-mail: jblankford@home.com

COMPUTER OPERATIONS AND SYSTEMS PROFESSIONAL

IBM PCs – Compatibles – Microsoft Office

DOS 5.0 and up – OS/2 2.0 and up – Windows 95 and 98

DSU/CSU – Routers – Hubs

QUALIFICATIONS SUMMARY

- Solid computer operations background involving installation, maintenance, and troubleshooting of PC hardware, operating systems, LAN and WAN equipment, and numerous software applications.
- Experienced as a technical trainer/instructor with strong knowledge in hardware repair and technical training.
- Ability to translate technical information and make it more easily understood by nontechnical audiences.
- Learn new systems and software readily. Strong desire to expand computer knowledge and apply it to improving business performance.

PROFESSIONAL EXPERIENCE

Field Engineer / Inside Sales Support..1995 – Present
DIGITAL COMMUNICATIONS, INC. – Hendersonville, Tennessee

- Configuration, installation, and troubleshooting related to connecting 120 LANs to WAN equipment in Birmingham for AmSouth Bank.
- Work with inside sales staff to determine customer needs and provide sales support.

Senior Field Engineer.. 1993 – 1995
TECH SYSTEMS – Marietta, Georgia

- Tested and repaired Packard Bell hardware for both personal users and small- to medium-sized businesses.
- Installed, operated, and troubleshot hardware and software, providing on-site support.

Personal Systems Help Center / Technical Support Group... 1990 – 1993
IBM – Marietta, Georgia / Research Triangle Park, North Carolina

- Provided information and technical support via telephone for users with software problems.
- Accurately and successfully identified customer problems and offered solutions.
- Served as an effective Team Leader and liaison between Technical Support Group and management.

EDUCATION

Bachelor of Science, Economics – 1990 ....Florida State University, Tallahassee

This individual's 10-plus years of directly related experience are summarized in brief "responsibility" statements, whereas his qualifications are presented "front and center" as his greatest selling points.

Joseph E. Boyce

7115 South Rosendale Drive • Franklin, Wisconsin 54315
Phone: (414) 487-2678 • Email: jeboyce@hotmail.com

PROFILE

Computer Operations & Systems Professional with 25+ years' experience. An extremely loyal and dedicated employee who has served as lead person for 10 years. Strong mainframe expertise; currently training for support of desktop systems. Commended for producing high-quality work with solid attention to detail. A team player with effective decision-making skills and the ability to operate independently.

TECHNICAL SUMMARY

- **Software:**   MVS, JES2, DOS, VM, CICS, TSO, DB2, Omegamon, Netview, Zeke, Autosys, UCC7, Windows, Word, Outlook, Exchange, Remedy

- **Hardware:**   IBM 3090, AS/400, IBM System 360 & 370, IBM Tape Robot, IBM 3480 & 3420 tape drives, Xerox Printers, IBM Printers

- **Languages:** JCL, COBOL

PROFESSIONAL EXPERIENCE

MIDWEST BREWING COMPANY, MILWAUKEE, WI   1973 to Present
(A subsidiary of Fortune 500 firm, with annual beverage sales in excess of $1 billion.)

Senior Computer Operator (1989 to Present)

Lead first shift computer operator within the Information Systems Department (ISD). Supervise and assist 2 other operators on IBM 3090 mainframe system utilizing MVS and JES2 operating systems. Generate reports in a timely manner and forward to ISD personnel. Ensure an effective overall operation by carefully monitoring hardware and software and responding as a first level of support. Maintain and control supplies inventory. Perform initial program loads and back up systems using established schedules.

- Promoted after serving as Junior Operator (1973-1979) and Operator (1979-1989).

- Recognized for maintaining a nearly perfect attendance record throughout tenure.

EDUCATION

Associate of Applied Science Degree—Computer Programming—1975
Waukesha County Technical College

The clean formatting and large type of this one-page resume make it highly readable. The two bullet points under the Professional Experience section describe notable achievements.

Jeremiah Best

32 Andrews Street, Livingston, NJ 07039
(973) 740-5555 ▪ jerbest@net.com

Objective	A technical support position in Computer Technology and Electronics

Education

April 2001   The Computer Institute, Rahwah, NJ
Certificate, Electronics and Computer Technology
- 60-week, 96-semester-credit-hour program
- GPA 3.93 / Executive List every semester
- Work part-time to fund education while taking classes

Courses

- ✓ Basic Electricity I & II
- ✓ Microcomputer Fundamentals
- ✓ Semiconductor Devices and Circuits
- ✓ Personal Computer Repair
- ✓ Integrated Circuits and Digital Logic
- ✓ Data Communications and Fiber Optics
- ✓ Systems and Networking

Technical Skills and Equipment

AC/DC Power Supply	PC Repair/Troubleshooting
Digital Logic Probe	Networking Media Installation
Bread Boarding Circuits	Networking Server Installation
Digital Voltmeter AC/DC	Workstation Software Installation
Oscilloscope	Data Communications
Function Generator	Microprocessing
DOS 6.22	Windows 95 / 98 / NT
Novell NetWare 3.12	Novell NetWare 4.0 / 5.0

Work History
1999 – present

Grand Central Theatre, Livingston, NJ
Kitchen Help / Concession Help

- Prepare fast food for theatre clientele, often cooking for 200-300 orders per shift per night, as part of a team of six kitchen and concession workers.

- Serve as cashier for concession sales, filling in for absent workers; proof out $3K - $4K in sales per night.

- Selected by Manager as "Employee of the Month" in October 2000 for cooperative attitude, perfect attendance and willingness to work double shifts on short notice.

Testimonials

"Jeremiah is an exceptional person, and I know that anything he is a part of will be a success."
– Ellery Williams, Managing Director, Grand Central Theatre

"Jeremiah is punctual and eager to work..."
– William McCarthy, Manager, Grand Central Theatre

This individual is a new graduate whose education and technical capabilities take up most of the resume. His work experience is less important; it is not technology based, but it does show strong capabilities and achievements. Note the effective testimonials at the bottom.

Lisel Roemmele

11034 Highway 1247
Waynesburg, Kentucky 40489
Voice (606) 555-1029
liselr@aol.com

"Lisel is at the top of her class, showing a great deal of insight and enthusiasm for networking, trouble-shooting, and administration.

"I feel she can be of considerable help in a school environment, as she has good people skills, is willing to work wherever needed, and is tenacious in solving problems that come up day-to-day."

- Roger Angevine
Chair, Physical Sciences and Mathematics

"If there is a network problem that is not easily discovered, Lisel is willing to go the extra mile to find and resolve it.

"She is quite knowledgeable and has the ability to troubleshoot many PC platforms. Her extensive knowledge of operating and network systems will be an asset to any company."

- Troy Schlake
Network Administrator, Bondtech Corp

PROFILE

Innovative, achievement-oriented computer professional with exceptional abilities in the areas of technical and systems support. Immediate goal is to provide comprehensive, high-quality support to meet the needs of a growing organization. Personal and professional strengths include:

- Microsoft Certification in Windows 98 and NT Server; NT Workstation 4 and Network Essentials pending.
- Conscientious and dependable in completing systems projects accurately and independently in zero error tolerance environment.
- Experienced in system management disciplines including disaster recovery.
- Proven ability to meet and maintain time requirements.
- Experience developing applications/solutions for ad hoc assignments.
- Quick learner; able to grasp and master new concepts easily.
- Equally effective working independently or as part of a team.
- Extremely hardworking; dedicated to enhancing personal computer skills.

PROFICIENCIES

Operating Systems:
Linux, Solaris 7 (Unix), Windows 95, Windows 98, NT Server, Workstation (Including User Manager), DHCP, WINS, MS Office, and Windows 2000.

Languages:
HTML and JCL; familiarity with CVB and C

INTERNSHIP EXPERIENCE

1999 - 2000   Somerset Community College   Somerset, KY
On-call Consultant. Installation of TCP/IP, IPX networks and workstation for lab units and associates as required. Strengths in troubleshooting and technical support.

EDUCATION

Network Information Systems Technology
Somerset Community College, Somerset, Kentucky
Degree anticipated — December, 2000

CERTIFICATIONS HELD

Microsoft Certified Professional, MCPID 1465546
NT Server Certified — 1999
Windows 98 Certified — 2000
NT Workstation 4 and Network Essentials Certifications pending

Excellent personal and professional references will be made available on request.

Appropriate graphics and an interesting layout make this resume attractive and fun to read. The testimonials in the left column are highly visible, yet they don't detract from the standard format of the rest of the resume.

RESUME 5: LAURA A. DECARLO, CCM, CPRW; MELBOURNE, FL

VANESSA BLYTHE

276 Wyndham Lane, Unit 10
Tallahassee, FL 32303
(850) 453-1211
E-Mail: vblythe28@prodigy.com

COMPUTER TECHNICIAN
System Set-Up / Repair & Troubleshooting / Networking

PROFILE

- Results-oriented professional with 10 years' experience with computers and software; possess Microsoft Certified Systems Engineer credentials.
- Strong technical troubleshooting and analysis skills balanced with strengths in communication, teamwork, and leadership.
- Key areas of knowledge, training, and experience encompass:

• Networking	• TCP / IP	• Local Area Networks (LAN)
• Windows NT	• Novell Netware Systems	• DOS
• Windows 3.1, 95 / 98	• Internet	• MS Office 97 & Works
• Mac OS	• MS Outlook	• MS Outlook Express
• Software Conversion	• System Upgrades	• Component Level Repair
• Hardware Installation	• Software Installation	• System Integration
• Computer Assembly	• Database Management	• End-User Training

EDUCATION

- **Microsoft Certified Systems Engineer Credentials**, Georgia Institute of Technology, Atlanta, GA
- **A.S. in Computer Engineering**, Manatee Community College, Jonesboro, GA

RELEVANT EXPERIENCE

Field Technician, ARCO Software Systems, Atlanta, GA — 1995 to 2000
Computer Consultant, Contractor, Atlanta, GA — 1997 to 2000
Computer Technician, ENVISION Microsystems, Atlanta, GA —1992 to 1995

- **System Design & Set-Up:** Built computer systems to customer specification for private clients, as field technician and as computer consultant at Atlantic Cellular.
  - Set up computer, forms, and database for Network Video and other private clients.
  - Assessed customer needs, ordered components, assembled computer systems, and installed and configured software and peripherals for ENVISION customers.
  - Installed and configured Mac-based desktop computers in a classroom environment.

- **System Repair & Troubleshooting:** Troubleshot and repaired computers to component and software level, establishing alternative repair procedures to meet customer needs.
  - Performed telephone and on-site troubleshooting for clients as field technician.
  - Performed Y2K system upgrades, and hardware and software upgrades as field technician.

- **Networking:** Set up local area networks for classroom projects.
  - Configured a multi-computer local area network (LAN) using Windows 98 for class project.
  - Learned to manage file systems, storage devices, network servers, and workstations.

Note the skills-based format of the Relevant Experience section, in which all positions are combined.

THOMAS LEMKE

5555 Dove Drive
Citrus Heights, California 95621
tlemke@att.net
(916) 788-9993

Computer Analyst

PROFILE

Over six years' combined experience in advanced computer diagnostics, continuing education, and ability to provide on-site system analysis and service. Effectively troubleshoot and install hardware/software, operating systems, networking strategy and direction. Proven capabilities in:

- Quality Standards
- Commitment and Reliability
- Interpersonal Relations
- Team Building
- Problem Solving
- Customer Service
- Purchasing
- Staff Training
- Business Solutions

TECHNICAL EXPERTISE

- Windows NT, 95, 98
- Technical Support/Service
- On-line Technology
- PC Hardware/Software & Networking
- Basic Integrated Circuit Repair
- Computer Peripherals/Equipment

RELATED EXPERIENCE

ASPER COMPUTER COMPANY, Sacramento, CA   1994 to Present
Field Technician/Lead Technician
Co-manage computer sales, service, and business processes. Assist as resource and problem solver for customers and local businesses to maximize benefit from equipment and applications development (*Holly Cleaners, Sacramento School District, Modular Buildings, Inc.*). Focus on providing a high level of customer service. Troubleshoot a full range of technical issues related to installations by telephone or in person.

Selected Accomplishments
- Supervised and developed highly involved, self-directed technicians.
- Worked closely with on-line technical support to ensure quality installation of hardware, operating systems, and software programs.
- Built strong reputation as Morris High School's resource for diagnosing and analyzing technical problems on the SASI program.
- Consistently planned and completed projects on schedule.

ALDA COMPUTER, Sacramento, CA   1993 to 1994
Manufacturing Associate
Highly motivated participant/team player of 20-member team. Focused on working together in problem solving and decision-making. Maintained safety standards and quality control for each job on production line.

EDUCATION

A+ Service Technician (1998)

Heald Institute of Technology, Sacramento, CA (1998)
Courses: Integrated Circuit Repair and Computer Science

This resume uses a very traditional format and clean typestyle to present quite a bit of information on one page without sacrificing readability. Note the attention-getting headline.

PENELOPE S. RICHARDS
4601 Arlington Drive, Baltimore, MD 21111
Home: (410) 521-4690
E-mail: oraclepro@hotmail.com

SUMMARY OF QUALIFICATIONS

- Computer Specialist with over 8 years' experience in IT / IS.
- Praised by superiors for Oracle expertise, ability to work as a team member and customer responsiveness.
- Proven oral and written communication skills; comfortable delivering presentations to large groups and training both technical and non-technical people in group settings as well as one-on-one.

TECHNICAL SKILLS

- Oracle
- PMRS
- HP900
- SunSparc
- JAM

- Delphi
- Windows 95 / NT
- Novell
- Banyan
- TCP/IP

- Enterprise Technologies 4.0
- MS IIS
- UNIX
- FTP

- TELNET
- ARCServe
- TM1 Database
- ADP

EXPERIENCE

COMPUTER SPECIALIST   **1998 – Present**
Web Hosts Unlimited – Baltimore, MD
Perform system accounts maintenance; change TCP/IP protocols for security purposes and manage IP address changes under Internet Information Server (IIS); maintain active server pages (ASP); provide user support; back up TM1 database using ARCServe Software; and monitor and install all Microsoft patches.

- Served as trouble desk coordinator, traveling on a moment's notice when necessary to provide onsite assistance.
- Wrote a database manual for onsite users to easily enhance the system and troubleshoot/solve problems.
- Recognized for Outstanding Performance.

COMPUTER SPECIALIST   **1994 – 1998**
Market Researchers, Inc. – Washington, DC
Served as Lead Senior Computer Specialist for design, development and implementation of two customized, complex database systems; worked as Lead Database Administrator (DBA) on and off site and trained Assistant DBAs; provided onsite user support in all areas of client/server software installation and upgrades.

- Designed, developed, tested and maintained four Oracle Version 7.3 databases on a SunSparc 2.0 server.
- Created, implemented and maintained forms, reports and program modules using JYACC JAM 6.3.
- Received Outstanding Performance award two years straight.
- Commended by the director for going the extra mile to troubleshoot and de-bug customized software for offsite operations systems.

COMPUTER SPECIALIST   **1991 – 1994**
Onsite Marketing, Inc. – Washington, DC
Provided application software and database support; supervised 16 personnel; installed patches; verified nightly database changes were run and synchronized with Honolulu location; and assisted switching stations with transmission validity.

- Conducted application software training classes for new personnel.
- Participated on the qualification board for personnel as the senior software engineer.
- Recognized with Outstanding Performance award.

EDUCATION

Northern Virginia Community College – Alexandria, Virginia
Computer Technology, Effective Presentation

The heading style in this resume is an attractive way of clearly distinguishing different sections of information. The right margin is justified to complete the clean look.

ANTHONY E. CALAVETTI
1501 Crosswicks Landing • Port Monmouth, NJ 07758 • 732-706-1341
E-mail: acala@aol.com

OBJECTIVE: Position in Technical Support

SUMMARY

- Experience installing and configuring a variety of operating systems, including Windows NT Workstation and Server, Novell Netware, Windows 95, and Windows 3.11.
- Familiar with network management tasks, including user and security administration, file / directory access, and remote access service; experience with TCP/IP and NetBEUI protocols.
- Self-directed, confident professional with effective troubleshooting, customer relations, interpersonal, and leadership skills.
- Strong academic performance (93% grade average) at a highly regarded technical school.
- Entrusted with highly confidential information; security clearance.

O/S: Windows NT Workstation and Server, Novell NetWare 4.11, Windows 95 / 3.1, MS DOS
Applications Software: MS Office 97 (Word, Access, Outlook, Excel, PowerPoint), MS Publisher, Lotus Smart Suite, Rhino, Front Page 2000, CAD Programs
Hardware: IBM-compatible PCs, Hard Drives, CD ROMs, Video Boards, NICs, Multimedia Devices, Printers, and SCSI Devices.

EDUCATION / HONORS

Computer Technical Support Program, 2000 • Computer Institute, Jersey City, NJ • 96% Grade Average
A.S. Business Administration, 1989 • Randall Community College, Randall, NJ

Technical / Leadership Achievements

- Performed network management and administration functions using Windows NT. Set up and managed user accounts, and handled security issues (file / directory access); configured print queues, network printers, and remote access service. Maintained registry profiles for local and roaming users and provided disk administration support.
- Designed an easy-to-navigate Web page for a retail company, using a version of Netscape Composer with limited capabilities; included a home page, product page, and order form, with strong graphics and hyperlinks.
- Installed and configured operating systems and applications.
- Assisted in network cable layout and installation.
- Recognized frequently as a team leader; selected to summarize project work and answer questions.
- Encouraged other students to focus on project objectives and provided technical guidance.

EXPERIENCE

Technical Support Representative, A.N.B., Inc., Irvington, NJ   1999 – Present
Provide hardware and software support for clients of a computer service and retail organization.

- Installed and configured computers and peripherals for clients throughout the Northeast.
- Performed a wide range of troubleshooting and repair work, including hard drive replacement, restoration of files, and video card replacement.
- Set up a peer-to-peer network with 5 workstations.
- Provided explanations for clients and demonstrated appropriate facets of system / software.

Secure Documents Handling Clerk, U.S. Army, VA   1997 – 1999
Entered, maintained, and tracked confidential information on 400+ military personnel, including personal records, achievements, salaries, benefits, and education. Supervised a data entry clerk.

- Reviewed records for accuracy and thoroughness, entered data into computer system, and submitted electronically to superiors for review.
- Instructed 12 trainees in various clerical functions.
- Received 2 awards for outstanding performance.

Administrative Clerk, U.S. Army, SC   1995 – 1997
Performed diverse clerical functions, including data entry, correspondence preparation, and record keeping.

- Assisted with installation of Novell operating system and applications software after a hard drive crash.

This individual has both recent education credentials and relevant work experience, so both are described in detail. Note how the Summary combines both overall qualifications and specific technical skills.

Mathew S. Michaels

417 Bettwork Street ➤ Port Orchard, WA 98366 ➤ 360-874-6519 ➤ pcpro@aol.com

PROFESSIONAL PROFILE

Technical expert with comprehensive knowledge of Computer Information Systems operation and administration. Documented skills in technical systems configuration, installation, maintenance, and repair. Extensive experience in software development. Recognized agency-wide as "go-to-guy" for immediate resolution of critical system problems.

TECHNICAL EXPERIENCE

> Trained in troubleshooting, diagnosis, installation, and modification of networked computer hardware and software components and programs.
> — Hardware: PCs and peripheral equipment
> — Operating Systems: MS-DOS, Windows 95/98/NT, UNIX, Novell, and LAN
> — Software: MS Word, Excel, PowerPoint, and Access

> Format and test system hardware; install operating systems and application software; replace boards; diagnose and correct hardware problems; install peripheral equipment; install PCs on network; install and upgrade hardware, software, and linkages for PC workstations.

> Set up, configure, use, and support Transmission Control Protocol/Internet Protocol. Use Windows utilities for diagnosing problems. Modify host files. Write batch files.

> Use computer-aided diagnostics and digital logic devices to locate malfunctions. Use testing equipment to troubleshoot equipment malfunction to system and board level.

> Provide user support for hardware, software, and operating systems.

SELECTED ACCOMPLISHMENTS

> As LAN Administrator, coordinated LAN consolidation with WAN to provide Internet/intranet access and e-mail capability. Consolidation significantly improved detachment efficiency and effectiveness and reduced system downtime and denial-of-service problems.

> Selected by Commander, Atlantic Submarine Forces, to implement, troubleshoot, and debug new automated inventory program. Successful implementation resulted in incorporation of program on ships fleet-wide.

> Consistently earned awards and accolades throughout career for technical and leadership abilities, including one of four Navy Achievement Medals for directing major Magnetic Disk File repair to missile fire control computer. Repairs allowed nuclear submarine to remain at sea and complete patrol.

COMMUNICATIONS

> Proven record of success working one-on-one with clients to identify and clarify product capabilities and recommend equipment and systems.

> Articulate in oral communications; clear and concise in written communications and technical documentation. Recognized ability to quickly generate trust and develop rapport.

> Professional and personable in demeanor and presentation.

> Successful instructor/trainer with ability to effectively convey technical information in an understandable format.

"...superior technical knowledge and supervisory skills...

...exceptional drive and 'can-do' attitude...

...brings maturity, experience, and technical knowledge to every endeavor...

...demonstrates the initiative, leadership, and drive to achieve exceptional results...

...meticulous administrator...

...possesses a great deal of energy, is highly industrious, and doesn't believe in idle time...

...level-headed and constantly uses sound judgment...

...strongly encourages development of teamwork...

...self-starter whose initiative and leadership skills stand out from his contemporaries..."

- excerpts from
Performance Evaluations

This is an intriguing format in which all employment experience is relegated to page 2, while the first page "sells" the candidate with extensive technical expertise, strong accomplishments, important "soft" skills, and effective testimonials.

Mathew S. Michaels   **Page 2**

CAREER HISTORY

Computer Systems Consultant
The PC Pro, Silverdale, WA   **1998 – Present**
➤ Concurrent to military service, provide consulting services to individuals and businesses on all aspects of computer operations, including:
  — system and component troubleshooting, testing and repair
  — hardware and software upgrades
  — setup of Internet ISP connections
  — networking solutions
  — system assessments and recommendations
➤ Design, write, test, and install software to meet customer requirements.
➤ Maintain and enhance existing system configurations to boost productivity.
➤ Manage all aspects of business: administer budget, monitor finances, process accounts payable/accounts receivable; research and order parts and equipment; develop marketing materials; promote business in local community.

System Administrator
Computer Program Configuration Coordinator
Nuclear Weapons Technical Inspector
Electronics Technician, U.S. Navy, Various Duty Stations   **1975 – Present**
➤ As System Administrator, conduct and oversee configuration, testing, troubleshooting, and maintenance of routers, hubs, switches, cabling, and other LAN equipment for 230-hub intranet system. Perform site surveys and prepare technical solutions for LAN installation and upgrades.
➤ Set up intranet system consisting of two servers and eleven units.
➤ Established, compiled, and managed a computer-based accounting system to automate over 1,400 classified documents, decreasing processing time by 40%.
➤ Troubleshot CPUs and Computer Maintenance Subsystem, preventing loss of training and correcting numerous equipment failures.
➤ Led training and qualification programs for seven diverse training groups. Success documented by numerous Outstanding ratings for major inspections. Student critiques cited instruction as creative, direct, and outstanding.
➤ Managed installation of shipboard security camera system consisting of over 3,500 feet of cable, 11 closed-circuit cameras, and 7 monitors. Authored 85-page system maintenance manual.
➤ Supervised performance of and presented formal training to electronic specialists performing operation, maintenance, and repair of missiles, fire control systems, launcher subsystems, and associated support and test equipment. Planned and conducted corrective maintenance, operation of test equipment, testing and repair of all subsystems and equipment.
➤ Assisted CEO in establishment of Command Management and Equal Opportunity Program.

EDUCATION and CERTIFICATION

1999 – Microsoft Certified System Engineer
1999 – Microsoft Certified Professional + Internet
1998 – Marine Computer Systems Degree (two-year program)
Trident Training Facility, Bangor, WA

TECHNICAL & SUPERVISORY TRAINING

Administering Windows NT 4.0	Digital Computer Basics
Internetworking TCP/IP on NT 4.0	Basic & Advanced Electronics
Windows NT 4.0 Core Technologies	Computer Program Configuration
Supporting Windows NT 4.0	Total Quality Leadership
Creating & Managing Web Server, IIS 4.0	Master Training Specialist
Networking Essentials	Leadership & Supervision

JASON DE MARCO

1030 Saddlehorn Drive
Hendersonville, TN 37075

Home: (615) 555-1097
E-mail: jdemarco@aol.com

A+ CERTIFIED SERVICE TECHNICIAN

Highly skilled technical professional demonstrating knowledge and skill with various PC-based operating systems, networks, and software applications. Trained to support end-users in a Windows environment via telephone and hands-on support. Diagnose and troubleshoot PC and basic network problems. Install and configure software onto individual and networked systems. Set up PCs, printers, modems, monitors, and other ancillary equipment and attach them to networks. An effective communicator with solid professional abilities, a strong work ethic, and a commitment to excellence.

TECHNICAL SKILLS

Operating Systems & Networks
Windows NT – Windows 98, 95, 3.x – DOS (all versions) – LAN

Applications
Expertise with Microsoft Office (Word, Excel, and PowerPoint)
Basic knowledge of Microsoft Access – Lotus 1-2-3 – WordPerfect

ABILITIES

- Help Desk Support / Customer Service
- On-Site Technical Support
- Installation / Configuration
- Troubleshooting / Repair

CERTIFICATIONS

A+ Service Technician Certification – August 1999
Career Blazers Learning Center – Delray Beach, Florida

PC Applications – May 1999
Edward Ross Career & Employment Institute – Deerfield Beach, Florida

EDUCATION

Degree Program: Associate of Applied Science (45 credit hours) – 1993 to 1996
Broward Community College – Fort Lauderdale, Florida

WORK EXPERIENCE

Computer Technician – 1999 to Present
Wireless Innovations – Nashville, Tennessee

- Perform troubleshooting, repairs, and upgrades for company's LAN system.
- Provide on-site software training and technical support to end-users using Windows 98, MS Word, and MS Excel.

Route Salesman – 1990 to 1999
Blanding Brothers – Fort Lauderdale, Florida

- Serviced commercial accounts, primarily supermarkets, delis, and convenience stores.
- Prepared daily log to track inventory, sales, collections, and payment receipts.

This individual successfully transitioned from a nontechnology sales job to a computer technician position and is ready for advancement. His resume highlights his solid and current technical skills.

RESUME 11: ANN BAEHR, CPRW; BRENTWOOD, NY

1159 Danlette Drive
North Bridge, NY 11703

EVAN FLANDERS

(631) 008-4000
eflanders229@aol.com

A+ Certified Technician seeking to expand career within the information technology arena

B.A. degree in Economics, continuing education in Information Technology, and a combination of technical and diversified administrative experience gained over ten years in positions of increased responsibility

Select strengths encompass . . .

Project Management / Help Desk Support / End-user Training / PC/LAN Service and Support
Systems Integration / Sales and Marketing / Procedural Documentation / Business and Technical Problem Resolution / Inventory Control / Procurement / Vendor Relations / Client Needs Assessment / Cost Management

PROFESSIONAL EXPERIENCE

PC/LAN Technician   1999 – 2001
FINANCIALLY SOUND, INC. (FSI), Merlin, NY

Technical Support

- Successfully rolled out NT 4.0/Windows 95 Workgroups and newly developed FSI software to 80 nationally based branch locations
- Installed and configured 50 NT workstations at Dallas branch office, providing comprehensive post-installation support including client training and provision of procedural documentation
- Attached corporate personnel to Novell and NT Network; performed scheduled network tape backups
- Provided remote and on-site end-user support on a broad scope of hardware/software problems and printing/network connectivity issues; delivered effective training and practical solutions
- Developed MIS procedural documentation to streamline and optimize departmental/company-wide workflow
- Built and maintained workstations and laptops; replaced and upgraded various peripherals and components
- Restored files utilizing Backup Exec and ARCserve for Netware and Windows NT
- Proficiently utilized diagnostic tools to assess and troubleshoot hardware and software performance to sustain the effective use of existing and newly implemented systems technology
- Retrieved borrower-related data for underwriters and processors through access of WAN and PC Anywhere

Office Management

- Sourced and negotiated with resale vendors, achieving total cost savings of $25,000 in license renewal fees for first and second quarters of 2000
- Handled all aspects of MIS cost center and inventory control at the corporate and company-wide level with direct responsibility for distribution of accurate and timely documentation to all impacted departments
- Created batch files to automate pulling of monthly pipeline reports for senior management review
- Maintained and updated equipment tracking data for accounting and reporting functions
- Supervised and maintained company-wide user activity to ensure the integrity of multiple licensing software

— continued —

The select strengths section combines with the technical skills summary on page 2 to create a strong "key word summary" for this individual.

EVAN FLANDERS
Page 2 of 2

ADDITIONAL WORK HISTORY

HH GROUP, Woodland, NY 1994 – 1999
New Accounts / Parts Administrator

RECOVERY HOME SYSTEMS, Centralville, NY 1991 – 1994
Administrative Assistant

COMPUTER / NETWORKING SKILLS

Operating Systems: Windows 98/95/3.x; Novell 3.x/4.x; NT 4.0 Workstation; MS-DOS 6.22

Protocols/Networks: TCP/IP, NetBEUI, IPX/SPX, Ethernet 10/100Base-T

Hardware: Hard drives, printers, scanners, fax/modems, CD-ROMs, Zip drives, Cat5 cables, hubs, NIC cards

Software:

Commercial:

Microsoft Office Modules, FileMaker Pro,
PC Anywhere, Norton/McAfee Anti-Virus, Ghost,
MS Exchange, ARCserve, Artisoft ModemShare

Industry-specific:

e-Credit, ICC Credit, Energizer, Midanet, Flood Link,
Greatland Escrow, Allregs, Echo Connection Plus,
Contour (Handler, Closer, Tracker and LP Module)

EDUCATION

CAREER CENTER, Garden Grove, NY
Fall 2001 enrollment: MCSE Windows 2000 Track

Completed Coursework, 2000-2001
Windows 98 and 95 / MS-DOS 6.22
Networking Technologies / Windows NT Workstation 4.0
Microcomputers I & II / PC rebuilding, upgrading, and repairing

THE UNIVERSITY AT OLD WESTERN TOWN, Old Western Town, NY
Bachelor of Arts, Economics, 1998
Graduated with honors — GPA 3.77

CENTER COMMUNITY COLLEGE, Bendwood, NY
Associate of Arts, Liberal Arts and Science, 1992
Graduated with honors — GPA 3.5

LICENSES / CERTIFICATIONS

A+ Certified Technician

New York State Notary Public

DALWIN E. TOOLMAN

1000 Court Place – Tyler, Texas 75700
(903) 999-8888 – dtoolman@etin.net

COMPUTER SYSTEMS TECHNICIAN / SPECIALIST

Utilizing cutting-edge technology and state-of-the-art components to build superior systems to meet needs.

▶ Highly efficient **COMPUTER SYSTEM SPECIALIST** with comprehensive knowledge and technical expertise in **PC fabrication, configuration, system networking, diagnostic testing, malfunction identification and repair.** Excellent **customer relations / service.**

▶ Proficiency in **surfing Internet** to **locate vendors** and **negotiate highest quality for lowest cost.**

▶ Customer satisfaction- and **challenge-driven.** Exemplary **integrity** and **work ethic.**

Hardware Installation	Operating Systems / Software Applications
PCs through Pentium III / K6 MMX/K6-3 3D	Windows 98 / 95 / OSR-2B2.5 / 3.x / DOS
Palm Pilots – Speaker Phones	MS-Office (Word, Access, Excel, PowerPoint)
Monster 3D Add-On Video Cards	Works – Outlook Express – Money – Encarta
Network Cards – Sound Cards	Publisher – Freelance Graphics – Adobe Photomaker
RAM and Video Memory	iPhoto Plus 4 – Lview Pro – Cheyenne Bitware
Multiple Hard Drives – Floppy Drives	Lotus 1-2-3 – Quicken – Turbo-Tax – Tax-Cut
Tape Drives – CD-ROM – CD-R	Parsons Personal Tax Edge – MS Internet Explorer
Printer / Parallel / USB / Mouse Ports	Netscape Communicator – Navigator – Eudora
Serial / Cable Connections – Modems	ICQ – Cute FTP – HTML (Web Page Design)
Power Supplies – Cooling Fans	Norton – Check-It – WinCheckIt Pro – Dr. Hardware
BIOS Upgrades – Batteries – Scanners	Ontrack E-Z Drive Diagnostics – Wintune – WinBench

PROFESSIONAL EXPERIENCE

A-OK COMPUTER — Tyler, Texas (1997 - Present)
Owner / Computer Technician

▶ Founded and progressed viable computer business from ground floor, managing all aspects of business.

▶ Establish trusting relationships with customers, provide high-quality, low-cost service, and "go beyond the call of duty" to ensure total customer satisfaction. Make service calls throughout East Texas.

▶ Build computer systems from shell up. Install, identify malfunctions through extensive diagnostics, and repair all types of components for multilevel systems through Pentium III/K6 MMX/K6-3 3D/Cyrix MII.

▶ Search the Internet to locate vendors and successfully negotiate lowest cost for highest quality.

▶ Frequently receive client kudos, such as: **"excellent service," "persistence to make it right," "honest/ fair."**

SPORTSMAN'S DEN TAXIDERMY / FISH CLONES — Tyler, Texas (1987-1997)
Owner / Manager

▶ Founded and built successful taxidermy business from ground level; hired, trained, and supervised up to five employees.

▶ Instructed seminars and judged competitions throughout the U.S.; served as board member / vice president of TTA.

▶ **Won over 140 state, regional, and national awards for excellence in taxidermy art.**

▶ One of eight in nation **certified by National Taxidermy Association in <u>all</u> categories** in 1995.

▶ One of **first in state of Texas** to achieve **"State Award of Excellence."**

This resume is visually appealing due to its appropriate graphic and triangle-shaped bullets. Note the "kudos" quoted in the final bullet point of the most recent position.

CHARLES SALONGO

2741 East Broadway
Phoenix, AZ 85048

(480) 555-0000
cslecky@home.com

SUMMARY OF QUALIFICATIONS

- Experienced Field Engineer with strong business, marketing, and customer service background, coupled with experience in troubleshooting, installing, and repairing electrical and electronic systems. Proficient in:

▸ System Installation	▸ System Development
▸ IS Service / Support Management	▸ System Troubleshooting
▸ Client Relations / Support	▸ End User Training

- Extensive technical hardware and software background, with ability to independently master new software and hardware, initiate troubleshooting process, and solve variety of technical support issues.
- Expertise in network design, configuration, and integration. Ability to assist in all facets of hardware and software conversion, including customization, support, cabling, training, and installation.
- Reliable member of team organization, assessing problems and system requirements, developing effective solutions to meet end user needs. Network with other computer experts via Internet regarding hardware and software problems.
- Education in Computer Science, with 3000 hours lab and theory training.

TECHNICAL EXPERIENCE

Systems:	Windows 98 & NT	Novell	IBM Platforms — AS400, RS6000
	DOS	UNIX	PC with Pentium Processor
	ZENIX / AIX	AS1 Series	Tiger
Software:	Corel Suite 2000	PC Anywhere	Penbase / PenDirect
	Microsoft Office 2000	Lotus Notes	Internet Browser / Plug-Ins
Certification:	Novel Certification, System Solutions, Tempe, Arizona — 1996		

PROFESSIONAL EXPERIENCE

Service Engineer — MYRIAD COMPUTER, Phoenix, Arizona — 1995 to Present
- Analyze and assess problems; recommend hardware, software, and office integration; determine use to make relevant recommendations on upgrading and networking, using LAN/WAN networks and out-of-office connectivity as appropriate.
- Train clients in all aspects of system, from basic instruction in operating hardware to more complex software applications.
- Purchase computer components, maintain and control inventory levels, and implement cost controls to ensure profitability.

Field Engineer — FIBERMESH SYSTEMS (Division of Visys, Inc.), Phoenix, Arizona — 1992 to 1995
- Served as primary contact for technical support to client base of 90 medical and 60 commercial clients. Supplied full integration between MS-DOS, Windows, and UNIX.
- Supported / operated 10BaseT, Ethernet, and personal computers for up to 700 end users and devices.

Field Engineer — HVM CORPORATION, Phoenix, Arizona — 1990 to 1992
- Developed and integrated electronic alarm control system designs and programs for gas distribution networks per client requirements.
- Installed diffusion equipment in U.S. and Mexico. Experience included diffusion furnaces, temperature / pressure indicators and controllers, relay / solenoid control, and programmable logic controllers integrated into Novell network for controlled shutdowns.

EDUCATION

Associate's Degree — Electronics Technology — 1990
LONG TECHNICAL COLLEGE, Phoenix, Arizona

The extensive Summary of Qualifications sells this candidate with a list of key words along with both an experience summary and "soft skills."

DON G. SHELLEY

65 Lake Green Circle ~ Stafford, TX 77477
Home: (281) 992-0663 ~ Office: (713) 565-4999 ~ dgs1159@mccn.net

NETWORK / PC TECHNICIAN

More than 10 years of broad-based experience encompassing installation, upgrades, troubleshooting, configuration, support and maintenance of third-party software applications, hardware, servers and workstations. Skilled at determining company and end-user requirements and designing architecture to meet or exceed those requirements. Effective leadership and training skills combined with extensive technical expertise. Highly organized, with the ability to efficiently manage projects and resources.

Competencies:

TROUBLESHOOTING, ANALYSIS & RESOLUTION ~ IMPLEMENTATION PLANNING & MANAGEMENT
END-USER TRAINING ~ SYSTEM UPGRADES ~ DATABASE ADMINISTRATION ~ IT PURCHASING
STAFF SUPERVISION & TRAINING ~ EXPENSE TRACKING & CONTROL ~ VENDOR RELATIONS

TECHNICAL SKILLS

Hardware: All relevant hardware, including LAN cards and Bay Networks switches, as well as fiber optic connections and network printers

Networks: Microsoft NT 4.0, NetWare 4.1

Operating Systems: Windows 95/98/2000/NT 4.0, NetWare 4.1, DOS 6.22

Software: Primavera Project Manager, Metaframe Citrix Software, Microsoft Office Suite, Aspen Plus Simulation Software, Bridge by Kemma, EPOCH, Engineer's Aid, Microsoft Exchange 5.5, Visio, Enterprise Administrator, Weather View 32, Performance 2000, WordPerfect 2000, Imagecast, Sybase SQL Anywhere, Visual Fortran 6.0

PROFESSIONAL EXPERIENCE

MODERN INFORMATION SYSTEMS – Houston, TX   1994 to Present
(Contracted to Sitico Chemical Corporation)

PC / Application Technician

Sole on-site technician with full accountability for hardware, software and network support for a manufacturing plant with 300 end users. Provide NetWare 4.1 system administration to include installations, maintenance, upgrades, troubleshooting and support for servers, fiber optics, printers, software applications and all workstations running Windows for Workgroups.

Manage installation and upgrade project schedules and work closely with management to control project risks involving schedule, technical issues and personnel. Communicate with vendors and suppliers to purchase parts and coordinate warranty service. Provide training to system users and new technicians. Set up and maintain individual user and group accounts. Work closely with Help Desk to ensure all issues are quickly resolved and to maintain optimal system performance.

- Managed the successful migration and data transfer from LAN Manager to NetWare 4.1 with no loss in productivity.
- Planned and managed migration project from NetWare to Windows NT.

This is a traditional, comprehensive resume for an experienced professional. Two full pages are devoted to his 15-year career. The Competencies listing and the Technical Skills section are effective key word listings.

DON G. SHELLEY ~ PAGE 2

PROFESSIONAL EXPERIENCE
(continued)

COMPUTER INNOVATIONS – Houston, TX   1993 to 1994
(A local computer manufacturer)

Service and Production Manager

Tested and troubleshot hardware and software problems of completed systems and corrected deficiencies in assembly or manufacturing. Supervised, scheduled and trained 20 technicians. Scheduled production, work flow and customer repairs to ensure a high level of customer satisfaction. Maintained and updated two Novell networks.

- Created database for tracking parts and service, which allowed for more efficient repairs and improved customer service.

JLM COMPUTERS INC. – Houston, TX   1989 to 1993
(A national computer manufacturer)

PC Evaluation and Test Engineer

Evaluated all new computer systems and internal peripherals before shipment to mass merchants such as Sam's Club and Wal-Mart. Supervised 14 production personnel. Provided installation, maintenance and support for systems at administrative offices. Installed and configured Microsoft's HCT (Hardware Compatibility Testing) on all systems to ensure complete compatibility with JLM systems. Installed EDI (Electronic Data Interface) to allow for more efficient and accurate communication with trading partners. Maintained current knowledge of major hardware and software manufacturers and technology changes.

TETRAMAX, INC. – San Jose, CA   1986 to 1988
(A plastics manufacturer specializing in fluorocarbons)

Process Engineer

Created and administered databases for all materials, log numbers and material properties for the Isostatic Molding Research and Development department. Interfaced all C.N.C. machines to a common terminal. Created bar and chart graphs to exhibit control limits for major companies such as Lockheed, Boeing and Hughes. Oversaw R&D development of the Isostatic molding process in order to improve material properties.

- Designed and built first machine on the West Coast to skive six-foot wide Tetrafluroethylene.

TRAINING

NETWARE 4.1 ADMINISTRATION – certificate

NT 4.0 WORKSTATION – certificate

MICROSOFT EXCHANGE SERVER – certificate

Please keep this inquiry confidential at this time.

ADAM TYLER, Austel Licensed No. 55555

220 Citizen Street, PCVILL 2615 ACT • 0404 555 555 • (02) 5555 5555 • adam@adam.com.au

"I can honestly say that Adam would be in the top 5 percent of people I have offered positions to and by far, the best installer/technician." Manager's Reference

Telecommunications/IT installation specialist with 9+ years' experience troubleshooting faults, installing systems and components, laying cables, restoring services, and refining technical expertise throughout. Poised for leading technician or supervisory role, where client interaction is integral to ongoing client retention and satisfaction.

- Cited by management for demonstrating high-level, enthusiastic customer service and willingness to achieve time-critical deadlines — resulting in increased productivity and business revenues.
- Exceptional track record for quality, safety, and team leadership.

KEY STRENGTHS

High-level technical competencies.
Install, repair, diagnose, and troubleshoot:
- Personal Computers & Networks
- Telecommunications Cables
- Security Systems
- Printers & Scanners
- Software
- Plotters
- Modems

Articulate in communicating problems and solutions to people at all levels. Noted for:
- Customer Relations Attitude
- Intuitive Hardware/Software Support
- Team Leadership/Team Building
- Rapid Conflict Resolution
- Safety & Quality Compliance
- Productivity in Deadline-Dependent Environments

QUALIFICATIONS & ADVANCED TRAINING

AUSTEL CABLING LICENSE (General Premises), *Australian Telecommunications Authority*

QUALIFIED ELECTRONIC SECURITY INSTALLER, *Australian Institute of Technology*

PROFESSIONAL EXPERIENCE

HEAD INSTALLER/NO. 1 TECHNICIAN, *ICU Home Security*   1998–May 2001

Installed, tested, maintained, and serviced security systems in domestic dwellings across Canberra. Despite no previous experience in this industry, attained security installer's certificate and was elevated to leadership role in recognition of technical expertise, thoroughness, and customer-focused communication style.

- Frequently requested to contribute fault-finding expertise on troublesome or complex project assignments; quickly gained reputation for ability to identify persistent and elusive faults.
- Instructed new customers on the use, operation, features, and benefits of security systems; shared information on emergency procedures, company policy, servicing schedules, and routine equipment care.
- Contributed to business revenues by recommending extended warranties and maintenance plans.

"Adam's honesty, integrity, work ethic, organization and people skills are to be envied by most…his workmanship has always matched his own personal high standards…this office constantly receives mail from Adam's clients heralding his praises." Reference Excerpt from Manager, ICU Home Security

FIELD ENGINEER, *Tekkoworld*   Feb 93–Feb 98

Hands-on technical role installing, configuring, and troubleshooting personal computers and peripherals (printers, scanners, plotters, modems). Established outstanding customer relationships, acquiring business-wide reputation for strengths in resolving the most complex of technical challenges.

"We found Adam to be responsive, efficient and meticulous in all his work activities. Indeed one of his skills lies in the rapport he had with our customers." Reference Excerpt from Managing Director, Tekkoworld

REFERENCES — AVAILABLE UPON REQUEST

"Because his hands-on work was repetitive (he installed only telecommunication cables and security systems), it was important that we get across his broader skills. He'd been cited frequently for his customer service focus, which would be a real selling point as a team leader where he'd have quite a bit of customer contact to 'put out the fires'—therefore, that's what I focused on."

KAMARRA E. MAHON

202 MAIN STREET • GRAHAM, NC 27253 • (336) 227-9095 • 1MAHON@TREX.NET

IT SUPPORT – ACADEMIC ENVIRONMENT

PROFILE

Technical Skills

- Hardware/software configuration, support and service
- System installation and networking (LAN)
- Multiuser Interface
- Operating Systems – Mac OS 9, Windows 95, 98, 2000
- Applications – AppleWorks, MS Office 98 for Mac, Adobe PhotoShop 5.0, PageMaker 6.5+, InDesign, MS Office Professional 2000 (Word, Excel, Access, PowerPoint, Publisher, Outlook), ACT!, WordPerfect, Draw 9, CAD
- Working on Network+ certification

Sales and Public Relations

- Key account management
- Client and vendor relationship development
- Detail and outside sales
- Problem solving, complaint resolution
- Trade shows, presentations and special events

Human Resources

- Hired, trained and supervised sales and technical staff
- Understand compensation, incentives, and benefits issues

Personal Strengths

- Self-motivated and dedicated
- Multitask oriented, versatile, and adaptable
- Quick and avid learner
- Organized and flexible
- Professional and diplomatic

EDUCATION

Alamance Community College, Graham, North Carolina
Currently enrolled in college transfer program

Newport University, Newport, Virginia
Completed 1 year in Computer Engineering curriculum
GPA 3.9

Oakville Community College, Chicago, Illinois
Associate of Arts degree, Space Planning
GPA 3.8

RELEVANT EXPERIENCE

COLLEGE AND UNIVERSITY COMPUTERS, INC.
Tanner College, Mason, North Carolina   01/99 - 08/00
Computer Store Manager (06/99 - 08/00)
Primary liaison with Tanner College IT Department. Acquired major accounts through outside sales efforts in addition to in-store sales and operations. Performed market research and sales forecasting, budget development, administration, and oversaw compliance. Achieved sales, margin, and inventory targets and minimized loss. Created and designed advertising communications, promotions, incentives, and special events. Served as service manager/technician responsible for hardware/software installations and repairs.
- Concurrent responsibility for new site development, build-out, budgeting and product line rationalization
- Co-authored store operations manual and new store set-up manual

Marketing Assistant (1/99 - 6/99)
Collaborated with a Marketing and Sales Team on projects including brochures, flyers, advertising, promotions, web development and trade shows.
- Developed a wide variety of multimedia promotional materials

Other Experience

THE GUILD HALL OF WILLIAMSBURG
Williamsburg, Virginia   07/96 - 05/98
Executive Assistant
Designed an inventory control system to track purchasing, receiving, on-hand inventory and P&L. Supervised receiving department. Project planning, development, implementation, and management. Hands-on administrative support activities.
- Restructured operations and wrote manual for receiving and front-end procedures
- Wrote job descriptions; retrained employees on new policies and procedures

HOMEBASE
Lacey and Vancouver, Washington   01/94 - 07/96
Interior Design Specialist

PREFERRED CARE NETWORK, INC.
Lincolnwood, Illinois   01/86 - 12/93
Client Relations Assistant

"Using this resume, my client got an interview with a school system that has a new Information Technology department that services the entire school system's network. She is an 'uneducated genius' who recently returned to school to get her degree in IT."

RESUME 17: DIANE BURNS, CPRW, CCM; COLUMBIA, MD

James M. Pantell

3409 Blue Tree Drive, Baltimore, MD 21047
Tel: 410.555-5555   Email: JMP@yahoo.com

Information Technology & Information Systems Technician
Clearance: TS/SCI

Certified through Microsoft: MCSE, MCP & MCP+I
Certified through Novell: CNA and CNE (Netware 4 & 5)
CISCO Certified Network Associate

Skilled Communications Technician incorporating fourteen years' in-depth knowledge of complex Communications, Computer, Network, Digital Imagery Processing, and local and worldwide Intelligence systems. Highly skilled with scores of network operating systems, hardware, software, networks, servers, workstations, LAN, WAN, fiber optics, and a wide variety of attached peripherals from military, commercial, and proprietary manufacturers.

Full scope of responsibilities include installation, integration, configuring, diagnostic testing, repair, and maintenance of systems, servers, fiber optic termination, worldwide data communications, Cisco routers, workstations, mainframes, digital, satellite, multiplexers, and cryptographic equipment.

Skills

Systems Administrator	Satellite Communications Systems	Encryption Equipment
Systems Analyst	Technical Hardware Support	Technical Authority
Secure Systems		Troubleshooting

Professional Experience

Bell Atlantic, Baltimore, MD   1995 to Present
Systems Field Representative (Europe)

- Currently participating in the implementation and administration of a Top Secret Windows NT 4 network integrated with the in-place UNIX environment.
- Manage baselining and daily desktop maintenance of Secret and Unclassified Windows NT 4 networks.
- Install and maintain Sun Enterprise Servers and Sun StorEdge storage devices, Sun workstations, and many personal computers. Plan and install fiber optics, Thinnet, and Cat 5 cabling.
- Efficiently provide residential, on-call, and deployed maintenance support throughout Europe. Maintain an extensive knowledge of complex U.S. military Command, Control, Communications, Computer, and Intelligence Systems. Conduct troubleshooting and maintenance on a wide variety of systems and provide technical hardware support.

Science of Computers International, Germany   1990 to 1995
Systems Administrator

- Provided technical support to four distinct networks (Novell NetWare 3.x, 4.x, and Microsoft Windows NT 4.x) utilizing three different Network Operating Systems (NOS) supporting classified and unclassified Local Area Networks (LANs).
- Conducted systems analysis on the networks, servers, and workstations. As a member of critical integration team, installed and configured new hardware and software into existing networks. Conducted a full range of testing and analysis of the compatibility of new and old components, configurations, functionality, and expandability, ensuring full support for the new system.

In this resume, extensive lists of technical training and proficiencies are relegated to page 2 to allow the individual's high-level experience to shine on page 1. Note the brief "a short list" notation under Technical Training; this is an effective way to convey only the highlights.

James M. Pantell, Page 2

Bell Atlantic, Baltimore, MD   1985 to 1990
Field Service Representative (Europe)

- Installed, integrated, and conducted diagnostic testing and repair at the European Node of the Joint Worldwide Communication System (JWCS). The system included secure high-speed data communications and simultaneous Video-Teleconferencing.
- Installed, tested, and repaired communication circuits and maintenance of three separate Video-Teleconferencing studios.
- Precisely calculated and ensured that the sparing level for the system was properly maintained.
- Installed and terminated fiber optic cables, Sun workstations and servers, and Cisco routers.
- Installed and administered several NET IDNX 20/70/90 Digital Exchanges for worldwide data communications.
- Instrumental in the critical installation and integration of an Ethernet LAN and ATM connecting over 150 Sun workstations.
- Ensured the security of highly classified materials by installing, testing, and repairing encryption devices.
- Managed a team responsible for installation, integration, testing, and repair of a prototype Sun-based classified message handling system. Ensured continuous, uninterrupted networks.

Education

A.A. in Computer Studies, Central Texas College, 1998

Technical Training

A short list

- *Certified through Comp TIA: Network+ Certification, 2000*
- *Certified through CISCO: CISCO Certified Network Associate, 2000*
- *Certified through Microsoft: MCSE, MCP, & MCP+I, 1999*
- *Certified through Novell: CNA 4 and CNE 4, 1997; CAN 5 and CNE 5, 1990*
- Windows NT Network Training, 1998
- Novell NetWare 4.1 Administration & Advance Administration, 1996
- Novell Service and Support & 4.1 Design and Implementation, 1996
- Novell NetWare 4 Installation and Configuration Workshop, 1996
- Fiber Optic Installation and Termination, 1995
- Cryptologic Equipment Limited Maintenance, 1995
- Rembrandt II/VP Maintenance and Operations, 1995
- IDNX 20/70/90 Installation, Operation and Maintenance, 1995
- LAN Cabling Systems, 1995

Computer Proficiencies

Software: Microsoft Office Suite, Novell GroupWise, Microsoft Exchange, Microsoft Exchange Server, Visio 5

Operating Systems: Microsoft Windows 95, 98, NT 4.0; Novell NetWare 3.xx, 4.xx, 5

Hardware Families: Sun Microsystems, SPARCstation 20, Ultra 1,2,5,10,30,60, SPARCserver 1000, Sun Enterprise Servers 450, Cisco Systems (2500, 4000, 7000, 7500 series routers), Catalyst 5500 Series Switch, Compaq, Proliant 6000 Servers, Network Equipment Technologies, IDNX 20/70/90

CHAPTER 5

Resumes for Computer Systems Professionals

- Computer Programmers
- Applications Programmers
- Programmer Analysts
- Systems Analysts
- Database Designers
- Database Administrators
- Software Engineers
- Systems Engineers

RESUME 18: ANN STEWART, CPRW; ROANOKE, TX

BRENT D. BOATMAN

1836 Tameria Drive, Dallas, TX 75234 · (214) 251-3415 · bboatman@texas.net

---

Game Programmer

C/C++	Open GL	Nintendo 64
Win32 API	3D Graphics	Nintendo Dolphin
MFC	AI	Sega Dreamcast
DirectX SDK	Console Development	Sony PlayStation 2
Assembly		Microsoft X-Box

PROFESSIONAL EXPERIENCE

1998 – 2000 **Koala Game Studio · Dallas, Texas**
Developer and publisher of entertainment software
Console Game Programmer

- Participated as a graphics programmer on a cross-functional development team that published a highly successful leading-edge sports game for Nintendo 64 and Sega Dreamcast. Recognized for strong individual contribution and emerging technical leadership.
- Represented company on team partnered with Microsoft that successfully resolved software incompatibility issues inhibiting game's development.
- Currently creating leading-edge graphics technology for next-generation platforms (Sony PlayStation 2, Microsoft X-Box, Nintendo Dolphin).

Manager's Comments: "very hard worker" ... "goes above and beyond to meet schedule" ... "instrumental in Nintendo 64/Sega Dreamcast versions of game" ... "very high-quality work."

1997 – 1998 **University of North Texas · Denton, Texas**
Computer Science Department
Student Intern

- Helped design and code an educational game under a research grant; incorporated graphics, sound, and network play into game.
- Assisted professor in innovative computer game development lab.

EDUCATION **University of North Texas · Denton, Texas**
Bachelor of Science, 1998
Major: Computer Science
Minor: Mathematics

Attended PlayStation 2 Developers' Conference, 2000

This resume is distinguished by the box design that sets off the technical skills and the manager's comments included under the most recent experience.

RESUME 19: JACQUI BARRETT DODSON, CPRW; OVERLAND PARK, KS

JUAN RONDON

1901 Pleasant Lane • Liberty, Missouri 64068 • 816-555-5555 Cell: 816-555-5123
jrondon@hotmail.com

SUMMARY OF QUALIFICATIONS

➢ Background in analysis, development and delivery of high-performance technology solutions
➢ Experienced administrator in Microsoft Back Office Server environment
➢ Readily adapt to new technology via education and implementation experience
➢ Maintain a consultative approach in business-to-business environments
➢ Exceptional relationship-building skills in communicating with all levels, front line to CEO
➢ Possess project planning expertise that propels smooth project delivery

INFORMATION TECHNOLOGY EXPERIENCE / KNOWLEDGE

Language / Development:	• SQL	• MS Access	• Visual Basic
Operating Systems:	• Windows NT	• Windows 98	
Packages:	• Microsoft Office		
Certification:	• Microsoft Solutions Development, 2001		

PROFESSIONAL EXPERIENCE

PREMIERE CONTRACTING, Kansas City, Missouri   10/97 - Present
$8 million roadway / parking lot striping company

Database Administrator / Project Manager

Notable Accomplishments:
• In collaboration with general manager, originated MS Access estimating database that was implemented office-wide, expanding estimating capabilities from one workstation to *all* workstations.
   Results:
   ➢ Slashed estimate production by 15 minutes per estimate, saving over 250 hours per year.
   ➢ Streamlined accounting reporting procedures to create instant accessibility to reports.
• Tagged as administrator for Microsoft Back Office Server that was implemented in 1/2000.
   ➢ Researched, purchased and instituted server and software and maintain smooth operations for multiple offices.
• Negotiated $546,000 in sales in 1999, delivering a 35% sales and 7% profit increase over prior year.

Responsibilities:
• Estimate / negotiate new projects for construction industry through plan take-off and site visits.
• Oversee 85% of company's total jobs (360+ jobs of 420 total) per year.
• Manage idea to implementation project scope: budgeting, hiring, job scheduling, vendor negotiations and customer communications.
• Supervise 3 foremen and 9 laborers in day-to-day project tasks; interface with construction companies, property owners / managers, estimators, project managers and field superintendents.
• Troubleshoot and resolve accounts receivable issues through tenacious follow-up.

SKY HIGH RENTALS, Evergreen, Colorado   5/95 - 10/97
Manager

EDUCATION

Bachelor of Science in Computer Science, 5/95: University of Missouri — Kansas City
• **Self-financed 100%** of tuition and living expenses

This resume is so attractive and easy to read due to a combination of formatting techniques—the boxed table, bold headings, and two bullet types. These techniques are also an effective way to make the Times New Roman font used for most of the resume look less "ordinary."

RESUME 20: LAURA A. DECARLO, CCM, CPRW; MELBOURNE, FL

TANYA KIRKPATRICK

578 14th Street, #3
Tampa, FL 33609

(813) 967-1408
tanya.kirk@browsenet.com

PROGRAMMER / SOFTWARE ENGINEER

PROFILE OF QUALIFICATIONS

Cited as *"a keen technical intellect who consistently makes the grade through innovation and the perfect eye for finding coding flaws."* - Jerry Drake, Director

- Results-oriented software engineer who adapts easily to requirements in mainframe and PC application development.
- Consistently commended for ability to work as a team member or independently while achieving critical deadlines. Strong project leader.
- Recognized for performance and project contributions. Consistently achieve highest rating in annual evaluations for top 2% of total company personnel.

TECHNICAL APPLICATIONS

- Programming Languages: C, C++, COBOL, SQL, CICS, Lotus Notes application development, FORTRAN, C-Shell, Java, HSPICE and Matlab.
- Platforms: Windows NT, Unix, OS/2, Windows 95 and Windows 98.
- Software: MS Word, Excel, PowerPoint and Access; various other programs.
- Experienced in developing Graphical User Interfaces (GUIs).

EDUCATION & TRAINING

B.S. in Computer Information Systems, University of South Florida, Tampa, FL
- Courses: **Coding for Tomorrow, Java, SQL and Images, Copyrights and the Web**

PROFESSIONAL EXPERIENCE

Senior Programmer, Carco Corporation, Orlando, FL - 1994 to Present
Performed multifaceted programming and analysis from code development through acceptance testing on a number of projects.

- Developed special applications in C++ to customize office business systems.
  - Enhanced existing software subsystems to accommodate new requirements.

- Developed a graphical user interface (GUI) for an analog design automation tool in a Unix environment.

  - Interface communicated with a range of C programs to transfer input parameters provided by user and to display programs' output on the screen.

Software Analyst and Programmer I, Carco Corporation, Orlando, FL - 1992 to 1994

- Analyzed all company-designed software programs for Y2K compliance.
- Led a consulting team in the analysis of customer operating systems and software applications. Made suggestions for software changes and customization to existing programs.

The attractive boxed headline and excellent testimonial are strong lead-ins to this resume.

JEFFREY J. VANBEEK

555 – 200 Masters Road West
Augusta, Ontario A2B 2B2

Phone: (905) 555-6666
Email: vanbeek@imail.com

Profile

Highly motivated and enthusiastic **IT professional** with proven experience in both team and project management capacities. Outstanding analysis, programming and debugging capabilities. Ability to work autonomously and as a team player, with demonstrated strengths in leadership and mentoring situations. Easily adaptable to change, with an eagerness toward learning and expanding capabilities. Industry expertise includes:

- **2D / 3D Graphing**
- **Speech Recognition**
- **Geometry Management**
- **Taxation Software**

Languages

C++, C, Visual C++, MFC, ATL, ASP, Java, COM, Windows SDK, Visual Basic, Delphi

Experience

C++ / ActiveX Template Library / Microsoft Foundation Classes / COM / ASP

1998 - Present

TECHNICAL PROJECT MANAGER — XYZ Group Inc., Augusta, Ontario

- Managed programmers, technical writers and release engineers from design and implementation through testing and delivery during several major release cycles.
- Produced charting and geometry management components for Windows developers.
- Researched and prototyped geometry management tool based on design by Chief Technology Officer.
- Led development of an ASP version of the charting components.
- Provided estimates and technical expertise to sales force to develop and close source code deals and arrange custom consulting work.

Visual C++ / Windows SDK / Microsoft Foundation Classes

1996 - 1998

SENIOR SPEECH RECOGNITION PROGRAMMER — VoiceTech Inc., Augusta, Ontario

- Used C++, MFC and Windows SDK to build a natural language interface to office productivity tools such as Microsoft Word, WordPerfect and Lotus 1-2-3.
- Controlled office tools through programmable APIs while processing speech input from programs such as Dragon Dictate and IBM ViaVoice.
- Highlight was VoiceMate for the Internet, which allowed control of Internet browsers, including Netscape, by voice control.

1996

SENIOR PROGRAMMER — Rybena Corporation, Pinehurst, Ontario

- Developed photo-realistic desktop communications centre using Visual C++, MFC and SDK.
- Mentored team members in MFC and debugging skills.
- Interacted with internal QA and usability groups to design and improve components.

continued...

This resume uses the attractive, clean, highly readable Tahoma font along with a clever design to make it a visual standout.

RESUME 21, CONTINUED

JEFFREY J. VANBEEK   (905) 555-6666 • vanbeek@imail.com   Page 2

1993 - 1995 | LEAD PROGRAMMER/ANALYST — TaxSystems Canada, Pinehurst, Ontario
- Guided UI subsystem development while building core tax calculation routines.
- Developed shared class libraries in C++ for personal, corporate and trust tax products.
- Connected TaxSystems' data structures to MFC's document/view architecture using a multiple document/multiple view interface (MDI).

DOS / C

1991 - 1993 | TAX SOFTWARE PROGRAMMER/ANALYST — TaxSystems Canada, Pinehurst, Ontario
- Conducted full overhaul of TaxSystems' system platform to improve performance and stability.
- Performed troubleshooting, maintenance, optimization and enhancements.

1990 - 1991 | TAX SOFTWARE PROGRAMMER/ANALYST — ABC Systems Corp., Medina, Ontario
- Reimplemented core of existing tax programs to rectify limitations caused by existing segmented architecture design.
- Highlight was design and implementation for "E-Tax," allowing preparation and transmission of electronically filed tax returns with Revenue Canada, Taxation.

Education
1988

University of Waterloo

Bachelor of Mathematics – Honours Computer Science / Information Systems option
Awards:
Brad J. Sokol Award for Student Leadership
Gates Foundation Scholarship 1987 – 1988
Réné Descartes Entrance Award

Training
2000 | **People Management Course**
- 3-day in-house program conducted by Canadian Management Association

1999 | **Microsoft Professional Developer's Conference**
1997 | **Project Management Course**
- 2-day in-house program developed for SHL and BC Tel

References

Personal and professional references available upon request.

Ryan F. Drury

1984 Maplewood Lane
810-555-9328

Saginaw, Michigan 48630
ryanfdrury@aol.com

Profile

◉ Experienced IT professional with expertise in programming and systems integration.

◉ Specific areas of interest include software construction and research & development.

◉ Strong communication skills include ability to interpret technical concepts for non-technical users.

◉ Adaptability evidenced by experience in diverse industries: automotive, food service/hospitality, photographic processing equipment, and banking.

◉ Personal strengths include an excellent work ethic, persistency, and strong organizational skills.

Highlights of Experience

◉ Developed applications for integrating customer systems with control systems and MMI.

◉ Created data collection applications using MS Access.

◉ Generated user manuals and technical documentation for applications.

◉ Collaborated with customers during project development; trained end-users in utilizing systems.

Technical Inventory

SOFTWARE

Programming Languages:
Borland C++ 5.0
MS Visual Basic 3.0/4.0/6.0
VisualAge C++ for OS/2

Operating Systems:
Windows NT Workstation
Windows NT Server 4.0
Novell 3.11/3.12/4.10
OS/2
OpenLinux 2.3
UNIX

DDE Servers:
Software Wedge/WinWedge 3.0
ModLink
WinLinx

PLC Programming:
PLC Workshop for
   Modicon PLCs
RSLogix

MMI Packages:
InTouch
Factorylink
PanelBuilder 1400e
PanelBuilder 32
Labview 4.0
RSView32

Applications:
MS Access 2.0/97/2000
MS Excel

HARDWARE
PLC-5
SLC500
PLC-2
Reliance A40
Modicon Compact 984

Sun SPARC Station
PanelMate
PanelView

Standard Register
   barcode printers

An unusual font, used judiciously, can effectively "spice up" a resume. Note the extensive Technical Inventory that takes up half of the first page, and how details of experience are not mentioned until page 2.

Ryan F. Drury   810-555-9328

Relevant Experience

AUTOMATED CONTROLS • Brighton, Michigan   1998-Present
Systems Engineer / Programmer
- Write PLC programs to control industrial processes.
- Develop operator interfaces for PC and industrial display terminals.
- Develop data collection applications using Microsoft Access.
- Oversee maintenance and back-up of Windows NT 4.0 fileserver.

Selected Projects:
- Designed and wrote C programs that were instrumental in the success of two projects.
- Installed and configured Windows-based UUCP mail server.
- Wrote Visual Basic program to record flaws found by engine block test stand.
- Developed Labview application to test fuel pump component.

GENERAL DATA • Detroit, Michigan   1995-1998
Software Engineer
- Developed C-based Windows programs for food service and hospitality management firm.
- Incorporated point-of-sale software, inventory management, and reservation systems.
- Wrote code for printing reports.
- Implemented module check-out procedure.

J. B. CROSS & ASSOCIATES • Ann Arbor, Michigan   1995
Simulation Engineer
- Developed simulation models for automotive paint and body shops.
- Collaborated with Simulation Group Manager to design and write a chain-pull program using Visual Basic.

QUALITY PHOTO PRODUCTS • Owosso, Michigan   1994-1995
Programmer
- Designed and maintained programs in C and FoxPro relating to photographic industry.
- Assisted with Novell LAN maintenance and troubleshooting.

NBD BANK • Lansing, Michigan   1992-1994
Computer Technician/Network Administrator
- Assisted in the installation of a Wide Area Network.
- Troubleshot Novell LAN/WAN.
- Maintained PC/LAN back-up schedule.
- Installed and configured software and workstations.

Education

SAGINAW VALLEY STATE UNIVERSITY • University Center, Michigan
Bachelor of Science - Computer Science   1994

References available on request

CHRISTOPHER WILLIAMS

2075 Exeter Road, #555
Augusta, Ontario A2B 2B2
Email: cwilliams@imail.ca

Home: (905) 555-6666
Mobile: (416) 444-5555

OBJECTIVE

Programmer / Analyst

TECHNICAL EXPERTISE

OPERATING SYSTEMS:	VERSIONS:	YEARS EXPERIENCE:
Windows NT	Server & Client	5
Windows	95, 98, 2000	5
Novell	4.1	5
OS/2 Warp	3.0, 4.0	2
SOFTWARE:	VERSIONS:	YEARS EXPERIENCE:
COM & DCOM	-	2
Visual Basic	5.0, 6.0	4
Crystal Reports	6.0, 7.0	4
Oracle PL/SQL	7.3	1
Oracle Stored Procedures	7.3	1
SQL Server Stored Procedures	7.0	2
OmniBuilder RAD Tools	2.9	2
OmniScript	2.9	2
COBOL	4.5	2

ADDITIONAL QUALIFICATIONS

- Motivated and hard working with the ability to adapt and work within tight deadlines.
- Highly skilled in troubleshooting, debugging, and problem analysis.
- Proven ability to complete projects according to specifications, on time and within budget.
- Equally comfortable and effective in both team member and team leader situations.
- Excellent verbal and written communication skills, ensuring the highest level of client service and relationship management.
- Effective time management and organizational skills.

PROFESSIONAL EXPERIENCE

PROGRAMMER/ANALYST
LCD Group
Technical Skills: Visual Basic, COM & DCOM, PL/SQL 7.0, Oracle 7.3, C++

1998 – 2000
Augusta, Ontario

- Led a sub-team of 6 developers in the design and development of a comprehensive operational database for NHLPA.
- Worked closely with program testers to ensure compliance with RFP (Request for Proposal).
- Successfully converted old dBASE programs to Visual Basic and ensured Y2K compliance for Ontario Hydro and CBC – all code tested to specs and user acceptance with no errors.

This resume effectively uses a table to display technical expertise. The Additional Qualifications section highlights important but less quantifiable attributes.

CHRISTOPHER WILLIAMS   PAGE 2

WEB DEVELOPER   1997 – 1998
PLATINUM SYSTRONICS   Peterborough, Ontario
Technical Skills: Oracle Web Server, PL/SQL, HTML, JavaScript, Windows NT 4.0 Platform

- Integrated a web site with an interactive database (Oracle 7.3) for Human Resources Development Canada (HRDC) – www.ititraining.com

SYSTEMS ANALYST   1995 – 1997
CABLESYSTEM SOFTWARE INC.   Pinehurst, Ontario
Technical Skills: COBOL

- Hired to write operating software program for local cable provider, managing all customer tracking, accounting, archiving, billing, etc. – program soon marketed to other small to medium-sized cable providers across Canada.
- Additionally wrote program to track all activities and correspondence between members of Canadian Cable Systems Alliance (CCSA) and cable signal suppliers.

APPLICATION DEVELOPER (Co-op)   1995
LCD Group   North York, Ontario
Technical Skills: Lotus Notes 3.0

- Proposed, designed, and developed internal client tracking system and re-engineered database.

ASSISTANT LAN ADMINISTRATOR (Co-op)   1995
Spotlight, Inc.   Pinehurst, Ontario
Technical Skills: Novell 4.0

- Provided primary technical support and troubleshooting for huge corporate network, responding to technical inquiries, resolving problems, and performing daily backups.
- Planned and installed Software Training Centre, including one server, 8 workstations, and all cabling.
- Repaired servers, PCs, printers, and cabling as required.

BUSINESS MANAGER/ CO-OWNER   1974 – 1992
Dubin Filtration Systems   Augusta, Ontario
Manufacturer of custom-made pipes, filters, and equipment for oil and water well-drilling industry. Clients throughout North America with sales of $10 million annually.

- Successfully built company from ground up, including all financing, premises, machinery, sales, production, and operational responsibilities.
- Responsible for managing all day-to-day operations to ensure quick production, product delivery, and client satisfaction.

PROFESSIONAL / TECHNICAL DEVELOPMENT

Java Development – Seneca College, Toronto, Ontario   Ongoing
MCSD Certification – Microsoft   Ongoing
Visual Basic 6.0 – ObjectSystems, Toronto, Ontario   1999
Oracle Development Seminar – Oracle, Mississauga, Ontario   1998
Computer Operations – Seneca College, Toronto, Ontario   1996

References available upon request.

LINDA SAGE

111 Vandermulch Street • Ridgewood, NJ 07450 • (201) 888-0066 • sage@aol.com

SENIOR PROGRAMMER ANALYST

Highly qualified IT professional with extensive experience in developing/supporting company-wide systems within a client-server environment.... Proven ability to work with a wide range of departments and levels of management, providing training and technical assistance.... Systems experience covers diverse functions within the broadcast field as well as financial and sales systems.

—— *Technical Skills* ——

Operating Systems	*Software*
Windows NT / Windows 98	MS-Word / Excel / Access / PowerPoint / Project
Languages	MS-SQL Server / SQL Xpediter / Crystal Reports
PowerBuilder / Visual Basic	RoboHelp / Visio2000 / Eicon Aviva

CAREER EXPERIENCE:

MEGA NETWORK, INC., New York, NY   1987-Present

Senior Programmer Analyst / Senior Systems Analyst — Advanced to progressively more complex projects, transitioning from Lead Programmer on mainframe systems to Senior Programmer Analyst within client-server environment.

Selected Accomplishments

- *Consolidation of New Company:* Part of team analyzing current computer systems with aim of integrating functionality and upgrading capabilities of newly merged company.
  Technology: PowerBuilder / MS-SQL Server Database
  Results: Converting business affairs from manual to automated contract date tracking system with projected time frame of six months.

- *Contract Information System:* Served as project leader for one of company's first client-server applications. Designed system to maintain contract information on TV shows, talent and future projects. Incorporated special features such as date tracking, contract life cycle and cost analysis.
  Technology: PowerBuilder; MS-SQL Server Database
  Results: Prompted staff regarding critical contract renewal dates, enabling company to make best possible deals with production companies and talent.

- *Research Reporting System:* Took over responsibility for supporting/enhancing a system that captures overnight ratings.
  Technology: Visual Basic; MS-SQL Server Database
  Results: Provided senior management and research departments on East and West coasts with most current ratings data, critical to the operation of the network.

- *Travel & Entertainment / Purchasing System:* Collaborated on supporting/enhancing two interrelated systems that initiated electronic submission of expense vouchers as well as automated purchase orders.
  Technology: Visual Basic; MS-SQL Server Database; MS-Access
  Results: Impacted company operations worldwide, substantially reducing processing time for A/P as well as for thousands of staff members and freelance personnel.

- *Network Sales System:* Team participant on this key long-term project, which automated the generation of proposals used to sell advertising time. Contributed new capabilities in management reporting such as cost analysis for reaching a target audience.
  Technology: IBM Mainframe System; Cobol; ADS/O; IDMS Database
  Results: Mega Network was the first national network to produce such an automated system. Provided sales force with the most accurate data to present to advertisers.

EDUCATION: Rutgers University, Piscataway, NJ — BA Degree

"This resume shows a way to group technology by projects rather than by traditional 'bullets,' especially effective for this candidate who has worked for one company her entire working life."

WALLACE GERNSTEIN

67 Meadow Rivers Pike, Greywood, Texas • (915) 987-5643 • Email: gernwal@tds.com

APPLICATIONS PROGRAMMING • DATABASE DEVELOPMENT

PROFILE

- **Computer Programmer** with hands-on experience developing numerous programs. Strong independent initiative and perseverance. Dependable. Core competencies:
  — object-oriented design using Visual C++
  — application-building using Microsoft Foundation Class (MFC) Library
  — development of client/server Internet messaging programs with Window Sockets
  — database management using Microsoft Access and Data Access Objects (DAO)
  — relational database programming with Visual C++/ActiveX Data Objects (ADO)
  — file processing (sort, search, retrieval algorithms, analysis)
  — data structure design/implementation (lists, queues, trees)
  — code maintenance   — Graphics Device Interface (GDI)
  — ASP familiarity   — design of Graphical User Interfaces
  — Visual Basic experience   — Web page development using HTML
  — Win32 API   — C/C++ on a UNIX platform

TECHNOLOGY

- Hardware: IBM PC, hands-on experience building Pentium-based machines
- Programming languages: Visual C++, MFC, Visual Basic, SQL
- Operating Systems: Windows 98, Windows NT, UNIX, DOS, Linux
- Software: MS Office Suite (Word, Excel, Access, Power Point), Photoshop, others
- Other: Access databases, Windows Sockets, ActiveX

EDUCATION

Bachelor of Science - Computer Science (Minor: Mathematics), 2000
Abilene State University, Abilene, Texas — GPA: 3.8/4.0

- Consistently received highest performance grades in all project-based work regardless of project difficulty, limited resources, or technical innocence.
- Proved strong work ethic through employment throughout college to fund expenses.

SELECTED ACHIEVEMENTS

CLASS PROJECTS

- Originated a series of client/server Internet messaging applications using Socket programming. After partner abandoned project, convinced professor to permit solo completion. Personally invested numerous hours to recover lost momentum and single-handedly secured an "A" on project. (Data Communications class)
- Served on a nine-person project team that designed an application to aid in the management of a Fantasy Baseball League. (Software Engineering class)
  — MFC-based program consisted of a moderate-sized database, an elaborate Graphical User Interface (GUI), and diverse functionality, allowing the user to manage information for a large number of league members.

INDEPENDENT PROJECTS

- Developed an Auto-Wallpaper Changer with Visual C++ that allowed a user to create a list of files (bitmaps and JPEGs) to be displayed automatically each day on the Windows desktop. This full-featured application included drag-and-drop capability for image application, a user-friendly GUI, and easy file storage and retrieval.
- Wrote program demonstrating how to stretch images using functionality provided by the Graphics Device Interface (GDI) for FreeImage, an open source project that aids developers who need to support popular image formats for multimedia applications.

"This resume was written for a 22-year-old, fresh out of college. Most of his programming experience was gained through class projects and independent projects. He rapidly landed a great contract IT job despite the fact that he had no previous IT employment experience."

Ahmed Malouf

2772 Wesleyan Road, Pinellas Park, FL 34877 — (727) 786-1258 — Mobile (727) 885-1132

OBJECTIVE

Employment with a progressive organization as a **Database Administrator** or **Computer Network Technician.**

EDUCATION

➢ Bachelor of Science, Mechanical Engineering ~ University of Central Florida, 1992
➢ Currently completing course work for Microsoft Certified Systems Engineer (**M.C.S.E.**)
  • **Network Essentials**
  • **Core**
  • **Enterprise**
  • **TCP / IP**

BUSINESS BACKGROUND

11/97-Present   Quick Cash Title Loans, Clearwater, FL   **Database Administrator**
➢ Prior to my employment, company was utilizing a spreadsheet in lieu of a database program. Using Access, I proceeded to create, test, and implement a database.
➢ Creating order out of chaos led to better control and allowed for expansion to 2 other locations, both of which were under my supervision.
➢ Database efficiency allowed for managing $35,000 per month in collections.

01/94-08/94   Integra Medical, Clearwater, FL   **Database Administrator**
➢ Designed, tested, and implemented a database system to record patient histories and track invoice payments, medical tests performed, and records of patient deductibles.
➢ System required extensive interface with various insurance companies such as AIB, AIG, and Fortune Insurance.
➢ Testing was normally performed in Miami, requiring field visits and liaison with software developers. This included downloading programs, making changes to the database management system, testing fixes, and generally bringing software up to speed.

8/94-3/96   Reconditioning Unlimited, Largo, FL   **Design Engineer**
➢ Designed and built automated pneumatic machines.
➢ Machined parts using drill press, lathe, welder, and various other machine shop apparatus.

01/93-08/94   AL&S, Houston, TX   **Assistant Engineer**
This company was a provider of digitized maps and wished to create software packages to market to tourists, car rental agencies, and hotels.
➢ Tested and designed software packages and worked with software designers to establish a user-friendly environment.
➢ Conducted ongoing training and supervision of 5 to 6 entry-level computer operators.

PERSONAL INTERESTS

Fitness, fishing, skiing, scuba diving

For this individual, an objective helps to define his current interests and reflects his ongoing MCSE training.

DAVID SUZUKI

Email: davidsuzuki@yahoo.com

145 West Rosecliff Court
Saukville, WI 53080

Office: (414) 629-3676
Res: (262) 344-3449

TECHNICAL PROFILE

A dedicated and loyal systems professional with 20+ years' hands-on experience as a **database administrator and application developer**. Solid understanding of relational databases. Excellent design, coding, and testing skills. Strong oral and written communication abilities.

Databases:	DB2, Oracle, SQL
Languages:	COBOL, IBM/AS, Visual Basic
Operating Systems:	VM, UNIX, DOS, Windows 95 and 98
Third-Party Software:	COGNOS, Impromptu, Informatica, Microsoft Access

PROFESSIONAL EXPERIENCE

Midwest Staffing Inc. Milwaukee, WI   1976 to Present
(A global employment services organization with annual sales in excess of $10 billion.)

LEAD DATABASE ADMINISTRATOR AND DEVELOPER
Lead mainframe and Oracle database administrator with 24/7 responsibility for performance, tuning, recovery, and planning. Use various utilities to transfer data to other platforms and build tables/indexes. Respond to end users' requests for information and resolve discrepancies in data reports. Research and interact with vendors in the purchase of third-party software. Train and supervise assistant DBAs. Write user manuals, operating procedures, and internal documentation.

Selected Database Development Projects and Achievements

- Administer mission-critical payroll and billing database that bills $5+ million per week.
- Designed, developed, and implemented Oracle databank—a duplicate of the mainframe databank. End users now have greater access to data using desktop tools.
- Developed and maintain franchise fee billing application.
- Developed Central Billing consolidation application that bills $5 million per month.
- Researched and recommended purchase of ETL Informatica PowerMart utility. Data movement to the data repository, the Internet, and databases is now accomplished in one step. Previously, data movement involved large amounts of development time.
- Developed mainframe processes using the ESSCON Channel (high-speed data transfer) to move data from the mainframe to the AIX platform. Compared to the old method using Outbound, this has reduced data transfer time by at least 50%.
- Selected by management to train assistant database administrator. Assistant is now a reliable backup on mainframe-related database issues.

EDUCATION

Oracle and Oracle Tuning, Certificate Courses, University of Wisconsin—Milwaukee, 1999

Note how your attention is drawn to the "Selected Database Development Projects and Achievements"—the hands-on experience that will sell this candidate.

JONATHAN P. WOODRIDGE

41 Chatham Avenue • Cherry Hill, NJ 08034 • 609-714-8020 • jpw@aol.com

Programming / Software Training / Technical Support

SUMMARY

- High-energy, self-directed professional with a technical / business academic background and 10+ years of successful business experience.
- Frequent recognition for outstanding performance in positions requiring strong planning, analytical, problem-solving, and customer service skills.
- C++ programming experience, using class functions and conversions, inheritance and dynamic memory location, I/O file streams, data files, and data structures: arrays, strings, address, and pointers.
- Developer of programs that integrated Visual Basic with Access.
- Extensive background in training and customer service; able to clearly convey information.
- Proven ability to assess and hurdle complex obstacles; viewed as a strong troubleshooter.

Programming Languages: C++, Visual Basic
Software: Excel, Access, PowerPoint, MS Word, Visio
Operating Systems: Windows 2000 / 98
Hardware: IBM-compatible PCs

EDUCATION / PROFESSIONAL DEVELOPMENT

A.S., Computer Science / Business Administration: Dumont County College, Dumont NJ

Professional Seminars / Training Programs: Customer Service, Training, Interviewing, Employee Relations / Coaching

SKILLS AND ACCOMPLISHMENTS

Programming

- Developed an amortization chart in C++ that allowed user to enter input to calculate payments, balances, and interest paid.
- In C++, created a bowling program that recorded score data input by user and stored it in an output data file for later use.
- Developed programs for the real estate and fast food industries that integrated Visual Basic with Access, utilizing the database in the interface and retrieving it using SQL statements.

Technical Writing

- As project manager, led a team of 6 in the development of a software manual.
- Conducted an analysis of the software program and typical users, assigned responsibilities, completed a task list, developed task completion dates, and performed frequent reviews to assess progress.
- Ensured clarity and integrity of document and use of appropriate terminology.

Planning / Leadership / Training / Troubleshooting

- Managed the operations of multimillion-dollar retail locations, with responsibility for sales, customer service, cost containment, recruiting, training, scheduling, and inventory.
- Received frequent regional and district recognition for sales volume and expense control.
- Evaluated problems at various sites and devised and implemented solutions.
- Trained managers throughout the region, while maintaining responsibility for store management.
- Conducted group orientation and training sessions for seasonal sales associates.

Customer Service

- Focused on creating customer-centered environments that inspired repeat business.
- Emphasized quality service with management trainees and staff.

PROFESSIONAL EXPERIENCE

Store Manager, The Man's Shop, Sea Girt, NJ   1992 – 1998
Store Manager, Carltons of California, Freehold, NJ   1985 – 1992

INTERESTS

Investing and Financial Management

This is one of the few purely "functional" resumes you'll find in this collection. Notice how the Professional Experience section is bare-bones, whereas the skills and accomplishments are categorized and explained in some detail.

Janet Jones

111 Flatlands Avenue
Brooklyn, New York 11111
(718) 444-4444 ▪ 1234@AAA.net

Systems Engineer ▪ Project Leader

Thoroughly experienced in the **development and implementation of business systems** within **mainframe** and **micro environments**. Areas of expertise encompass:

- ➢ **Data Model / Logical Design**
- ➢ **Coding**
- ➢ **Needs Analysis**
- ➢ **Functional / Design Documentation**

- ➢ **Module / Class Specifications**
- ➢ **Data Security**
- ➢ **Batch / Online Systems**
- ➢ **Test Management**

Technical Summary

➢ **Mainframes**

Languages:	COBOL / COBOL II, ISPF Dialog Manager, REXX, SQL (DB2), BMS / SDF / SDF II, Script / GML
Databases:	DB2, VSAM / IDCAMS / ICCF
O/S:	MVS / XA, CICS / INTERTEST
Other:	TSO/ISPF, SPUFI, PRO-EDIT, DATA-XPERT / FILE-AID, LIBRARIAN / PANVALET, ENDEVOR

➢ **Micros**

Languages:	Basic (MS and Visual), C/C++ (MS and Visual, Solaris), MS Access, xBASE (dBASE, Clipper), Microfocus COBOL, REXX, SQL (XDB, SYBASE, Watcom)
Databases:	SYBASE, MS Access, Btrieve / Xtrieve, XDB, Watcom, dBASE (III and IV), Clipper
O/S:	MS-DOS (3.x to 6.x), Windows (3.x, WFW, 95 and NT), UNIX (Solaris)
Other:	Galaxy, Rogue Wave Tools.h++, Window Widgets, Crystal Report Writer, PVCS, TLib, Visual SourceSafe

Sample of Accomplishments

➢ As a consultant for **Software, Inc.,** participated in a number of major projects within the Financial Services community:

Columbia Bank / Big Apple Bank *(post-merger)*:

- Enhanced SAS-based Reorg Letter Writing System to accommodate changes in business environment, resulting from a prior merger. System subsequently integrated into the Corporate Action Letter Writing System, due to further merger activity.

- Added new vendor data feeds to a Corporate Action Reporting facility, which involved changes to both the batch and online processing.

- Member of team that designed, developed, tested and implemented PC client / server system for the Corporate Action Letter Writing System to replace existing SAS-based system. Developed GUI workstation using Visual Basic 5. Interfaced with the Data Base Administrator (DBA) for the physical design, creation and maintenance of all Sybase-stored procedures.

- Participated in the design, development and implementation of an automated input system for the Global Securities Area using COBOL II in a DB2 SQL Batch/CICS environment.

- continued -

"Ms. Jones is continuing to look for project-management positions, capitalizing on her systems engineering experience. Major projects are highlighted, showing her technical skills as well as industry expertise."

Janet Jones

111 Flatlands Avenue
Brooklyn, New York 11111
(718) 444-4444 ▪ 1234@AAA.net
Résumé - Page Two

Sample of Accomplishments

Big Apple Bank:

- Involved in the development of a Visual Basic interactive interface of a Securities Lending and Asset Management System. System functions included file maintenance of the underlying MS Access database, daily trade processing, data transmission and reporting. Reporting functions were created using Crystal Reports for data access and printing.

Mellon Brothers:

- Developed audit application written in C++, with Galaxy as the GUI interface and Sybase as the underlying database. The application processes daily delta files downloaded from the mainframe and produces a variety of reports based on user-generated ad hoc report requests.

Bank of the Americas:

- Participated in the development of the Global Custody component of a client / server project designed to provide the customers with an integrated Reporting and Inquiry System and an easy-to-use integrated workstation for entering and modifying global instructions. The system was developed under Windows / NT using C++, Galaxy and Sybase on a Sun platform. The Accounting System was a Novell-based system written in Microfocus COBOL using BTRIEVE.

➢ As technical project leader at **Monolith Insurance Company**, supervised programming staff, streamlined systems, oversaw enhancements and modifications:

- Within Actuarial / Statistical Reporting Area streamlined an annual maintenance effort by replacing common hardcoded file and table definitions by COPYLIB members, and utilized PERFORMS to replace hardcoded loops and common field suffixes to identify usage and/or derivation.
- For Schedule F Reinsurance Reporting System replaced the existing Batch Interrogation System with online IMS System.
- Redesigned and enhanced Automatic Statistical System, which resulted in the merging of the 5 systems into 3 new systems with an approximate 30% additional savings in operational resource requirements.

Professional Experience

SOFTWARE, INC. (SAI), New York, New York   1996-Present
Consultant

MONOLITH INSURANCE COMPANY, New York, New York   1990-1996
Technical Project Leader

MEDICAL INSURANCE CORP., New York, New York   1985-1990
Technical Project Leader

Education

ROCHESTER INSTITUTE OF TECHNOLOGY, Rochester, New York
B.S., *Cum Laude*, Computer Studies

RESUME 30: KRISTIE COOK, CPRW; OLATHE, KS

TIMOTHY BUNT

SOFTWARE DEVELOPER / SOFTWARE ENGINEER / APPLICATION DEVELOPER

- Energetic IT professional with specialty in software development.
- Excellent problem-solving and abstract thinking skills with proven ability to identify a problem, analyze possible solutions and determine the best course of action to meet stated objectives.
- Demonstrated oral and written communication skills; bilingual in German and English.
- Member – IEEE Computer Science Society.

TECHNICAL SKILLS

- MS Visual Basic
- C, C++
- Fortran
- Pascal

- SQL
- Object-Oriented Programming
- Windows 95 / 98 / NT 4.0
- Assembler

- Proprietary Script Language (CCL)
- MS Word, Excel, Access
- Internet
- Mathematica

EDUCATION

BACHELOR OF SCIENCE – COMPUTER SCIENCE AND MATHEMATICS (1999)
Pittsburg State University – Pittsburg, Kansas

- GPA: 3.59; Dean's List
- Named "Outstanding Computer Science Graduate"
- Funded 50% of tuition and housing through scholarship and employment.

EXPERIENCE

APPLICATION DEVELOPER – Major Corporation, Kansas City, Missouri   1999-PRESENT
Maintain code, troubleshoot and fix bugs, provide technical support to clients and implement new functionality for three programs running as one product. Provide input to Technical Writer for online documentation. Applications are three-tiered client/server written in Visual Basic on the front end and communicating with programs in CCL, a Major-owned script language, on the back end.

- Initiated Major's new Off-Cycle-Distribution (OCD) process into the team and provided training and support to team members in using the process; process allows full documentation of bug fixes and new code distributed to clients.
- Awarded raise in less than one year due to performance and contributions.
- Worked directly with customer to troubleshoot product issues.

OFFICE ASSISTANT – Pittsburg State University, Pittsburg, Kansas   1998-1999
Wrote database queries with MS Access, developed publications and forms and handled general office duties for the housing office.

CONTRACTOR – A+ Temp Agency, Des Moines, Iowa   1998
Contracted by a major health provider's Central Billing Office to create Excel spreadsheets and perform general office tasks.

CONTRACTOR – ABC Contract Services, Atlanta, Georgia   1997
Contracted to Lucent Technologies to track inventory of their on-site computers and electronic equipment.

4489 NW 122nd St. Kansas City, MO 66211	Email: bunt.t@ieee.org	Home: (816) 521-5683 Mobile: (816) 523-2675

The unusual placement of contact information at the bottom allows strong focus on this candidate's expertise and skills. Because his degree is recent, it is placed toward the top of the resume.

RESUME 31: WANDA McLAUGHLIN, CPRW; CHANDLER, AZ

MARY G. RODRIGUEZ
4411 East Maryland Avenue — Gilbert, AZ 85234
(480) 555-0000 — MRodriguez@aol.com

FOCUS   Position as **Software Engineer** where B.S. Degree in Computer Science, experience in Object-Oriented Programming and knowledge of Internet Technology are desirable.

TECHNICAL EXPERTISE

Program Design / Development / Maintenance

Database & Network Administration

System Upgrades & Enhancements

Hardware & Software Evaluation / Support

Programing Languages / Platforms:
Java 1.2, C + +, Visual C + +, HTML, JCL, CICS, SQL, COBOL, PASCAL, BASIC, NATURAL, FORTRAN, MS DOS, Windows, Unix

Software:
MS Office, Corel Draw, Harvard Graphics, Pagemaker, WordPerfect, Quattro Pro, Novell Network

RELATED EXPERIENCE

Programmer / Analyst   STATE OF ARIZONA, Phoenix, AZ — 1998-2000
Used 4GL programming languages to develop interdepartmental programs. Analyzed data and wrote basic requirements documentation to create databases and programs. Assisted in training end users.
   Achievements:
   — Member of team that brought existing system, programs and databases successfully into Y2K compliance.

Programmer   ANALYTICAL RESEARCH, INC., Sacramento, CA — 1997-1998
Directly accountable for all facets of programming and system maintenance for market research company providing services for major travel and leisure accounts throughout the world, including America West Airlines, Lufthansa, United Airlines and Ritz-Carlton Hotels.

Developed and implemented custom marketing research programs; administered 30,000+ database; coordinated user additions, deletions and system back-up functions for Novell network. Participated in all phases of hardware and software upgrades, enhancements and maintenance. Occasionally supervised temporary employees.
   Achievements:
   — Developed presentations for visual aids and company books utilizing a variety of graphic packages, including Harvard Graphics, Corel Draw, ACROSS and Windows.
   — Assisted in upgrading 20-system linked network in Novell.
   — Managed 200+ slide presentation to major clients.

Desktop Publisher   ARTISTRY, INC., Los Angeles, CA — 1993-1996
Assisted customers in the development of visual graphic presentations for custom brochures and marketing materials. Determined client requirements, assisted in selection of special graphic designs and programs, designed and processed orders.
   Achievements:
   — Developed strong skills in computer operations and creative design.

EDUCATION / TRAINING

Bachelor of Science in Computer Science – 1997   CALIFORNIA STATE UNIVERSITY, Northridge, CA
Emphasis: Software Engineering & Computer Mathematics

Coursework: Java, Intermediate Java, C + +, Visual C + + SCOTTSDALE COLLEGE, Scottsdale, AZ
— Currently attending
— Developed Mortgage Calculator utilizing Java Applets

This efficient, one-page format uses good organization and formatting to clearly communicate the individual's qualifications. The Focus statement at the top is another way of stating an objective.

Teresa D. Fisher

8585 Barbara Avenue • Sacramento, CA 95916   (916) 321-5505 • tdfisher@golden.com

SOFTWARE DEVELOPMENT • PRODUCT MANAGEMENT • TECHNICAL SUPPORT

PROFESSIONAL EXPERIENCE

GOLDEN COMMERCE, Sacramento, Texas   1998–Present
A global provider of end-to-end, Internet-based electronic commerce solutions.

Product Manager – Exchange Payment Business Unit (EPBU), Feb. 1999–Present

Promoted to oversee the Cash Management product line—*Exchange: Banker, Exchange: ACH, Exchange: Advice,* and *Exchange Banker for the Internet.* Manage 4 programmers in software development and support activities for these products providing payment systems solutions in and from the client corporation through to the payment network (Federal Reserve Bank, Value-Added Network, or Value-Added Bank).

- Served as effective cross-functional liaison across technical support, sales, development, finance, and management, as well as customer interface for product direction, bug fixes, and enhancements.

- Maximized productivity of high-wage development staff, improved customer satisfaction, and achieved faster project turnaround. Accomplished by working with technical support manager and establishing a process for escalation and tracking of product issues, whereas before support staff routinely escalated problems to Development before validating that the issues were not operator- or environment-generated.

Client Services Consultant – Financial Electronic Data Interchange (FEDI), Aug. 1998–Feb. 1999

Conducted onsite installation, training, and support of FEDI software, including EDI mapping and systems integration. Worked with large financial institutions that market and license the software to their own clients.

- Provided valuable, first-hand knowledge of bank operations to help consultants customize installation and implementation of Exchange products for a better fit with the institutions' operational needs.

- Assisted with product testing and guidance of leading-edge *Exchange Banker for the Internet.*

FIRST FEDERAL BANK, Fresno, California   1995–1998
A leading statewide financial services organization offering state-of-the-art electronic technology to process customer and internal transactions.

Unit Supervisor – Technical Support Unit, Electronic Banking (1996–98)
Electronic Banking Technician (1995–96)

Managed operation, development, and maintenance of sophisticated electronic banking systems that included commercial electronic transactions, telephone transactions, and internal processing. Led the installation of *Exchange: Banker* software and network, customizing the application to interface with existing systems. Supported entire electronic banking department in use of software and hardware, and served as contact with vendors to initiate modifications. Played key role in assessing system upgrades. Directly supervised 3 technicians responsible for hardware and software support functions.

Selected Achievements:

- Spearheaded technological upgrade that attracted significant new business to the organization due to convenience, efficiency, and ease of use.

- Integrated commercial financial services software *(Exchange: Banker)* into existing host system using Novell 4.x network. Customized programming with batch files and host link interface, File Express, and script languages to move files to and from host. Examined business workflow to determine how systems would interact for maximum efficiency/reliability.

This is a classic, well-designed resume that includes all pertinent information in an easy-to-skim layout that emphasizes career advancement and accomplishments.

Teresa D. Fisher

(continued)   (916) 321-5505 • tdfisher@golden.com

PROFESSIONAL EXPERIENCE (cont.)

- Promoted to unit supervisor to lead implementation of more sophisticated and broad-based technology.
- Supervised expansion of customized *Businesslink* system, increasing total active users fourfold.
- Upgraded hardware and software for *Firstline* telephone banking and information system, and accomplished maintenance using Intervoice programming language. Managed system security and generated utilization reports.
- Conducted development for a PC Banking system allowing retail customers access via home computer.
- Served (by invitation) on Golden Commerce's User Advisory Committee for *Exchange: Banker* software to provide user feedback, prioritize system modifications, and interact with developer on support and future planning for the product. Identified need for code changes by the Federal Reserve and Golden, as well as a security upgrade and other minor modifications that were implemented by software vendor.

NATIONAL BANK OF NORTHERN CALIFORNIA, Modesto, California   1988–1995

Programmer / Analyst (1993–95), Computer Operator (1990–92), Data Control Clerk (1988–90)

Initiative and rapid assimilation of technical knowledge resulted in fast-track promotion to network administration position providing network and desktop support for 380 internal customers using Microsoft Office and financial services software Maxxus ACH.

- Developed applications using DOS, Visual Basic, and QBasic, and designed a Novell menu system.
- With limited resources, improved availability of support for host applications with a remote access pool.
- Served as primary point of contact on help desk, adjusting communication with users to accommodate their level of technical knowledge.

RETAIL SALES – COMPUTER AND ELECTRONICS EQUIPMENT, Sacramento, California   1982–1988

EDUCATION & TECHNICAL TRAINING/SKILLS

Electronics Technology: Modesto Community College Coursework (32 credits)

Hardware: PC, modems, peripherals, modem pools, host interface cards, voice cards, Token Ring MAUs, routers, bridges, remote access pool, tape backup devices

Operating Systems: Novell 3.x and 4.x, Windows NT Workstation, Windows 9x, DOS, OS/2, Sun/Unix

Software: Word, PowerPoint, Excel, Exchange: Alliance Electronic Data Interchange (EDI)

Programming: DOS QBasic, Visual Basic, ProComm scripting

DEBORAH WOOD

4209 Brower Road, P.O. Box 325, Anderson, MA 56209
Phone: (345) 555-555 ▪ Mobile: (345) 555-5555 ▪ E-mail: dwood@aol.com

SOFTWARE DEVELOPMENT MANAGER / SENIOR SOFTWARE ENGINEER
20+ years' experience in all phases of software development life cycle

Exceptionally well-qualified senior software engineer and manager with sophisticated programming skills and a sincere passion for resolving complex problems and business challenges through technical innovation. Solid portfolio of vertical market software products proving expert hands-on ability in all phases of the software development life cycle – conception to customer delivery and support. Dedicated, results-driven, and energetic leader; extensive experience in small start-up environments. Core strengths in:

- Product Conception, Design, & Development
- Project Management
- Product Quality Assurance
- Troubleshooting & Customer Support
- Contract & Licensing Negotiations
- Custom Software Engineering
- Team Building & Leadership
- General Business Management

TECHNICAL QUALIFICATIONS

Languages:	Borland Delphi, Borland C++ Builder, MS C/C++, MS Assembler, MS VC++, MS Visual Basic, Mark Williams C, Basic, Borland C/C++, Turbo Pascal, HP Assembler, Z80 Assembler, Access, dBase, Clipper
Libraries & APIs:	Windows 16/32 API, ActiveX, Inso OEM Viewer API, Quick View, Aztec Copy Protection, Cimmetry AutoCAD API, TurboPower Series, Raize, LMD, WPTools, Dream Inspector, Topaz, Rainbow Technologies Hardware Lock, Essentials Series, Genus Series, Greenleaf, and more
Development Tools & Applications:	Wise InstallMaster, MS Visual SourceSafe, Multi-Edit, EC, DOS Batch files, WinBatch, CodeView Debugger, CodeSmith Debugger, MS Office (Word, Excel, PowerPoint, Outlook, FrontPage, Project) MSIE, Adobe Acrobat, Norton Utilities, PowerDesk, Paint Shop Pro, Photoshop, Netscape, and more
Operating Systems:	Windows 3.1, Windows 95, Windows 98, Windows NT/Server, Windows 2000/Server, Mac OS, DOS 2-7

CAREER HIGHLIGHTS

Alsiksek Software Solutions, Boston, MA   Nov 1997 – Jun 2000
New Technologies, Inc., Boston, MA   Jan 1987 – Oct 1997

VICE PRESIDENT OF ENGINEERING / DIRECTOR OF PRODUCT ENGINEERING

Cofounded New Technologies, Inc., and directed all software product development, shipping, and customer support efforts. Conceptualized, designed, and managed the development of vertical market software products targeted to the industrial and manufacturing industries. Formulated and implemented quality assurance policies, procedures, and methodologies. Negotiated favorable contracts and licenses for third-party software modules and libraries. Led teams of up to 7 programmers and technicians.

Retained by Alsiksek as Director of Product Engineering following acquisition of New Technologies in 1997. Continued in previous product engineering, project management, and support role; focused on refining and upgrading the cutting-edge document management product developed by New Technologies.

- Conceptualized, designed, developed, and delivered a full line of software products meeting industrial and manufacturing industry needs for computer-based training, file organization and document management, troubleshooting, and shop floor utilities.
  - Products included Trainer Series, Assistant Series, Technical Toolbox, Portable HGR, and the company's most notable product, Virtual Library.
- Earned professional reputation for exceptionally solid, high-quality, and supportable software products through stringent oversight of specifications, code version control, code reuse, documentation, and testing.

Extremely appropriate for a senior software engineer, this resume includes a detailed profile, lengthy technical skills summary, and experience that highlights accomplishments and contributions.

RESUME 33, CONTINUED

DEBORAH WOOD – Page 2

- Invented, designed, and integrated new technologies within software products, utilizing special talent for analyzing customer requirements and creating new, marketable products to meet needs.
- Specified and developed troubleshooting products and played an instrumental development role in custom computer-based training covering a wide range of general and specific industrial topics for Allen-Bradley, GE Fanuc, and Reliance Electric. Assisted in structuring third-party reseller licensing agreements with Rockwell Software and Taylor Software for New Technology's products.
- Productized and delivered fully functional software applications; oversaw licensing enforcement, setup utility development, documentation and packaging creation, and manufacturing/shipping processes.
- Developed a minimally intrusive licensing enforcement/copy protection strategy that enabled the ability to meter software product users in a multiuser environment.
- Redesigned, upgraded, and enhanced Virtual Library for the Windows 32-bit platform, achieving complete backward compatibility and the ability to coexist with earlier versions.
- Created totally innovative feature for Virtual Library that utilizes dynamic pointer technology to provide an advanced, non-database-driven document revision control system with e-mail support for companies seeking to achieve and maintain ISO-9000 status.

Wood and Associates, Inc., New York, NY   Jan 1984 – Jun 1987

PRESIDENT / PRINCIPAL SOFTWARE CONSULTANT

Built and managed this software consulting company, working under contract with Allen-Bradley to handle CNC custom software engineering engagements as well as support customers through troubleshooting and enhancements for previously developed custom software. Directed a 10-person team of subcontractors. Simultaneously managed other computer consulting projects for a wide range of clients.

- Designed, developed, and tested "Merlin" - Allen-Bradley's first PC-compatible hardware platform for the CNC line; implemented to improve the human interface front-end to the 8200AT CNC. Created and integrated new features such as real-time task scheduling and task switching.
- Conceived and developed Desktop PAL, the first and only third-party software product for developing and documenting 8200 and 8200AT CNC PAL on a PC-compatible computer.

Allen Bradley Co., Highland Heights, OH / Dusseldorf, West Germany   Mar 1972 – Dec 1983

CNC SOFTWARE GROUP SUPERVISOR, MILLS AND ROBOTICS (1981 – 1983)
CNC SOFTWARE QUALITY ASSURANCE SUPERVISOR (1980 – 1981)
COMPUTER CENTER SUPERVISOR (1979 – 1980)
SOFTWARE ENGINEER / TECHNICIAN (1972 – 1979)

Advanced rapidly through positions of increasing responsibility as a software engineer and supervisor to final management position, leading a team of 5 directly reporting supervisors and approximately 70 indirect reports. Managed all standard and custom software development projects for mill and robotics applications.

- Measurably improved "as shipped" software quality through the implementation of new policies and procedures for testing and shipping. Analyzed and isolated problem areas and developed an innovative preventative method to eliminate problems in new shipments.
- Developed a fully operational and self-sustaining CNC computer department in Dusseldorf, West Germany, achieving corporate goal of establishing a local CNC software development engineering presence in Europe. Completed assignment in just 19 months, 5 months ahead of schedule.
- Designed, developed, tested, and debugged CNC executive software, focusing on operator interfaces, PAL special features, basic control logic, servo control, axis motion, and system configurability.

EDUCATION

COMPUTER PROGRAMMING
Institute of Computer Management, Boston, MA – 1972

Extensive continuing education includes college-accredited courses in software development languages/ techniques, operating systems, and network administration, as well as vendor training with Microsoft, Borland, and IBM/Lotus. Certified as ISO-9000 Facilitator Specialist through Cleveland State University.

CHAPTER 6

Resumes for Technology Support Professionals

- Help Desk Administrators and Analysts
- Technical Call Center Representatives
- Technical Support Technicians
- Data Library and Warehousing Specialists
- Technical Training Specialists
- Technical Writers
- Technology Sales and Marketing Professionals
- Technology Business Development Professionals

laKeisha Carter
7742 Eagle Eye, Melody, New York 11763 ◆ (631) 999-2660 ◆ lakeisha419@aol.com

entry-level
HELP DESK SUPPORT

Qualifications

A+ Certified Technician
MCP Certification
Bachelor of Business Administration degree
Professional Help Desk Support training
Nine years of combined experience in Customer Service and Office Support

Computer Skills/Training

LONGTRAIL BLAZERS TECHNICAL CENTER, Merlin, New York
Certificate of Completion, Help Desk Support Professional, 2001

Gained comprehensive, hands-on computer help desk training in the following areas:

PC Building: Installation, Configuration, Troubleshooting and Maintenance
Installation, Configuration and Upgrading of Computer Hardware and Software
Installation, Configuration, Troubleshooting and Maintenance of DOS and Windows 3.1/95 Environments
Installation, Set-up and Configuration of Network Printers
Set-up of File System Security
Diagnosing and Troubleshooting Computer Problems and Modem/Network Connectivity Issues
◆ ◆ ◆
Windows 98/95/3.1; DOS 6.22; NT 4.0
MS Office 97 (Word, Excel, PPT, Access), Lotus Notes 4.5

Education

DANCLERY COLLEGE, Overton, New York
Bachelor of Business Administration - Marketing, 2000

CENTER COMMUNITY COLLEGE, Bendwood, New York
Associate in Applied Science - Business Administration, 1998

Work History

Call Center Representative, DIRECT CALLS, East Slip, New York	1/00 - 3/01
Reservationist, USA TRANSPORTATION CO., Boatherson, New York	7/99 - 1/00
Sales Associate, XOXO, Allentown Mall, Garden Gates, New York	8/98 - 4/99
Sales Associate/Cashier, LIZ'S STYLES, Riverboat, New York	11/92 - 8/98

Because this candidate is a new graduate, her computer skills and training are emphasized and her work history (mostly unrelated to a career in technology) is played down.

Furkhunda Rizvi

57 Hofstra Boulevard
Port Jefferson Station, NY 11772
631-555-2425 • frizvi@yahoo.com

Overview

Skilled **Helpdesk Analyst** with 7 years of experience providing PC and CLIENT/SERVER TECHNICAL SUPPORT. Experience in diagnosing and resolving difficult problems in the area of hardware, application, and operating systems. Interface with end users handling inquiries regarding system configuration and operating systems. Effectively render technical advice to non-technical personnel. Keen ability to address technical issues and close out customer tickets in a timely manner.

Technical Capabilities

Operating Systems:			
	■ Windows NT	■ Windows 95/98/3.11	■ Unix
	■ DOS 5.0/6.0/6.2	■ Novell Client	■ AS/400

Applications:			
	■ Windows NT	■ Microsoft Office Suite	■ PC Anywhere
	■ WordPerfect	■ Lotus 1-2-3	■ Netview
	■ Lotus Notes	■ Arbiter	■ Tandem
	■ Oasis 4.5	■ Deja Win	■ Outlook 2000

Hardware:			
	■ HP Brios/Vectras	■ Okidata Printers	■ Digi Boxes
	■ HP Printers	■ Cisco Routers	■ Multiplexors
	■ Serial Connectors	■ CATS Cables	■ NIC Cards

Professional Experience

Helpdesk Analyst, Federal City Bank, Littletown, New York **1995-Present**
Provide technical support to over 2,000 branches, back offices, and ATM computer-based systems.

- Provide expedient and appropriate commands to incoming inquiries regarding system malfunctions.
- Dispatch appropriate second-tier support or vendors to solve hardware complications.
- Maintain complete documentation of all daily site outages, LAN outages, and application alerts allowing corporate headquarters to identify high error frequency locations.
- Identified possible technological glitches and offered solutions for a newly installed GUI program.
- Executed, as part of a team, the technical integrity of two computer systems during a merger.

Helpdesk Representative, Cable USA, Northport, New York **1993-1995**

- Resolved daily systematic and operational malfunctions, ensuring minimal loss of work productivity.
- Directed support for complex problems to next-level support, simultaneously keeping users informed as to the status of open calls.
- Assisted end users with connectivity problems, computer lockouts, and printer problems.

Education

Associate of Science – Computer Information Systems, Briarcliffe College, Patchogue, New York, 1995

The clean, attractive look of this resume is achieved through font selection, horizontal lines at top and bottom, and the three-column format of the Technical Capabilities section.

William Regale

8/37 Prince Henry Street, Carlton 3053
email: regale@bigpond.com.au
(03) 9889 3711 (W) or (03) 9743 3130

CAREER OBJECTIVE

To work in a client support role where my skills in information systems, data processing and librarianship can be utilised in resolving information management problems through data processing.

SUMMARY OF SKILLS

Computing

As manager of one of the largest Australian corporate library's computer systems for the last 6 years, I have gained experience in:

- PC systems, particularly communications and word processing packages
- the VAX VMS operating system and DCL programming
- programming in the INFO language

As part of my studies in the Graduate Diploma in Business (Data Processing) at Victoria University of Technology, I have gained experience in:

- programming in Cobol, Pascal and Prolog
- relational database systems
- system analysis and design
- data communications and communications networks

Management

As manager of this corporate library with a staff of six and an annual budget of $600,000, I have gained experience in:

- budgeting and the strategic planning of resources and service needs
- management of staff including their performance appraisal and personal development
- written communications including many user manuals and guides
- marketing a service function to 35 operating units and subsidiary companies
- time management

Experienced Librarian

As a librarian for over 14 years, in both private and public sectors, I have gained considerable experience in:

- design and management of computerised information retrieval systems including reference databases and videotex
- library management and associated systems

This resume demonstrates some of the differences between resumes in the U.S. and other countries—in this case, Australia. The resume starts with a career objective, freely uses the pronoun "I," and includes

William Regale   **Page 2**

TERTIARY QUALIFICATIONS

- Completed to date two-thirds of Graduate Diploma in Business (Data Processing) at Victoria University of Technology

- Graduate Diploma in Information Services, Royal Melbourne Institute of Technology, 1983

PROFESSIONAL DEVELOPMENT

- Management Development Program, In-house

- Performance Appraisal and Personal Development Review, In-house

- Interpersonal Communications Program, In-house

CAREER EXPERIENCE

1996 to November 1997	Manager, NAB Infoservices, Corporate HQ
1991 to 1995	Senior Information Officer, NAB
1990	Travelling Overseas
1985 to 1989	Senior Information Scientist, MIM
1984 to 1985	Librarian, State Office Block Library

PROFESSIONAL ACTIVITIES

- Member of the Library Association of Australia. Have held several executive positions in interest groups of the Association since 1988

- Member, Institute of Information Scientists (UK)

REFERENCES WILL BE PROVIDED ON REQUEST

some language that might be baffling in the U.S. job market. Yet it's entirely appropriate and effective in the Australian employment market.

Jayne Wharburton

3213 Zenith
Blairsburg, IA 50010

(515) 238-1875
Jaynewharb@prairienet.com

SUMMARY OF QUALIFICATIONS

Solution Center professional with two and a half years of experience interacting face-to-face with students, faculty, and staff. Able to clearly understand problems and find positive solutions through use of problem-solving skills, knowledge, and consultation with other technical support staff. Excellent knowledge of policies and procedures. Willing to learn new skills to continue serving the best needs of the customer and Solution Center.

TECHNOLOGY SKILLS

Knowledge of Solomon bookkeeping program, Fox Pro reference library program, Microsoft Word, Excel, Internet, and E-mail systems.

WORK EXPERIENCE

Iowa State University, Ames, IA, 1980-present

Computation Center, Clerk III, 1999 – present
Interface with walk-in customers (students, faculty, staff) on a daily basis. Explain technical procedures in a clear, precise manner using personal knowledge and expertise, consulting with other support staff, or referring to senior-level technical staff. Distribute handouts on setting up Internet access.

→ Understand and apply the Center's policies and procedures.
→ Explain Internet access registration to students, faculty, and staff.
→ Direct appropriate set-up of Ethernet for dormitories and off-campus modems.
→ Verify Vincent accounts and enter information into database.
→ Develop excellent client relations with internal and external departments.
→ Prepare invoices and process charge orders, sales, and reference materials.
→ Maintain inventory of computer supplies necessary to meet customer needs.

Extension Distribution Center, Clerk III, 1995 – 1999
Balanced cash reports to sales on a daily basis, prepared billing and credits, maintained up-to-date database, and processed orders.
→ Applied problem-solving skills to resolve complicated orders in a timely manner.

EDUCATION

Bachelor of Science, Iowa State University, Ames, IA, 1997
Major: Social Work

Note how this individual transitioned from a degree in Social Work to a career in technology! The resume does a good job of defining her technical activities along with problem-solving and customer-service skills.

ALEXANDER V. MATTESON

1234 Winterberry Crescent
Winter Park, Florida 32793

407-678-1234
E-mail: AVM123@hotmail.com

OBJECTIVE   Entry-level technical support/programming position utilizing strong computer skills.

QUALIFICATIONS

Programming Experience:

- Utilized dBase to create inventory/sales analysis tool for retailer. This program identifies customer buying trends and allows user to project sales of various product lines.
- Designed and implemented Just-In-Time ordering system utilizing dBase and EDI to directly interface with book publishers' electronic ordering systems. This innovation reduced inventory on hand by 36% for these product lines.
- Familiar with UNIX and dBase; learning C/C++.

Software Skills:

- Implemented and administered UNIX-based integrated inventory, purchasing, and point-of-sale system for local retailer. System handles 100,000 transactions per year and has substantially streamlined inventory/ordering procedures.
- Installed, revised, and administered "One-Write" accounting system.
- Proficient in DOS, Windows 3.1, and Novell Network.

Business Management Experience:

- Administered payroll, accounts payable/receivable, and all tax filings for retail business.
- Managed $120,000 securities portfolio.
- Restructured organization for retailer, redefining job descriptions and reclassifying job responsibilities.
- Reviewed business insurance policies and instituted changes resulting in 34% savings in annual premiums.
- Reduced costs of direct-mail advertising campaign by 43% through analysis of mailing list and programming designed to minimize postage costs.

EMPLOYMENT HISTORY

1991 - Present   **Operations Manager/Financial Manager**
Enchanted World of Toys, Inc., Orlando, Florida

EDUCATION

Graduate School of Business Administration
University of Miami, Coral Gables, Florida
Coursework in Accounting and Economics

1991   **Bachelor of Science, Aeronautical Studies**
Florida Institute of Technology, Melbourne, Florida
Dean's List — 5 Semesters; G.P.A.: 3.4/4.0

PERSONAL   Sergeant-at-Arms, Orlando Rotary Club
FAA Certified Commercial Pilot

References Available Upon Request.

The lengthy Qualifications section, subdivided into three distinct areas of expertise, places the focus squarely on these essential qualifications while de-emphasizing the candidate's current combined operations/financial management position.

RESUME 39: LYNN P. ANDENORO, CPRW, CCM; SALT LAKE CITY, UT

KATY F. BERGEN

2564 South 1800 East ▪ Salt Lake City, Utah 84106
(801) 245-9607 ▪ katyfbergen@aol.com

PROFILE

TECHNICAL TRAINING PROFESSIONAL
Hospital Information Systems / End User Training & Support
Needs Analysis / Systems Installation & Testing / Financial Applications

Results-driven professional with solid experience in the delivery, evaluation, and customization of effective hands-on instructional programs that improve efficiency, increase productivity, enhance quality, and strengthen financial results. Combine strong analysis, planning, and organizational abilities with effective problem resolution and relationship management skills. Proven expertise in hospital information software, accounting/finance applications, and system installation, upgrade, and support.

VALUE OFFERED

☑ ***In-depth knowledge*** of AS400-based SMS financial software for hospital operations. Provide installation, training, and follow-up support for custom systems. Strong background in accounting/bookkeeping. Proficient with Windows 95/98, Word, PowerPoint, and Lotus Notes.

☑ Deliver ***intensive hands-on training programs*** at client sites using live systems. Ensure that clients understand system functions and can manipulate software to produce desired results.

☑ ***Consistently receive highest possible ratings*** for training effectiveness. Frequently requested by clients to provide training for add-on products and new employees.

☑ ***Analyze business needs***, recommend procedural changes/software customizations, and ***adapt training program content*** and level for specific end user training requirements. Provide detailed feedback to software development team.

☑ ***Highly articulate and effective communicator***. Excellent team-building and interpersonal skills; work well with individuals on all levels.

☑ Organized, take-charge professional with ***exceptional follow-through abilities and detail orientation***; able to oversee projects from concept to successful conclusion.

☑ Effectively prioritize a broad range of responsibilities to ***consistently meet tight deadlines***. Demonstrated success in surpassing productivity and performance objectives.

PROFESSIONAL EXPERIENCE

HEALTH SYSTEMS CONSULTANT
Shared Medical Systems (SMS) ▪ Salt Lake City, UT   1997 to Present

$1.1 billion provider of information system solutions for worldwide healthcare industry. Serve 5,000+ customers in 20 countries in North America, Europe, and Asia Pacific, including hospitals, physician offices, clinics, and major health provider networks and organizations.

Consult on new system implementation for clients in small- to medium-sized hospitals across the U.S. Work with software development team to analyze customer business objectives and develop customized integrated systems to facilitate financial transactions and reporting.

This attractive format—combining a wide, gray-shaded left column, check-box bullet points, and a clean sans serif font—creates a very professional resume for an experienced technical trainer. Note the unusual Value Offered section.

KATY F. BERGEN   Page Two

PROFESSIONAL
EXPERIENCE

HEALTH SYSTEMS CONSULTANT
Shared Medical Systems (SMS), *continued*

Travel to customer sites for 4-week installation jobs. Deliver, install, and test systems; interface with hospital administrators and technical staff for troubleshooting and performance assessments. Train end users on live system, providing on-the-job support/Q&A during final week. Compile thorough reports for management and development team on installation events and training outcomes.

Recent accomplishments:

- Successfully completed training for 35 users at hospitals in 8 states and the Caribbean during 2000. Provided on-site installation, training, and support for 42 weeks of the year.

- Consistently earned *excellent* and *exceeds requirements* ratings on student and supervisor performance evaluations.

- Selected for SMS Installer's Achievement Club —1 of 20 consultants chosen by management among 150 installer/trainers company-wide.

- Assisted 10-member team in documenting policies and procedures for remote computer operations. Wrote hidden command-line policy for AS400 system, including user profiles and upgrades. Provided feedback to team on hospital environment/situations, staff responsibilities, and trainer interactions.

- Worked with 12-member Process Improvement Team to rewrite extensive SMS system implementation methodology.

- Mentored 3 new SMS trainers. Routinely served as resource person for colleagues, providing materials and advice on training methods.

PRIOR
EXPERIENCE

BOOKKEEPER
Affordable Fabrics ▪ Omaha, Nebraska

RADIO NEWS & PROMOTIONS DIRECTOR/WRITER/BROADCASTER
KLO-AM, Ogden, UT ▪ KSIT-FM, Rock Springs, WY
KTRS-FM, Casper, WY ▪ KALL-FM, Salt Lake City, UT
AEROTRAFFIC, Salt Lake City, UT ▪ KRVI-FM, Salt Lake City, UT
KYNN-FM, Omaha, NE

OFFICE MANAGER
Spring Air Mountain West, Inc., Salt Lake City, UT
Norm Bishop Volkswagen, Boise, ID

EDUCATION
AND TRAINING

Boise State University, courses in Business Administration, Boise, Idaho

Professional Development:
Completed 100+ hours of SMS training annually. Courses included Consulting Skills, Business Writing, Interviewing Skills, Listening Skills, Communications, Sexual Harassment, PowerPoint Presentations

Bonita Thomas

27851 Altadena Street, Cacillo, CA 91384 • 661 538-9331 • bearsys@aol.com

Technical Expertise

- Windows 3.0
- Windows NT 4.0
- Windows 95
- Windows 98
- MS Works
- MS Word
- MS Excel
- MS PowerPoint
- Netscape Navigator
- Internet Explorer
- Freelance Graphics
- Ascend 5.0
- Lotus 1-2-3 5.0
- Lotus Notes
- LAN
- WAN

Community Volunteer

- Big Sisters of Los Angeles
- Santa Clarita Shelter
- United Negro College Fund
- Delhaven Community Center
- Adult Tutor, California Literacy

Systems Training & Technical Support Professional

Dynamic, passionate, creative, dedicated, and results-driven Training and Support Specialist with proven record of achievement in computer systems training and technical support (groups and individuals). Outstanding project management, networking, presentation, and follow-up skills. Solid abilities in technical training, team building, management development, and customer service. Extensive background in sophisticated networking, client/server, and telecommunications technologies. Excellent troubleshooter; persuasive communicator; superior motivator. Flexible; loyal; strong work ethic; quick learner.

Professional Experience

CACILLO INSURANCE • Southern Valley, CA • 1986 – Present

Senior Fire Claim Automation and Procedures Specialist (3 years)
Senior Auto Claim Automation and Procedures Specialist (2 years)
Auto/Fire Claims Procedure Training Specialist (2 years)
Agency Field Specialist (7 years)

Consistently promoted based on performance.

As designated **Instructor,** design instructional system and manage training program. Train claims employees in the use of automated computer system for effective handling of client claims. Conduct group sessions either in office or at central training facility. Perform work flow analysis on clerical support, professional (claims representatives), and management units in each office: interview and watch them perform, then review common errors occurring in different situations; lead monthly discussions with superiors and report findings directly to corporate HQ. Keep meticulous records as to who (300+ employees) was trained, when, and in which applications.

In **Technical Support** role, manage, support, troubleshoot, and maintain claims system for five offices. Provide on-site training and telephone support (MIS Help Desk) for multiple offices/departments (clerical, administrative, accounting, claims, agency administration, management). Produce computerized/multimedia presentation materials for employee meetings and other functions. Involved in development, testing, and training of new software programs distributed throughout the region.

- Instrumental in diagnosing major system problem and implementing solution in regional offices affecting 100+ employees. Resolved numerous issues and made recommendations that were adopted office-wide.

- Member of system conversion team when Claim Master Record software superseded Claim Service Record; conversion from mainframe/dumb terminal to distributed client/server PC-based system.

- Lead project team in setup and operation of Disaster Operation Offices for handling of claims. Set up computers (hardware), train and supervise temporary/permanent staff to process claims.

Education
Bachelor of Arts: University of Redlands, Redlands, CA
- Major: Communications; Minor: Education
Microsoft Office User Specialist Program
IIA (Insurance Institute of America) Designation
Department of Insurance, State of California
- Fire and Casualty Broker/Agent, Life Agent

This resume packs a lot of information onto one page, yet in a highly readable format thanks to clear, bold headings, brief bullet-point lists, and a readable serif font. The computer graphic adds interest and helps to break up the text-rich sections.

MELINDA A. PETERS

4000 West Low, Tyler, Texas 75700
(903) 555-9999
melinda.peters@ramsey.net

"Melinda is able to present training material in a manner understood by the entire spectrum of corporate employees. This style of presentation has proved to very effective in training almost 3,000 employees from diverse industries with a wide variety of needs."
— Written by John Clark; Published in SVITraining Newsletter

PROGRAM DEVELOPMENT & MANAGEMENT ◆ COMMUNICATIONS FLOW MANAGEMENT

HIGHLIGHTS OF QUALIFICATIONS

◆ Dynamic **COMMUNICATIONS PROFESSIONAL, CORPORATE TRAINER, & PROGRAM DEVELOPER** with diverse experience and proven success in:

Corporate Training ◆ Communications Flow Management ◆ Sales & Client Growth
Public Relations & Public Speaking ◆ Strategic Planning & Development
Program & Systems Design, Implementation, & Management

◆ **Registered CBIS Trainer in customer service.** Created new training manuals for CBIS upgrade version, which was incorporated as company's standard training manual. Designed and formulated corporate training materials.

◆ **Savvy in communications technology systems design and layout.**
Hardware: A/S 400; IBM PC; Macintosh
Operating Systems: Novell NetWare; Windows 98/95/NT
Applications: Microsoft Office (Access, Excel, PowerPoint, Word); Lotus SmartSuite (WordPro, Lotus 1-2-3, Approach, Freelance Graphics); Corel WordPerfect Suite (WordPerfect, Quattro Pro, Presentations, Paradox); E-mail: Groupwise, MS Exchange, Schedule+, Outlook, MS Mail, Lotus Notes; Internet: MS Internet Explorer, Netscape Navigator, MS FrontPage

◆ Optimize training success by strategically planning and organizing effective programs, cultivating trusting relationships with people of diverse levels and personalities, and exercising immense patience and understanding.

PROFESSIONAL EXPERIENCE

COMPUTER NETWORK TECHNOLOGIES – Tyler, Texas (1995-Present)
Director of Training & Application Training Specialist

Challenged with developing, coordinating, launching, marketing, and conducting corporate training program for major full-service East Texas computer firm. Developed marketing plan to promote new program. Designed computerized system to track and maintain all aspects of program.

Selected Achievements & Projects

• **Escalated sales 200+% and client base 900%** through restructure/redevelopment of primitive training program and effective corporate training and public relations.

• Mastered challenge of executing massive hospital-wide conversion and training program for the University of Texas Health Center at Tyler; included converting mainframe platform to PC and developing and presenting five-month training program for 612 users.

• Developed and coordinated all aspects of training during conversion for major law firm (Potter, Minton, Roberts, Davis, & Jones, P.C.), which encompassed converting Windows 3.1 with WordPerfect 5.1 to Windows 95 with Microsoft Office 97. Designed customized material used in training. **Successfully completed training of each group in two days** (total 45 users).

• Executed **Windows NT/Microsoft Office 97 conversion** and **training program** for Kilgore Division of Texaco (100 users).

• **Managed Windows 95/MS Exchange conversion** and **training program** for 225 corporate headquarters employees of The Trane Company.

~ ~ ~ Continued on Page Two ~ ~ ~

This resume starts off with a "bang"—a highly complimentary quote that came from a published (thus perceived as highly credible) source.

MELINDA A. PETERS

Page Two

CABLE TV – Tyler, Texas (1990-1995)
Corporate Field Trainer

Planned, coordinated, and delivered software training of highly confidential, specialized, and sensitive nature to corporate executives nationwide for 12th largest cable company in North America (out of over 3,000) at 65 national offices. Designed and authored training materials. Researched procedures and customized software for each system office. Provided in-house and field training in areas of Customer Sales, Billing Software Operations, Special Needs Reports, Bad Debt Collections, System Marketing, Time Management, Organizational Communication, Commercial Account Maintenance, and Interpersonal Communications.

Selected Achievements & Projects

- **Managed field training of Corporate Communications Overhaul Project**, which encompassed A/S 400 billing software conversion for entire company with 350 users at 65 locations. **Successfully completed 50 systems in 7 months.**
- **Coauthored manual for CBIS Upgrade Version** that was implemented as company's standard.
- Analyzed and identified system and software malfunctions and developed strategies/programs to resolve inefficiencies.

BROSANG'S – Dallas, Texas (1984-1990)
Director of Banquets and Special Events

- Independently coordinated all aspects of banquets and special-event parties (in-house and outside); activities included negotiating pricing, purchasing, subcontracting, floral arrangements, design, planning, and coordination of weddings and receptions, business meetings, social affairs, and seasonal parties with costs of $3,000–$5,000 each.
- Marketed retail merchandise in gift shop. Created enticing merchandising/displays and superior customer service.

EDUCATION

UNIVERSITY OF TEXAS AT TYLER – Tyler, Texas
Bachelor of Science Degree in Speech and Communication
Emphasis: **Public Relations**

PROFESSIONAL AFFILIATIONS/HONORS

Member, UNIVERSITY OF TEXAS ALUMNI ASSOCIATION

Recipient of **"Musician's Award"** (1997) (presented to the **"Most Dedicated Christian Musician"**)

KYO TANAKA

75 Hillcrest Drive • East Haven, CT 06512 • (203) 469-2320 • kyotanaka@netzero.net

PROFILE

Experienced technical writer / trainer with demonstrated skill in documenting software used for both non-technical users and technical support staff. Recognized for producing consistently clear, coherent documentation within deadline and with minimal supervision. Accustomed to collaborating closely with programmers during development and testing as an integral part of the software development team.

- ❑ Strengths include communication skills (both oral and written), organization and planning, meticulous proofreading, and project / schedule management.

- ❑ Experienced with computers and, in particular, with word processing programs and authoring systems (Corel WordPerfect, Microsoft Word, RoboHelp).

EXPERIENCE

MAAX INDUSTRIAL AUTOMATION AND CONTROLS, New Haven, Connecticut
AUTO-CONTROLS CORPORATION (purchased by Maax IAC 4/99)
HIGH RIDGE CORPORATION (purchased by Auto-Controls 6/97)

Technical Writer / Trainer, 1996 – May 2001

Wrote detailed on-line and print instruction manuals for Windows NT-based and OS/2-based industrial gauging equipment.

- ❑ Manuals included a technical reference for setting up and maintaining the hardware as well as in-depth software documentation for daily use and system setup.

- ❑ Involved in each product during the development cycle and contributed significantly to software testing.

- ❑ Provided software training classes, for both an historical product and newer products, to customers and technical support personnel.

Technical Writer, 1994-1996

Researched, wrote, and often illustrated industrial-gauge manuals.

- ❑ Manuals include theory, safety requirements, installation and setup procedures, operator guides, and maintenance requirements.

- ❑ Also wrote detailed instructions for the computerized electronics or personal computers used to operate the gauges.

"With this resume, Kyo rapidly moved on to a new technical writing position after the company relocated its headquarters out of state."

KYO TANAKA

Page 2

FREELANCE

Writer / Proofreader / Trainer, 1993-Present

Independently generate diverse professional assignments. Recent sampling includes:

- ❑ Teach word processing (Corel WordPerfect and Microsoft Word) classes in the Southern Connecticut Community Education program.

- ❑ Taught Windows NT, basic and intermediate, to employees of Kelly Staffing Service, 1999.

- ❑ Revised Policies & Procedures manual for Pratt & Whitney Credit Union, 2 versions, 1997 and 1998.

- ❑ Summarized market research interviews, edited and consolidated findings into structured reports for Angus Consultants, 1994.

- ❑ Wrote travel article published in *Yankee* magazine, 1999.

- ❑ Feature article writer for local Habitat for Humanity newsletter (volunteer).

YALE-NEW HAVEN LIBRARY, New Haven, Connecticut

Indexer, January 1992 - May 1993

Assisted with the development of a local history index generated from newspapers dating back to the early 1800s. Focused primarily on individuals and their connections to events.

BUILDERS REVIEW, INC., Derby, Connecticut

Managing Editor, March 1989 - November 1991

Wrote and assigned feature articles, "spotlights" on local home builder associations, and news items, as well as promotional material for the company. Proofread both the Xerox and blue-line of the 20-plus magazines and all printing assignments. Established the editorial, feature, and production schedules for all the magazines.

EDUCATION

UNIVERSITY OF CONNECTICUT, Storrs, Connecticut

Bachelor of Arts, Biology, May 1989

Minors in both Communications and English. Worked Sophomore, Junior and Senior years as a Resident Assistant for the University Housing Department. Served one year as a Peer Assistant. Active in intramural sports.

ACTIVITIES

- ❑ Senior Member of the Society for Technical Communication.

- ❑ Marathoner (qualified for Boston Marathon 2001).

NATHANIEL (NICK) JOHNSON

882 Berkinshire Drive
Austin, Texas 78664   http://www.careerfolios.com/nickjohnson

Home: 214-555-1212
Fax: 214-555-1212

SALES AND MARKETING PROFESSIONAL
FOCUS: TECHNOLOGY / SOLUTIONS / SERVICES

Results-oriented, customer-focused executive with over 10 years' experience leading sales and marketing initiatives to increase market share and build revenues. Visionary leader with strong management and team-building skills used to motivate staff and develop business partnerships. Excellent communication skills used to inform, educate, persuade and motivate a variety of persons including industry leaders, managers, engineers, government officials and sales staff.

- Competitive Market Analysis
- New Product Launch
- Market Positioning
- Client Needs Assessment

- Sales Cycle Management
- Profit and Revenue Growth
- Quality Control
- Contract Negotiations

- Business-to-Business
- Business-to-Government
- JIT
- Customer Satisfaction

CONTRIBUTIONS AND ACCOMPLISHMENTS

- Earned "Preferred Supplier" designation from key customer through consistent product quality and on-time delivery.
- Negotiated 5-year contract with industry leader to supply product for major government defense project as well as subcontracted sales.
- Delivered significant results in increased sales throughout employment history.
- Built positive vendor relationships allowing company to negotiate improved cost-of-goods resulting in increased profit margins.
- Utilized management strategies to enhance company communications and improve sales and operations systems.
- Planned East Coast territory expansion for established company; developed business plans to gain market share in a highly competitive industry.
- Opened new markets and gained access to new industries.
- Developed partnerships with other vendors to maximize market share and revenues.
- Coordinated sales and engineering teams in successful effort to achieve vendor status and product approval with major buyer.

PROFESSIONAL EXPERIENCE

ASLO INDUSTRIES - Columbus, OH, and St. Petersburg, FL
Sales and Marketing Director (2000-2001)
Supervised 12-15 persons in sales and marketing for wire and cable manufacturer and distributor. Worked with General Manager to improve plant efficiency and devise system to improve shipping performance. Reduced cost-of-goods through enhanced vendor relationships. Established employee training system to assure consistent service and adherence to company policy.
- Increased sales 20% in 8 months.
- Initiated management committees to improve communications and operations.

Branch Manager (1991-1996)
Directed sales and warehouse operations. Managed customer inventories, technical support, new product design and quality control. Created sales proposals and pricing structures.
- Increased sales over 100% three consecutive years.
- Negotiated $4 million contract with McDonnell-Douglas; structured contract to gain additional subcontract sales, increasing revenue and net margins.
- Maintained 98% on-time delivery and 95% quality ratings; led to "preferred supplier" status with key customer.
- Awarded 1993 *Employee of the Year* designation.

For sales and marketing professionals, success is all about numbers, and this resume showcases the candidate's strong accomplishments in technology sales. Note that the key word list in the summary

NATHANIEL (NICK) JOHNSON

RÉSUMÉ - PAGE 2

ALBRIGHT ELECTRONICS CABLE (formerly NetScope) - Dallas, TX
Regional Sales Manager (1998-2000)
Directed sales activities and technical support for 13 states in central U.S. territory. Developed creative proposals to gain market share. Supported engineers in product design. Initiated recruitment and hiring of manufacturer's representatives to increase sales.

- Introduced new product to previously untapped industry and effectively gained access to this market.
- Achieved approved vendor status and first-ever product approval by Bell Helicopter.
- Reduced critical distribution lead times by creating ready-to-ship inventory plan.
- Gained significant market share through partnership of supply chain segments.
- Initiated negotiation of $1.7 million contract.

ELECTROMARKET - Orlando, FL
District Sales Manager (1997)
Hired to open East Coast sales territory in highly competitive market of passive electronic components, wire and cable and electronic materials. Consulted with senior management in market strategy and territory development. Developed and implemented expansion plans.

A.E. PETRIE, INC. - Hartford, CT
Sales Representative (1989-1991)
Managed large sales territory including New York, New Jersey and Connecticut for leading U.S. wire and cable distributor targeting the aerospace industry. Introduced Just-In-Time (JIT) inventory proposals and quality control measures. Analyzed client needs through direct interaction with design engineers.

- Increased sales over 200%.
- Expanded sales of products to previously untargeted industrial and energy markets.
- Improved sales through modification and product specification to meet specific client needs.

U.S. MAJORITY LEADER, DICK ARMEY - Washington, DC, and Lewisville, TX
Consultant / Director / Legislative Assistant / Organizational Director (1984-1988)
Joined Mr. Armey's campaign for Congress as Organizational Director to recruit and direct campaign volunteers. Promoted to subsequent leadership positions with Mr. Armey's organization based on performance and ability to interact with political leaders. Assisted with development of proposals for federal legislation. Directed first reelection campaign including writing reelection plans, financial oversight, fundraising, volunteer recruitment and organization, media planning and execution.

- Increased re-election percentage 18%.
- Recruited over 700 volunteers for initial campaign; doubled volunteer base for reelection.
- Exceeded fundraising goals by 35%.

EDUCATION AND CERTIFICATIONS

CERTIFIED MEDIATOR, **Southern Methodist University**, Plano (2000)

BA - PUBLIC ADMINISTRATION, **Stephen F. Austin State University**, Nacogdoches (1983)

PROFESSIONAL ORGANIZATIONS

SOUTHWEST CONFLICT RESOLUTION NETWORK, **Founding President** (1999)

PC-Proficient with MS Word, Excel, PowerPoint, ACT, Internet and Email

emphasizes sales and marketing language rather than technology skills, because this is what's most important for this individual.

LOUIS M. DIAMOND

515 Bay Drive
Residence: (732) 295-9803

Brick, New Jersey 08724
Mobile: (201) 609-2520

email: lmdiamond@home.com

TECHNOLOGY SALES / MARKETING AND BUSINESS DEVELOPMENT

Asia, Europe, Middle East and United States

Solid executive career leading start-up and fast-track growth of high-technology companies. Expert in business development, product positioning and market expansion with strong operating, financial and HR skills. Strengths include forging cooperative working relationships, identifying and formulating strategic, revenue-generating partnerships. Proven "intraprenuer" with a track record in championing new organizational initiatives and employing "out of the box" thinking.

CAREER HISTORY

XYLINK CORPORATION, San Diego, CA (2/96-Present)

Director of Business Development, 7/99 to Present

Full strategic and tactical responsibility for creating and leading a worldwide business development team in the sale of high-technology products, including security software, standalone WAN / LAN appliances, modules and components. Accountable for planning and orchestrating aggressive market and business development initiatives throughout emerging global markets for this $400 million corporation. Captured vertical industries such as telecommunications (network equipment manufacturers and carriers), health care (payers and providers) and wireless (e-merchants and solution providers). Performed financial evaluation of business development opportunities, including NPV and IRR calculations. Conceived and developed new product distribution channels that increased market penetration.

Accomplishments:

- Evaluated competitive activity, competitive products, emerging technologies and new markets to determine the corporation's global market position. Performed financial evaluation of business-development opportunities, including NPV and IRR calculations.

- Built and led a global business development and sales organization. Spearheaded business development initiatives and marketing strategies that spanned four continents. Trained new sales recruits in international liaison, marketing and business development skills.

- Negotiated an annual $4 million technology license contract with L3 Communications.

- Performed due diligence and negotiated an OEM contract with DICA technologies for the sale of an ISDN product into the Japanese market; captured $3.5 million in annual sales revenues.

- Negotiated and signed a global purchasing agreement with AT&T Solutions, resulting in $6 million in annual sales revenues.

- Established multichannel distribution networks to expand product reach in health care, wireless and telecommunications markets.

- Negotiated strategic alliances and signed multiple co-marketing agreements, including the establishment of partnerships with SYMANTEC and IBM/Tivoli.

- Developed Marconi Communications and ADTRAN as a reseller channel for VPN products; estimated annual revenue of $6.5M.

- Developed business partnership with Nokia and Ericsson to provide wireless security technology.

Global Account Manager, 2/96-7/99

- Drove international sales revenues, launched new business development initiatives and profitably directed account development programs throughout emerging markets worldwide, including such accounts as Citigroup, AT&T Solutions, MBNA, Chase, Bankers Trust, Credit Suisse / First Boston and Fidelity Investments.

- Increased sales revenues by 200% over two-year period.

(Page One of Two)

More than half of the first page of this resume is taken up with sales-related accomplishments. As in resume 43, technical qualifications are included only within the context of sales achievements.

LOUIS M. DIAMOND
Page Two

CAREER HISTORY (Continued)

CINCINNATI ELECTRONICS CORPORATION, Mason, OH (1/95-2/96)

Regional Sales Manager, Eastern United States

Responsible for regional profit and loss, distribution network management, and the coordination of marketing and sales activities within a territory extending from the Caribbean to eastern Canada. Boosted both market penetration and company brand recognition. Increased sales by more than 90 percent. Revamped regional coverage to maximize productivity and enhance efficiency of the distribution network. Tracked sales and analyzed trends and market conditions to develop annual forecasts. Generated market analysis reports. Developed and implemented application-specific seminars and presentations for value-added resellers. Interfaced with advertising and public relations agencies to maximize marketing efforts.

HUGHES AIRCRAFT CORPORATION (FLIR Systems, Inc.), Carlsbad, CA (12/89-11/94)

District Sales Manager, Northeast Territory

Managed and coordinated infrared imaging system sales to Fortune 500 companies throughout New Jersey and extending to eastern Canada. Cultivated this territory by developing and implementing comprehensive marketing strategies. Increased sales by 74% within a five-year period. Hired and trained independent factory representatives to exceed targeted sales quotas. Tailored an incentive program to optimize productivity.

AGEMA INFRARED SYSTEMS, Secaucus, NJ (9/87-12/89)

Sales/Service Representative

Introduced thermal imaging systems to the medical marketplace. Performed market research prior to product introduction.

DATAGRAPHIX, New York, NY (7/86-9/87)

Customer Engineer

Responsible for the installation and maintenance of complex microfiche systems.

EDUCATION

RUTGERS, THE STATE UNIVERSITY OF NEW JERSEY, Newark, NJ

Executive MBA, Finance Concentration

Bachelor of Science Degree, Marketing

GAVILAN COLLEGE, Gilroy, CA

Associate Degree, Electronic Technology

MILITARY HISTORY

UNITED STATES NAVY (Honorable Discharge), 9/80-6/86

Cryptologic Technician Maintenance E-5; received Top-Secret SBI Clearance

References Furnished Upon Request.

Dwight D. Stephenson

1082 South Street • Natick, Massachusetts 01760
Tel: 508-555-9876 • Fax: 508-555-1234 • dstephenson@mailcity.com

IT PROFESSIONAL SERVICES / TECHNOLOGY SALES

- 20 years of experience – information technology and professional service sales
- Consistently achieve or surpass quota
- Proficient in learning and selling technical products to sophisticated clients
- Exceptional ability to build a region through prospecting and missionary selling
- Strong "closer" with emphasis on strategic selling to major account market
- Leadership qualities and a team player

PROFESSIONAL EXPERIENCE

TECHNOLOGY FOR YOU – Boston, MA   1999 – Present
Regional Sales Manager – *IT professional services to Fortune 500 accounts*
- Place teams of consultants to identify/solve issues of client, e.g., enterprise systems management, Y2K compliance, software distribution, etc.
- Exceeded quota ($3 million) with sales to large corporate and government accounts.

SOLUTIONS, INC. – Boston, MA   1995 – 1999
Account Manager – *Mainframe and PC development tools and Year 2000 solutions for major accounts in the New England marketplace*
- Closed sales with large corporate accounts, including BankBoston, Fidelity, UNUM and Allmerica.
- Exceeded quota with fifty percent of the business coming from new accounts. Developed strong CIO / CTO relationships with client companies to achieve long-term company success.
- Rebuilt Fortune 500 direct end-user account base in New England.
- Established and managed new systems integration partners throughout New England.

RBN ASSOCIATES, INC. – Boston, MA, and Providence, RI   1993 – 1995
Account Manager – *Routers, bridges and other internetworking products*
- Built State of Rhode Island territory from $400K ('93) to $2.5 million in sales ('94).
- Top producer of new account business in Eastern Region.
- Successfully maintained key end-user accounts including Fleet Bank, GTECH, Textron and State of Rhode Island.
- Developed numerous new accounts and reseller channels.

With a bold, italic description of specific technologies and environments following each job title, it's very clear that Mr. Stephenson's expertise is in technology sales. Note how sales "buzz words" (quota, prospecting, missionary selling, strategic selling, and so forth) are included in the summary.

Dwight D. Stephenson, 508-555-9876
Page 2

DATATEL, INC. – Boston, MA   1990 – 1993
Senior Account Executive – *Networking management systems, multiplexers*

- Represented company products in the public and private sectors.

- Established strong relationships with new WAN and LAN customers, including State of Massachusetts, BBN, Raytheon, Lotus.

- Rookie of the Year, 1991

ENTERPRISE DATA SYSTEMS CORP. – Boston, MA   1987 – 1990
Account Manager – *IBM plug-compatible CPUs and data storage systems*

- Produced over $10 million in sales to commercial, education and public sector accounts.

- Developed relationships with highest levels of MIS management in Boston.

- Achieved status as highest producing representative in Boston District.

- Awarded 1990 Sales Contest Winner (#5 out of 135).

VITEM CORPORATION – Albany, NY, and Boston, MA   1983 – 1987
Sales Representative – *Plug-compatible storage equipment and 3270 communication products*

- Sold successfully to Albany-area commercial and New York State government accounts.

- Developed significant volume of new accounts; established strong contacts with 50 area data-processing industry executives.

- Managed all sales functions of remote office.

- Achieved Quota Club status: #1 ('84) and #2 ('85). Sold over $2 million/yr. '84 - '87.

SOFTWARE UNLIMITED – Boston, MA   1979 – 1983
Account Manager – *IBM - 34/38-type minicomputers and software for the manufacturing and distribution industry*
Consistently exceeded quota objectives ('81 through '83). Acquired excellent product and industry training.

TRAINING, SEMINARS and WORKSHOPS

Holden Associates	– Power-Based Selling (1995)
Target Marketing Associates	– Target Account Selling (1992)
Miller-Heiman	– Strategic Selling (1988)
	– Conceptual Sales (1988)

EDUCATION

MBA, 1985, Bentley College – Waltham, MA
Bachelor of Arts, Economics, 1979, Roger Williams College – Bristol, RI

Darrell Jahari
SENIOR TECHNICAL SALES / MARKETING CONSULTANT

555 Straley Avenue
Las Vegas, Nevada 89104

(702) 555-5555
jmdoe@yahoo.com

CAREER PROFILE

*Strategic Marketing Positioning / New Product Launch / New Market Development
Market Research / Multimedia Communications / Sales Forecasting / Trend Analysis
Total Quality Management / Telecommunications & Network Solutions*

Dynamic sales and marketing management career delivering state-of the-art technology nationwide. Track record of achieving strong and sustainable revenue, market and profit contributions through expertise in business development, organizational development and performance management. Keen presentation, negotiation, communication and cross-cultural skills.

EXPERIENCE AND ACCOMPLISHMENTS

Pre-Sales Marketing Support Representative   1999-2001

Silver State Technology, Las Vegas, Nevada

Pre-sales and post-sales technical support for the new IBM Thin Client Networkstation. Territory required 75% travel throughout 9 western U.S. States and western Canada. Marketed and installed the IBM Thin Client Networkstation and its software on multiple system platforms — Windows NT 4.0 PC, IBM AS/400, IBM RS/6000, IBM S/390 — in various industries including manufacturing, finance, retail, government, distribution, and transportation.

- Provided technical proof of concept by installing the IBM Thin Client Networkstation on clients' existing network and demonstrating its features and functions in addressing the customer's requirements.

- Delivered personalized presentations, customer briefings, and product education.

Senior Sales Representative   1997-1999

Los Peros Technical Consultants, Las Vegas, Nevada

Guided the entire sales cycle management process, from initial client consultation and needs assessment through service presentation, price and service negotiations, and final sales closing. Consistently exceeded monthly enrollment goals by successfully executing sales negotiations and favorably positioning sales closing against competition. Applied sales forecasting, trend analysis, and market research in the conceptualization, implementation and documentation of profitable business operations that increased enrollments and revenue.

Marketing Sales Manager   1994-1997

Booz & Grady, LLC, Las Vegas, Nevada

Evaluated new product opportunities and directed strategic development of business plans, financial projections, marketing plans and field sales teams. Presented product, reference and price suggestions in strategic planning sessions in cooperation with top-level executives, sales and marketing managers, product line managers, manufacturing director and other key management staff. Surveyed customers in the direction of the copywriting and graphic design of multimedia communication pieces.

Starting off the Career Profile with a list of key words is an effective way to position this individual "right off the bat." The list is followed by a concise summary and results-oriented job descriptions.

Darrell Jahari — Page 2

Product Marketing Manager 1992-1994

Citrus Technology, Sunnyvale, California

Utilized Total Quality method to manage a fully integrated customer service function composed of 8 personnel from graphic design, domestic and foreign public relations, and accounting; also oversaw budget in Product Development Department. Evaluated competitive market trends and implemented product positioning strategies to ensure long-term and sustainable growth. Increased customer satisfaction ratings with the implementation of customer-driven account management and sales retention strategies. Directed multimedia production and supplied personnel with materials to create an integrated campaign management strategy.

- Exploded market penetration of Fortune 500 companies, securing 11 new corporate accounts and driving significant gain in revenue.

- Directed market launch of new 4745 front-end processor, delivering total revenues of more than $47,000,000 in FY93.

Telecommunications Marketing Specialist 1980-1992

Western Telcom, San Francisco, California

Marketing executive with full responsibility for the design, development and implementation of marketing IBM telecommunication products. Fast-track promotion through four increasingly responsible assignments to final position as Telecommunications Marketing Specialist. Telecommunications support to IBM marketing branches in six states, providing planning, configuring and networking designs. Managed new single domain (mid-range systems) to multi-domain (large systems) of corporate and government accounts.

- Appointed to oversee the creation of 9 new product demonstration booths as Project Leader for the TEXPO 88 trade show at San Francisco Moscone Center.

- As a member of merger acquisition team, structured and executed asset purchase of Wes-Tel-Co Corporation and launched new Wes-Tel-Co 9750 CBX.

CIVIC LEADERSHIP

Certified mediator for Clark County and State of Nevada.

Direct strategic planning committees of the American Cancer Society, the Volunteers of America, and the United Way's fundraising campaigns.

TECHNOLOGY SKILLS & EXPERTISE

IBM Thin Client Networkstation	Local Area Networks (LANs)
Microsoft Windows NT 4.0 Terminal Server	Citrix Metaframe 1.8
TCP/IP	Cisco Routers/Bridges
Voice, Data, & Video Telecommunications	IBM Cabling Systems

Michael Roy

5 Fairway Court • Burlington, Ontario, Canada L7M 2S8

(905) 336-5454 • (905) 336-1999 (FAX) • mroy@hotmail.com

IT BUSINESS DEVELOPMENT PROFESSIONAL

Experienced business development executive with 17 years of success in formulating and implementing high-level strategic business directions within the Pharmaceutical, Healthcare and Financial Industries. Innovative professional with proven ability to successfully analyze client business issues, recommend IT solutions and convert to sales opportunity utilizing:

- Program Development & Management
- Product Development & Marketing
- Client Training & Management
- Team Leadership

Demonstrated skill in assimilating new concepts and technology and capitalizing on the primary competencies of technical and design teams.

TECHNICAL SKILLS

Project Management Tools	**Special Operating Systems**	**Network/Infrastructure**
Visio 5.0	Document Imaging	LAN/WAN
Microsoft Project 98	Automated Workflow	Wireless Cardiac Telemetry
Microsoft Office 98/NT/2000	Electronic Medical Records	Monitoring Systems

CAREER HIGHLIGHTS

Compusolutions, Washington, DC   2000 – Present
Regional Vice President—Business Development
Manage a multidisciplinary team of technical professionals in offshore/onshore outsourcing of Software Development to leading-edge technology firms.

- Increased Software Development outsourcing contracts by $30M in 6 months within the domains of ERP, CRM, Document Imaging, Workflow, Airline Reservation Systems, and e-learning.
- Collaborated with local and international project leaders to achieve "best practices" in software development life cycle.
- Provided management leadership to multiple teams of professionals such as project managers, business analysts, technical architects, web developers, and quality assurance resources.

ELT, Ottawa, ON   1998 – 2000
Senior Business Development Executive
Assumed responsibility for software sales (in excess of $10M) and professional services in an eight-state account base for a Fortune 50 Healthcare Information Systems company.

- Collaborated with implementation team to successfully install clinical information, document imaging, and workflow systems in 15 larger hospitals.
- Developed cost benefits and return-on-investment analysis demonstrating the effectiveness of document imaging and workflow on clinical and financial environments.
- Won the approval of key executive stakeholders (CEO, CFO) to convert ROI analysis into sales opportunity.

This resume includes a summary that hits all the right notes to connect with technology companies looking for an experienced business-development professional. The position summaries are brief and results oriented.

Michael Roy   Page 2

HighNet Systems Inc., Houston, TX   1996 – 1998
Technical Account Executive
Consulted with key executives in utilization of IT to solve business issues for a developer of document imaging and workflow systems for the Financial and Healthcare Industries.

- Participated in maintenance of various accounts and projects within the financial and healthcare industries.
- Worked effectively as a team member to assemble new technology and information.

SYmPiatic, Ottawa, ON   1991 – 1996
Director—Information Technology
Provided technical leadership to a company of 850 employees whose areas of expertise centered on clinical information systems for the healthcare industry.

- Designed, implemented, and maintained the LAN environment at the corporate and seven regional offices across Canada.
- Successfully coordinated corporate selection of Customer Relationship Management (CRM) solutions provider.

Technis Ltd., Toronto, ON   1984 – 1991
Technical Service Engineer
Designed and implemented LAN/WAN-based diagnostic and monitoring systems for hospital critical-care environments.

- Collaborated in the management of multiple complex projects, providing support profit growth from $2M to $10M in 1 year.
- Provided project management and technical support, on-site diagnosis and troubleshooting of LAN and wireless cardiac telemetry monitoring systems installations.

J&R Testing, Windsor, ON   1983-1984
Design Engineer
Worked on all phases of design and development of various industrial and pharmaceutical testing equipment.

- Consulted with development team on architecture and development tools that enabled the on-time, on-budget development of the Hepatitis Testing System.

EDUCATION & PROFESSIONAL TRAINING

- **Electrical Engineering Technologist:** Algonquin College, Ottawa, ON
- **Electrical Engineering Technician:** Seneca College, Toronto, ON
- **Project Management Skills:** DigitalThink, Inc.
- **Data Communication and Networking:** Learning Tree International, Ottawa, ON
- **Financial and Management Accounting:** Toronto University, Toronto, ON
- **Executive Presentation Skills:** Communispond Inc., Chicago, IL

REFERENCES AVAILABLE UPON REQUEST

CHAPTER 7

Resumes for Network and Systems Technologists

- Network Administrators and Analysts
- Network Engineers
- PC and Computer Specialists
- Systems Administrators
- Systems Engineers and Analysts
- Certified Professional Systems Engineers

RESUME 48: LAURA A. DECARLO, CCM, CPRW; MELBOURNE, FL

Charles Cartlett

1001 Bellgrade, Athens OH 44820
(740) 341-8977 • cartlett@coastalnet.com

IT professional with key skills as:
NETWORK ADMINISTRATOR / TECHNICIAN & PC SUPPORT PROFESSIONAL

MICROSOFT CERTIFIED SYSTEMS ENGINEER (MCSE) with extensive and diverse technical experience in the IT field, emphasizing network administration and PC support. Excellent problem solver with strong communication, teamwork, and interpersonal skills. Skilled supervisor and manager. Experience includes:

• Network Planning	• System Integration	• Switches & Hubs
• Frame Relay Networking	• Software Configuration	• Router Configuration
• Telephony & Fiber Optics	• TCP/IP	• Network Firewalls
• Internet Information Server	• Hardware Configuration	• ISDN / T1 Lines

- **Operating Systems:** Windows NT, Windows NT Server, NT Terminal Server, NT Workstation, Windows 2000 Pro, UNIX Sun, and Mac
- **Software:** MS Office (Word, PowerPoint, Excel, Access), MS Outlook, and Norton

EDUCATION & TRAINING

Microsoft Certified Systems Engineer Curriculum, Herzing College, WI – 1999
Bachelor of Science in Computer Information Systems, University of Wisconsin, WI – 1994

PROFESSIONAL EXPERIENCE

IT SYSTEMS MANAGER, Sortex Systems, Inc., Athens, OH   1997 to Present
Directed a team of PC Technicians, a Network Administrator / Analyst, and two Help Desk personnel in the management of all facets of information technology for this 2000-person financial firm.

Provided support and planning for critical requirements including:
... Network Administration ... Computer Builds ... Software Loads ... Product Testing
... Telephony ... End-User Support & Training ... Vendor Relations ... Project Management

Critical contributions included:
- *Networking:* Planned and integrated a 12-office Windows NT 4.0 Domain with over 800 computers. Administered primary and back-up domain controllers, file servers, print servers, proxy server, and e-mail server. Introduced thin client technology through dial-in connection for remote administration.
- *Computer Network Security:* Implemented policies for employee use of Internet and e-mail. Utilized Geotech Firewall and monitored proxy server.
- *Telephony Administration:* Integrated voice-over IP to reduce phone bills between offices. Equipment paid for itself in six weeks, and introduced a monthly savings of $6K. Managed Audix phone system.
- *Technical Support:* Provided technical support and end-user training to internal and external customers on network, software, and computer systems.
- *Vendor Relations:* Negotiated all hardware and software purchases for company, successfully saving thousands during new network integration.

PC TECHNICIAN, Sortex Systems Inc., Athens, OH   1994 to Present

The MCSE logo at the top is a nice attention-getter. The resume itself is concise and focused on technical skills and "critical contributions."

Myra C. Landers

1256 GEYERS LANE, ELLICOTT CITY, MD 21046 — 301.555.5555 — MCL@HOTMAIL.COM

Network Administrator / Systems Analyst

Tech Profile

- ▶ PC Hardware & Software Configurations
- ▶ DOS
- ▶ LAN/WAN
- ▶ Windows NT Workstation (4.0 & 5.0)
- ▶ ADP
- ▶ Microsoft Products

Awards

- ▶ Received a number of notable awards for excellence in managing computer operations, professionalism, and team leadership. Please inquire as to the nature of the awards.

Profile

- ▶ Expert knowledge of all Microsoft products.
- ▶ Microsoft Certified Professional, NT Workstation 4.0, April 2000.
- ▶ Ten years' direct experience supervising critical computer operations.
- ▶ Troubleshoot operations, processes, and networks; determine accurate and timely solutions. Apply quality assurance measures.

Experience

UNITED STATES ARMY, 1993 to 2001   *Top Secret Clearance*
Network Administrator/Systems Analyst, Germany   **1996 to Present**

- ▶ Supervise two personnel supporting critical computer requirements and ongoing operations. Effectively manage daily operations in a network with 50 computers, two servers (40 offices), and 250 clients.
- ▶ Implement upgrades and policies regarding network security. Excellent ability to research and figure new ways to make applications run smoother. Skilled problem solver. Provide quality service to all customers. React quickly and thoughtfully to ADP problems, applying an experienced knowledge of computer systems to ensure minimal computer problems/downtime. Keep all automation systems free from viruses. Analyze problems/glitches and recommend or implement viable working solutions.
- ▶ Maintain a comprehensive, working knowledge of Windows NT 4.0 Server Workstation and Exchange Server 5.0. Proficient knowledge of PC server hardware and software configurations and LAN/WAN networking.
- ▶ Start new accounts for secure Internet access. Manage and issue PKI email encryption software to best secure military email.
- ▶ Selected by senior management to co-lead a diverse team in providing daily customer service and network administration. Instrumental in getting a new server on-line.

SPECIFIC PROJECT

- ▶ Developed a system policy and implemented network security upgrading software, ensuring compatibility with the fast-paced civilian sector, which was running dual operating systems. Ensured the DOS-based programs operated correctly, then installed more server-based software and services enabling server-based administration of the network, significantly enhancing initial response time to the client.

Power Generation Section, Team Leader, Kentucky   **1993 to 1996**

- ▶ Supervised a team of six mechanics. Performed direct support, maintenance, repair, overhauling, and rebuilding of power generation equipment.
- ▶ Trained, guided, and offered assistance to a team of mechanics to ensure full mission capability at all times. Reviewed operator's equipment licenses.
- ▶ Conducted troubleshooting of mechanical, electrical, and hydraulic systems and determined faults.
- ▶ Prepared status reports for senior management on equipment and parts tracking. Managed inventory and parts tracking databases. Administered quality control measures.

Education and Training

- ▶ AA in Computer Science, Central Texas College, 1995
- ▶ Microsoft NT Server 4.0 Core Technologies, New Horizons, 1999 (Certificate of Training)
- ▶ Internetworking Using MS TCP/IP, New Horizons, 1999 (Certificate of Training)
- ▶ Primary Leadership Development Course, U.S. Army, 1995
- ▶ Power Generation Management, U.S. Army, 1993

This attractive, unusual format does a good job of organizing and presenting the information in this resume so that it remains highly readable. The left column effectively highlights important and distinguishing qualifications.

CONFIDENTIAL

Mary Hudson
1000 Green Meadow Drive
Montgomery, Alabama 36100   mary@Hudson.com

Ø [334] 555-5555
[334] 555-6666 (Mobile)

MY VALUE TO CHRONOS INSURANCE AS A NETWORK PROFESSIONAL: _____

> **Expertise** to keep ahead of users' demands

> **Business sense** to control costs

> **People skills** to help teams want to succeed

RECENT WORK HISTORY WITH SELECTED EXAMPLES OF SUCCESS: _____

> **Regional Marketing Director,** Gorrilla.Net, Montgomery, AL   Feb 00 – Aug 01
> *Gorilla.Net – an ISP with 13,000 subscribers and $4M in annual sales – purchased my company.*

Results: Designed and wrote the program that allowed Gorilla.Net to integrate **3,000 new customers in less than a week.**

Targeted our six top accounts for upgrades that gave us the highest profit margins. **Results:** Major account **multiplied** his capability **24-fold.**

> **CEO and Cofounder,** The Bridge, LLC, Montgomery, AL   Dec 98 – Feb 00
> *My ISP generated annual sales of $750K with fifteen employees.*

Built this business from the ground up with nearly no money. **Results:** 3,000 customers in just two years.

Used shell scripts to develop **optimized billing** and user accounting **systems.** Installed, managed, maintained and **improved WAN and LAN** network traffic. **Results:** Tight control costs. **Optimized revenue flow.**

Found ways to get, and maximize, vital phone capacity fast. **Results: Saved** nearly **$7K** in installation costs, then used the money to rent office space for a year.

Smoothly handled network crash that came at the worst time, Friday at 5:00 p.m. at a site 100 miles away. **Results:** Short-term fix done at once. Long-term solution ready in six weeks at **minimal cost.** Went on to **double our subscribers in seven months.**

Worked diplomatically through "gatekeepers" to **persuade product line manager** of startup company to give us vital equipment at the lowest price. **Results: $8.4K savings.**

> **Computer Programmer,** United States Air Force, Montgomery, AL   Nov 90 – Nov 98
> *Helped maintain 30-year old programs supporting accounting and finance systems.*

Chosen by VP over 14 other eligibles (some with 30 times my experience) to help keep the Department of Defense's accounting system from failing. **Results:** Solved the problems **one month early. Flawless operation** from then on.

Mastered complex, next-generation report generator in my "spare time." **Results:** Senior decision-makers chose me as one of two to **train** Air Force **people nationwide.**

CONFIDENTIAL

Broad and deep computer capabilities and education ↝

"The goal here was not to show this candidate as overqualified. Nor did I want to show her as 'jack of all trades and master of none.' So the cover letter [not shown here] blends her strengths to portray her as a productivity enhancer."

C O N F I D E N T I A L

Mary Hudson **Network Professional** [334] 555-5555

COMPUTER CAPABILITIES:_____

> TCP/IP Networking:
>   > *Expert*: POP3, DNS, Telnet, FTP, SSH, HTTP; *Proficient*: SNMP, TFTP, Radius; *Working knowledge*: BGP4, RIP (versions 1 and 2), SMB, NTP

> Firewall rule creation and administration: *Working knowledge* of UNIX and Cisco

> CGI Programming: *Proficient* in C, Perl, Shell scripts

> Configuration:
>   > *Expert*: Sendmail, Bind (DNS), Apache, Squid; *Proficient*: Apache-SSL

> Operating systems:
>   > *Expert*: UNIX (Linux, xBSD, SUN, HP, Digital, Unisys, IBM), Unisys OS 2200, Windows NT 3.51+, Windows 95/98, Windows 3.1+, MS-DOS, Macintosh; *Proficient*: Cisco IOS 9.x+

> Ascend Communications Equipment: *Expert* in Pipeline 50/75/130, Max 4004/4048/TNT lines

> Cisco IOS Products: *Proficient* with models 1600, 2500, 4500, AS5200

> UNIX Shell Scripting: *Expert* in bash, ksh, csh, sh, tcsh

> Technical HTML Design: *Expert*

> WAN Technologies: *Expert* in T1/PRI Provisioning and ISDN configuration

> LAN Design and Implementation: *Expert* in Ethernet including collision domain setup and multicast routing

> Programming languages:
>   > *Expert*: COBOL, PASCAL; *Proficient*: Assembly (Intel 80X86 and IBM 360/370), C, LISP, Visual Basic; *Working knowledge*: C++

> Database retrieval languages:
>   > *Expert*: LOUIS, LOUIS II, LOUIS/Link; *Proficient*: Oracle

EDUCATION AND PROFESSIONAL DEVELOPMENT:_____

> *Pursuing* B.S., **Math** and **Computer Information Science** (double major), Troy State University at Montgomery, Montgomery, AL, **GPA 3.8+** *Paying my own way. Attended night classes while working up to 100 hours a week.*

> A.A.S., **Computer Science Technology**, Community College of the Air Force, Maxwell Air Force Base, AL, 96

> *Pursued* B.S., **Hardware Engineering**, University of Connecticut, Storrs, CT, 94 *Completed 136 semester hours while working at nights and on the weekends.*

> **Computer Programmer**, USAF Technical School, Keesler Air Force Base, MS, 92 *The only honor graduate in this 15-week class.*

C O N F I D E N T I A L

Page 2

Nicholas H. Fittsimmons, Jr.

400 Red Lion Road, Apt. E • Philadelphia, PA 19114 • 215-249-8001 • fittsimmonsjr@rcn.com

PC Specialist / Network Administrator

Experienced PC maintenance technician, with a combination of skills in network administration, PC technical support, and operations. Strong background in software management, installation, user training, and help desk.

Areas of Expertise: LAN Administration, LAN Implementation, Server Installation, Performance Tuning, Troubleshooting, Quality Assurance, Disaster Recovery / Network Backup, and Data Warehousing.

Operating Systems:	DOS, Windows 3.x, 95, 98, 2000
Hardware:	HP 3000, Novell, NT Server, PC, PC cards
Software:	MS Excel, MS PowerPoint, MS Word, WordPerfect, Reflections Terminal Interface w/ Mainframe, McAfee Anti-Virus, Norton Anti-Virus, Client32
Databases:	dBase, FoxPro, MS Access
Network Essentials:	LAN, Windows NT, Novell 3.x, 10BaseT, Cisco Router, Hubs, ISDN, Routers, Servers, TCP/IP, T1

Employment

TECHNICAL SUPPORT REPRESENTATIVE, Industry Dimensions, Inc., Philadelphia, PA   **1979 to Present**

Software vendor warehousing and managing property and casualty insurance data.

Network Administration: Manage the 100+ user multi-protocol Windows and Novell operating systems, supporting DOS and Windows 95, 98, and 2000. Established and configured Windows NT 4.0 and 5.0 with TCP/IP and DNS. Install, configure, and manage all software and hardware across the multi-file server LAN. Arrange remote software demonstrations using PC Anywhere. Establish and maintain email accounts on PCs and servers.

Troubleshooting/Maintenance: Performed installation and maintenance on internal PC devices. Troubleshoot software such as MS Office, PC desktop operating system matters, and computer virus issues.

Operations: Assist in operating and processing mainframe computer systems using HP MPE/ix 5.5 series HP 3000 system. Perform system backups and restore data. Schedule batch jobs and process client reports; prepare data files and reports for CD and diskette distribution to clients and associates, as well as for network transfer. Assist operators with operating systems issues pertaining to report production. Assist in troubleshooting terminal interface and mainframe operations.

Technical Support: Visit client sites to troubleshoot server, connection, or software difficulties. Provide remote support to users nationally.

Contributions:

- Provided key support in the upgrade and transition from the Honeywell mainframe to the HP: established JCL to be read by the new system directly from the old one; assisted programming staff in the data conversion.

- Re-established cable and network connections for a 75-user system after a major building renovation. Completed the reconnections, testing, and troubleshooting under extremely tight time constraints to maintain a zero productivity loss.

ADMINISTRATIVE SPECIALIST, U.S. Army, Darmstadt, Germany   **1975 to 1978**

Education

B.S., Computer Science   The University of Pennsylvania, Philadelphia, PA   1975

This resume is visually attractive due to the use of a readable, contemporary font, justified text, judiciously used underlining, and a variety of type enhancements.

Edward A. Battaglia

14 Jordan Road, Tewksbury, MA 01876 • (978) 694-6242 • ebattaglia@javanet.com

OBJECTIVE

Network administration / technical support position utilizing current training and experience in hardware, software, and network technologies.

SUMMARY

- NT/A+ Certified Technician with excellent diagnostic and problem-solving skills.
- Ten years' experience building, upgrading, and installing computer hardware, software, and peripherals.
- Utilities/software proficiency includes Norton, Mijenix Fix-it 99, Checkit Pro, Power Quest, Drive Copy and Partition Magic, Norton Ghost, PcAnywhere, MS Office, Adobe Photoshop 4.0, Corel Draw 8, Canvas 5, Ray Dream Studio, Internet Explorer, Netscape Communicator, FTP Voyager.
- Exemplary work history of on-time project completion and customer satisfaction.

EDUCATION AND TRAINING

Boston University Corporate Education Center, Tyngsborough, MA
(1998 Winner of the Microsoft Award for Educational Excellence)
Certificate in Windows NT Administration

Franklin Institute of Technology, Boston, MA
Certificate of Proficiency in Automotive Technology

TECHNICAL EXPERIENCE

Technology Consultant   1996 – Present

Install, maintain, and support PC systems and networks for several small companies and individuals Diagnose and correct system hardware and software conflicts. Perform end-user technical support.

Experienced with a broad range of installations and support, including:

- Complete system set-up (hardware, software, and upgrades), service packs, and peripherals.
- Installation and configuration of MS-DOS, Win 3.11, Win 95/98, Win NT workstation, Linux. Multi-boot systems. Software configuration for Internet and email access.
- Peer-to-peer networks, administration of user privileges and shared resources on NT and 95/98 networks. Ethernet networks.
- Component installation including motherboards, video cards, network cards, drive controllers, SCSI controllers, MPEG decoders, I/O cards, internal and external modems.
- Drive set-ups including IDE/SCSI hard drives, DVD/CD, CD-RW, Zip, and tape drives. Hard drive replacement using Norton Ghost, Drive Copy.
- Peripherals including hand scanners, flatbed scanners (LPT/SCSI/USB), monitors, printers.

ASE Certified Master Technician – Nashua Volvo, Nashua, NH   1994 – Present

Perform diagnostic services on a PC-based system, specializing in electrical and electronic systems diagnosis. Use well-developed troubleshooting skills and technical experience to efficiently analyze and solve performance problems, with the ultimate goal of satisfying the individual customer.

Administer the NT-based network and install software upgrades. Provide technical assistance and training to system users.

Certified Master Technician (BMW) / Certified Technician (Mercedes) –
Auto Engineering, Woburn, MA   1986 – 1994

Part of a high-level, experienced team providing diagnostic and repair service in extremely busy operation. Gained a reputation as a specialist in electrical, electronic, and computer diagnostics. Participated in ongoing certification and training by BMW and Mercedes engineers.

"This interesting client is a career changer who took his strong technical diagnostic skills honed over 15 years as a precision automotive technician, combined them with a rigorous and highly regarded NT administration certificate program, and moved into the high-tech world."

JUSTIN WILSON

Phone: 510.524.2557
Mobile: 510.653.7542

Email: jwilson@worldnet.att.net

45 N. Winding River Road
Oakland, California 94605

Microsoft Certified Professional / Certified Internet Architect / A+ Certification

3.x, 4.x, 5.x, Master CNE / Cisco Certified Network Associate

QUALIFICATIONS SUMMARY

➤ Results-oriented technology engineer with over 18 years of experience in electronics, computer technologies and digital commerce.
➤ Extensive customer service background worldwide.
➤ Expertise in multiple protocols and platforms.
➤ Extensive training and experience using Novell's Directory Services for Directory Tree design and repair (NDS).
➤ Excellent team development, management and leadership skills.
➤ Multicultural and multilingual. Fluent in German, French and Italian.

PROFESSIONAL EXPERIENCE

TECHNO-SUPPORT USA, La Jolla, California   1997 to Present
The largest independent provider of technology support for the digital world.

Senior National Technical Support Engineer

Oversee the development and execution of customized solutions to help established businesses adapt their IT infrastructures to the changing requirements of the rapidly evolving digital marketplace. Assist major providers of broadband, DSL, cable and wireless technologies meet demands for deployment and support. Manage a team of 92 Technicians in a 24/7 operation.

• Manage Sabre Travel information support for Novell 3.x and 4.x server-based and Win95 peer-to-peer-based networks including modem and frame relay connectivity.
• Provide direct second-level support for Novell Inc. under contract including all aspects of client and server, issues dealing with design and repair of directory services (e.g. 700 servers for the State of California).
• Managed a series of customer service and quality improvement projects to improve customers' experience and create loyalty.
• Conduct monthly classroom instruction in Novell Certification courses.

MEMOREX TELEX, Fresno, California   1990 to 1997
Product Test Supervisor (1992 to 1997)

Oversaw testing of more than 12 state-of-the-art technology product lines and 30+ technicians.

• Developed and created test plans, organized test resources and schedules, managed execution and oversaw quality control procedures and processes.
• Interfaced with project leads and engineers to define test requirements and develop a database for streamlining processes.
• Interfaced with customers, engineers, technicians and senior executives to resolve and improve productivity, efficiency and quality.

With strong technical credentials leading off this resume, it is sure to catch the attention of employers. It is particularly well written and inviting in appearance.

JUSTIN WILSON

Page 2

MEMOREX TELEX (Continued)

Electronics Technician (1990 to 1992)

Instrumental member of an elite electronics team designing and troubleshooting electronic circuits for technologically advanced systems for a series of new product releases.

- Drew schematic circuit diagrams using PC software, designed and built mechanical enclosures, produced drawings for outsourcing and prepared layout of circuits using PCB layout software.
- Oversaw assembly of fine pitch surface mount components and ball grid arrays on printed circuit boards used in oscilloscopes, digital multi-meter, soldering iron, microscope and vacuum operated de-soldering equipment.

TELETECH/AMERICA ONLINE, Stockton, California   1986 to 1990

Technical Lead

Supervised a group of 32 technicians providing customer service and technical support to incoming callers using America Online, CompuServe, and Internet Mail software.

- Worked with various operating systems and applications including Vantive, Windows 95, NT, DOS, Lotus AmiPro, Microsoft Office, Microsoft Works and Word Perfect.
- Assisted users worldwide in a diverse range of technical support issues.

BURTEK INC., Sacramento, California   1983 to 1986

Senior Field Service Engineer

Supervised in-house and on-site assembly, test and customer acceptance of flight simulation training devices to British Air, PSA, TWA and Eastern Airlines.

- Provided close customer contact to resolve product performance issues in a timely fashion.

U.S. NAVY   1979 to 1983

Electronics Technician

Served as communications liaison in NATO fleet exercises. Supervised work of radar and communications technical group, NAS Whiting field. Top Security Clearance. Recipient of numerous awards, medals and commendations.

EDUCATION

BBA, Computer and Information Science, University of California, 1993
AAS, Industrial Engineering, TCC Tulsa Community College, Oklahoma, 1983
AAS, Computer Science, TCC Tulsa Community College, Oklahoma, 1980
Graduate, US Naval Electronics School, Great Lakes, Illinois

Completed 48 technical training, application, systems and technology courses and seminars. Amplified training addendum available upon request.

PROFESSIONAL AFFILIATIONS

NPA (Network Professionals Association)

NUI (NetWare Users International)

JARED C. LEWIS, CNA
1701 Hatteras Way, Raleigh, NC 27606
Telephone: (919) 568-9425 ◆ E-Mail: JLewis@internet.com

NETWORK ENGINEER · NETWORK ADMINISTRATOR · MIS MANAGER

Accomplished network administrator and computer support professional skilled in all facets of desktop and network systems planning/design, programming, installation, configuration, and maintenance. Highly proficient in establishing user accounts, implementing network security protocols, and evaluating/monitoring system and network performance.

Analytical thinker with exceptional project management, organizational, and communication skills. Solid interpersonal and communication skills as well as a demonstrated ability to manage multiple priorities in fast-paced environments.

COMPUTER EXPERTISE

Protocols: TCP/IP, IPX/SPX, NetBIOS
Network Operating Systems: Windows NT Server 4.0/3.51, Novell Netware 3.12
Desktop Operating Systems: Windows 2000, Windows 98/95, MS-DOS 6.2
Software: MS Office (Word, Excel, PowerPoint), Proxy Software, Trading Applications
Hardware: IBM-Compatible Systems, NT Servers, Switches, Hubs, Cabling, Printers, Related Peripherals

PROFESSIONAL EXPERIENCE

NETWORK ENGINEER, RALEIGH FINANCIAL GROUP, Raleigh, NC (1997-Present)

Direct all facets of local area network/server administration, software installation, TCP/IP configuration, hardware upgrade, and troubleshooting for a busy financial services day-trading firm. Supervise project teams during all phases of application upgrades and coordinate activities with network cabling technicians to ensure connectivity. Monitor network resources, install proxy servers, configure new devices, enable LAN/WAN interconnectivity, load client applications, build user groups, establish network permissions, create log-ins and scripts, and devise IP addresses.

Control a $50,000 annual purchasing budget, negotiating favorable contract terms with service providers like Bloomberg, Reuters, Instinet, and Com-stock. Supervise ongoing customer support for multi-protocol environments, including TCP/IP, IPX/SPX, and NetBIOS.

◆ Orchestrated the design and installation of a LAN comprised of 200+ personal computers. Supervised office relocation to a new 15,000-square-foot area.

◆ Tripled client service capacity by planning and executing set-up of additional trading rooms.

◆ Spearheaded development and implementation of a comprehensive back-up procedure for the LAN.

◆ Improved system performance by engineering upgrade of LAN connections from traditional cabling methods to use of fiber optic links.

◆ Recouped significant savings through research and investigation into a vendor's erroneous billing.

◆ Improved productivity by introducing a new e-mail system company-wide.

NETWORK ENGINEER, WAKE INTERNET SERVICES, Raleigh, North Carolina (1996-1997)

Oversaw installation, maintenance, upgrade, and troubleshooting of personal computers for internal and external clients in LAN/WAN environments. Controlled purchasing of hardware, software, and network components, managing a $75,000 budget. Teamed with sales executives to assess client needs and prepare quotes and sales presentations.

EARLY EXPERIENCE in sales/marketing and payroll services management.

EDUCATION

Associate in Arts — Business Administration: Capital Community College, Columbia, SC
Novell Certified Netware Administrator: Career Blazers Learning Center

Clear headings and strongly contrasting bold type help important areas to stand out. Note the Early Experience summary that alludes to but does not elaborate on prior, nonrelevant work history.

RESUME 55: DIANA C. LEGERE; SALT LAKE CITY, UT

RICHARD TAYLOR

937 Hillside Avenue, Worcester, NY 12197 • Phone 607-555-5555 • taylor@computerspring.com

LOTUS NOTES / NETWORK ADMINISTRATOR – COMPUTER CONSULTANT
(Network Installation, Configuration, Computer Installation/Setup, User Training)

Microsoft Certified Professional (MCP)
Certified Novell Administrator (CNA)
Certified Lotus Notes System Administrator
Certified Lotus Notes Application Developer

Innovative and talented computer professional with an impressive record of achievement in data center operations including technical and systems support covering both Microsoft and Novell systems.

PROFESSIONAL PROFILE

- Results-driven expert skilled in all phases of computer technologies including **installation, configuration,** PC Network backup, virus detection and removal, and **system upgrades.**
- Accomplished technical professional skilled in building customer rapport, **troubleshooting,** and **problem resolution.**
- **Strong communication skills.** Able to interact with varied personality types from trainees to executives.
- Proven ability to develop procedures to streamline and improve daily operations.
- Extensive experience in a variety of **desktop technology** environments, operating systems, and PC applications including **Lotus Notes** and **Microsoft Exchange.**

TECHNICAL SKILLS AND QUALIFICATIONS

Hardware:	Compaq/Dell, Servers and Workstations
Operating Systems:	MS-DOS, Windows 3.1, Windows for Workgroups, Windows 95/98, Windows NT 3.51/4.0, Novell NetWare, IBM OS/400
Programming Languages:	Domino Fax Server, Lotus Pager Gateway, Sametime Server, Rumba, LotusScript, JavaScript
Network Applications:	Domino Fax Server, Lotus Pager, Gateway, Lotus Sametime Servers
Client/Server Applications:	Lotus Notes 3.x/4.x/5.x, Microsoft Outlook, Microsoft Exchange Server, Microsoft SMS, Novell Application Launcher
PC Experience:	Software Installation, Hardware Configuration, PC Repair
NT Experience:	Enterprise Networking, Domain Model Planning, Workstation Troubleshooting, Server Troubleshooting
Networking Experience:	TCP/IP Configuration, TCP/IP Troubleshooting, Internet Mail Routing, Web Hosting, Network Configuration, Network Troubleshooting
Software:	Microsoft & Office Products, Lotus SmartSuite Software

PROFESSIONAL EXPERIENCE

1999-2000   American Universal, Oneonta, NY
LOTUS NOTES ADMINISTRATOR
- **Streamlined rollout of Lotus Notes** using Network Application launchers resulting in reduced manpower of 700 hours per rollout.
- **Pioneered and implemented procedures to establish Help Desk System,** which strengthened end user support.

This resume fits the first few lines of important professional experience on page 1, while giving most of the space to technical and professional qualifications.

RICHARD TAYLOR   PAGE 2

(Professional Experience continued)

- Administered and maintained **Lotus Notes e-mail system** for over 1400 system users.
- Developed and **conducted training programs** for daily support of Lotus Notes for up to eight desktop services team members.
- Planned, designed, and **implemented an internal intranet strategy** using Domino Web Servers. Confer with programming department to develop and maintain website used by over 7000 field insurance agents.
- Successfully **implemented Domino Web Mail, SSL, and Java Servlet Manager.**

1996-1999   **Mutual Medical Systems,** Worcester, NY
                     PRODUCT ANALYST (1997-1999)
                     SR. CUSTOMER SERVICE ACCOUNT REPRESENTATIVE (1996-1997)

- **Coordinated technical pre-sales support** for GroupWare Sales Team including training and development for new interns.
- **Directed Lotus Notes infrastructure planning** and implementation for clients.
- **Installed NT Servers, Lotus Domino Services, and Lotus Notes** and maintained NT Server Administration.
- Proficient in applications including **Fax Gateways and Pager Gateways** both internally and for hospitals across the country.
- Provided **customer support for over 40 hospitals** having purchased products from SMS GroupWare Services team.
- Primary Support for **MedSeries 4 Optical Archiving** and **AR/ADT Purging application** running on AS/400.

1993-1996   **Jennings Oil Company,** Middleburgh, NY
                     MANAGER

- Managed all phases of store operations for multiple store locations.
- Coordinated processes of accounting, inventory management, training up to seven associates, and customer service.

EDUCATION

Enrolled in BS Psychology program – **Oneonta Community College**
Completed 2 years in **Computer Information Systems** – SUNY at Cobleskill – 1998-1999
BA (Business Information Systems) – SUNY at Cobleskill – 1997

ANDY DeSALVA

20825 Spinning Circle Drive ◆ Germantown, MD 20874
E-mail: adesalva@hotmail.com ◆ (301) 542-3333

IT PROFESSIONAL

Self-directed technical management professional with over 10 years of progressive experience in **network administration**, **UNIX systems administration** and **Windows NT administration**. Combine strong analytical, troubleshooting and technical acumen with solid leadership, project management and team-building skills to consistently deliver productive technological solutions. History of commitment to bottom-line objectives and professional achievement. **MCSE / MCP+I Certifications.**

CORE COMPETENCIES

- **Network Administration**
- **Technical Troubleshooting**
- **Systems Administration**
- **Customer Technical Support**
- **Network Installation**

- **Disaster Recovery**
- **Quality Assurance**
- **Y2K Compliance**
- **Network Troubleshooting**
- **Staff Technical Training**

PROFESSIONAL HISTORY

UNIX SYSTEMS ADMINISTRATOR
Adco Research Laboratories — Adelphi, MD (January 2000 to April 2001)

Maintained UNIX system accounts on Silicon Graphics Onyx and Sun Sparc servers for this government research facility with 250+ employees. Provided UNIX support to division, including maintenance of hardware and software on several Silicon Graphics workstations, Linux workstations and X Window support.

- Guaranteed consistent operations of print queues and print software and ensured daily backups of software and research data.
- Updated operating systems with latest upgrades and patches and created accounts for new users.
- Provided support to research team with installation of software applications and created / maintained NFS file systems on 5 different UNIX systems.
- Credited with replacing backup script and customizing it to work with an automated DLT tape changer.

IT CONSULTANT II / LEAD CONSULTANT
Impact Visions Group, Inc. — Columbia, MD (June 1996 to November 1999)

Charged with providing IT support to U.S. Naval Medical Information Management Center projects for this $35M IT consulting firm.

- Configured and deployed client/server system for U.S. Navy hospitals worldwide, known as Ambulatory Data System (ADS), consisting of Information Database, 1–5 application servers and X Window terminals at each clinic. System was designed to retrieve patient appointment data and store information about patient procedures prior to billing insurance provider.

The highlight of page 1 of this resume is the boldface Core Competencies section that includes all relevant key words.

ANDY DeSALVA
Resume, Page 2 of 2

Continued...

- Led installation and configuration of SCO UNIX on 2–10 servers at 7 Navy sites and performed extensive UNIX troubleshooting at each site.
- Provided on-site technical support to resolve applications software and network projects and assisted personnel in integrating ADS system with existing medical system.
- Performed testing of upgrades to ADS system and also performed the actual upgrades to most sites including Bethesda National Naval Medical Center.
- Saved government thousands of dollars in travel and lodging expenses by developing UNIX shell scripts that were used to perform remote system upgrades.
- Co-led a $1.5M project to research, develop, document and deploy 53 Y2K-compliant UNIX servers in U.S. Navy hospitals and clinics worldwide. Migrated from Interactive (Sun) UNIX operating system to SCO UNIX 5.0.4., exporting data from MUMPS database and importing data into newer version of MUMPS.
- Provided on-site project support to Naval Medical Information Management Center including serving as Webmaster for 3 Navy projects and UNIX system administrator for 2 Bethesda Naval Hospital Information servers; configured NT servers for shipment to remote sites.

COMPUTER REPAIR TECHNICIAN
University Computing Services (Student Intern) — Baltimore, MD (June 1995 to May 1996)

Primarily responsible to diagnose, repair and install workstation platforms of Macintosh, DOS, Windows 3.x/95 and Silicon Graphics workstations for student labs and faculty. Maintained Novell 3.12 server, hardware and software of university PC and Macintosh labs and SGI lab hardware.

QUALITY ASSURANCE TECHNICIAN
U.S. Army Information Systems Engineering Command — Germany (September 1990 to August 1993)

Responsible for the continued operation of the Wide Area Network for the Army European Command. Accountable to diagnose and repair faulty components of the European Defense Data Network including Cisco routers, switches, PADs and modems. Provided numerous quick response technical assistance efforts and served as lead tester of Digital Interface to Autodin Host (DINAH) system which included workstation, specialized software and digital encryption device.

- Awarded Army Commendation Medal for consistent quality, performance and service.
- Selected as lead technician on technical assistance efforts based on extensive knowledge of systems.
- Coordinated and conducted network performance testing of military communications circuits at communications centers throughout Europe.

EDUCATION

BS, Information Systems Management, 1996
University of Maryland, Baltimore County

Army Communications Computer Systems Repair Course (Computer Technician) — 7 months
Telecom Troubleshooting Seminars

SARAH LANCER

155 Crystal Road, Hilltop, New York 11787 • (631) 222-0102 • lancer523@earthlink.net

Manager of LAN Administration with CNE, MCSE and MCP+I certifications seeking continuous challenge with a progressive organization. Core strengths encompass:

— LAN Administration
— Project Management
— System Conversions
— Help Desk Support

— Technical Writing
— Business/Technical Solutions
— Planning & Development
— Team Leadership

— Expense Control
— Procurement
— Inventory Control
— Vendor Relations

PROFESSIONAL EXPERIENCE

MILLER-STENSON FINANCIAL ADVISORS, Miller Place, New York   1/95 - present
Manager, LAN Administration   1/00 - present
LAN Administrator   1/95 - 1/00

Project Management

- Report directly to the Vice President of Information Services; charged with overseeing the technical support needs of 200 corporate users and 40 users throughout seven remote branch locations.
- Manage the performance of LAN-based hardware and software as it relates to multiple versions of NetWare and Windows NT Servers, to support the management of critical financial data. .
- Provide technical expertise and support for multiple Microsoft products encompassing Office Suite 97/2000, Outlook, Exchange, Internet Explorer and various hardware, inclusive of printers, scanners and Palm Pilots.
- Directed the complexities of a Corporate Human Resources system conversion involving the purchase, installation, configuration and migration of confidentially sensitive information to a NetWare 4 Server.
- Guided several mass deployments of corporate-based systems through implementation of Novell's ZENworks, and provided post-installation support with client connectivity issues.
- Collaborate with Sprint concerning service issues, user access privileges and firewall protection for the corporate web site, and monitor the integrity of on-line ethics.
- Remain on call to expeditiously diagnose and troubleshoot a broad scope of technical problems, and serve a key role in the execution of disaster recovery plans 24 hours a day, seven days a week.

Office Administration

- Requisition the purchase of hardware and software, and monitor data and company-wide user activity reports to track equipment and the use of multiple licensing software.
- Participate in NCUA audits to ensure LAN activities are fully compliant with regulatory procedures.
- Develop technical manuals and documentation for technical teams and company-wide personnel.
- Prepare biweekly status reports for management review.

— continued —

This resume uses bulleted style to present diverse experience and accomplishments. It is extremely readable in 12-point Times New Roman font.

SARAH LANCER

— Page 2 —

OLYMPIA UNIVERSAL, Lake Calverton, New York   4/94 - 12/94
Technical Support Engineer

- As part of a team of Technical Support Engineers, provided post-installation systems support to 6,000 field service engineers, salespeople and customers for approximately 1,000 networks servicing nationally based medical professionals.
- Diagnosed and supported an extensive product line of Olympia video imaging equipment, printers and voice recognition software utilized during medical procedures.
- Prepared tradeshow exhibit materials, developed technical documentation, and planned LAN designs.
- Compiled field data, maintained activity logs and prepared monthly reports for management review.

GLOBAL AVIATORS, INC., Unionville, New York   5/87 - 6/93
Network Administrator

- Traveled internationally to collaborate with management on the planning of technical breakthroughs.
- Supported diversified network requirements for multiple corporate locations, established data communications capabilities and implemented data backup procedures.
- Guided the analysis, testing, implementation and conversion of multiple entities to an A/P and G/L system to facilitate the preparation of budget forecasts, financial statements and monthly reports.

COMPUTER / NETWORKING SKILLS

Operating Systems: Windows NT 2000/98/95; Novell NetWare 3.x/4.x/5.x
Hardware: Extensive hardware and peripheral installation and maintenance
Software: Installation and troubleshooting of various Microsoft applications
Protocols: TCP/IP, IPX/SPX
Cabling: Ethernet 10/100Base-T

EDUCATION

COMPUTER TRAINING SOLUTIONS, Miller Place, New York
Microsoft Certified Systems Engineer (MCSE), 2000

NAUTICAL HEIGHTS COMMUNITY COLLEGE, Miller Place, New York
A.A.S., Computer Information Systems, 1993

CERTIFICATIONS

Microsoft Certified Systems Engineer, 2000
Microsoft Certified Professional + Internet, 2000
NetWare 5.x Certified Novell Engineer, 1994

BRIAN JONES
4/23 Smith Street, Rocklin, California 95677 • Mobile (407) 555 6666 • jonesbrian@bigworld.com

SYSTEMS ANALYST • SYSTEMS DEVELOPER • SYSTEMS SUPPORT MANAGER • TECHNICAL SUPPORT MANAGER

SUMMARY

Accustomed to supporting large multi-user networks, driving system design and architecture improvements to meet changing business needs, and determining technical, operational, and financial viability of producing client-focused solutions. Specialist knowledge of financial systems, team leadership and training, providing a balanced mix of business and technical expertise.

SELECTED ACCOMPLISHMENTS

- Strategically planned, coordinated and led complete divisional relocation to new site, establishing new structure and developing customer-responsive network; multi-phased relocation process successfully completed over 3 separate stages, on time and on budget.

- Spearheaded and rolled out multi-level training program to raise staff competency levels in using Microsoft Office 2000 integrated product suite; reduced burden on desktop support areas for rudimentary technical information.

- Coordinated major booking system implementation; oversaw diagnostics, testing, rollout, and end user training.

- Designed, planned, and implemented new network hierarchy.

- Instrumental in the career progression of 5 IT trainees.

TECHNOLOGY SKILL SET

Key Credentials
- Network Management
- Systems Design & Development
- Accounting Systems
- Formal Documentation for Systems Development

- System Upgrades
- Software & Hardware Support
- Network Security
- Critical Problem Solving
- Staff & End User Training

Software/Hardware
- Windows 9x, 2000 & NT workstations
- Microsoft Office 2000
- Visio
- Adobe Photoshop
- Visual Basic 6
- Integrated Accounting Packages

- Filemaker 5
- Novell Networks
- TCP/IP
- Unix Servers
- NT Server

CREDENTIALS & TRAINING

CERTIFIED NETWORK ADMINISTRATOR, *ADTD Training*
DIPLOMA IN ACCOUNTING PRACTICES, *University of Rocklin*

- Visual Basic 6
- MS Access (Advanced)
- Filemaker 5

Brian Jones   Page 1   Continued Page 2

Professional experience doesn't appear until page 2, whereas key attributes and accomplishments take center stage on page 1 of this well-organized, attractive resume.

CAREER EXPERIENCE

SYSTEMS COORDINATOR, *Training & Development Section, Department of Education*   1996-Present
Systems manager leading team of 6 in supporting, creating, developing, and managing systems at the Education Development Center at Rocklin.

Accountable for overall strategy including technology acquisitions and integration, hardware/software support, quality control, vendor selection, scheduling, safety, team training and support, and daily operations.

- Contribute technical expertise in resolving customer hardware/software support issues; provide personal attention to 60+ people across 6 units; troubleshoot and advise customers on technical problems achieving maximum system utilization.

- Administer Novell and NT servers.

- Established and maintained new computer-training classroom initiative.

BUSINESS & IT MANAGER, *Vallejo Community College*, Los Angeles   1990-1996
Challenged to demonstrate fiscally responsible financial decision-making, driving information technology enhancements school-wide. Streamlined financial reporting processes, and improved the quality/caliber of financial data.

- Spearheaded the integration of technology advancements; installed and administered Novell network; updated software/hardware, and contributed technical support to IBM and Mac end users throughout administration and classroom areas.

- Coordinated and supervised Unix server installation.

ASSISTANT ACCOUNTANT/IT MANAGER, *Mega Manufacturing Works*, Australia   1986-1990
Large manufacturing company. Supervised Unix server, hardware, and software installations. Provided user support for all mainframe and workstation issues.

Actively participated in planning, implementing, and installing integrated accounting system to streamline tasks, boost productivity, reduce labor costs, and diminish potential for duplications and errors. Dual accounting role. Analyzed and reconciled accounts, prepared journal entries, calculated monthly summaries, led month-end closing and analysis, and prepared financial statements.

ASSISTANT ACCOUNTANT, *FTRE Enterprises*, Australia   1984-1986
Financial management accounting. Compiled and produced accounting reports for 2 Victoria-based companies for presentation to Sydney headquarters.

REFERENCES

Available upon request.

JACK A. HOLMAN, CNA, CNE

190 East Sidewater Lane ▪ Austin, Texas 77000
(512) 999-7666 ▪ jaholman@spirit.net

QUALIFICATIONS SUMMARY

■ Efficient **CERTIFIED NOVELL ADMINISTRATOR / CERTIFIED NOVELL ENGINEER / MIS SPECIALIST** with **computer operation** expertise using variety of mainframes and printers and encompassing console operation, tape mounting, documentation. Experienced in utilizing CA-1 to monitor and control scratch, vault, and disaster tapes; CA-7 to monitor and control batch job processes, schedule run flows, and abend jobs; CA-11 to restart abended jobs.

■ Proficiency in **system troubleshooting, malfunction identification**, and **problem-solving**; assist programmers and users in resolving software and hardware problems.

■ Excellent **team leadership, instructional, communication**, and **interpersonal** skills; effectively train, supervise, and motivate operators; interface well with people of diverse levels, backgrounds, and personalities. Work well independently or as productive team member.

■ College academic studies with concentration in **Computer Science** and **Computer Networking**.

■ High level of accuracy with attention to detail. **Career-** and **goal-oriented**.

HARDWARE EXPERIENCE

IBM 9672 MVS/ESA	9395 DASD	4635 Xerox Laser Printer
IBM 3090 MVS/ESA	3390 DASD	9700 Xerox Laser Printer
3490 Cartridge Tape System	IBM RS6000	IBM Printers (4224, 4248,
3480 Cartridge Tape System	1900 Forms Separator	4234, 6262, 4246)
3420 Reel-to-Reel System	2000 Forms Counter	3174 Controllers

SOFTWARE EXPERIENCE

JCL	CICS	RAPS	Netview	Windows 95/98
MVS	CA Products (CA-1,	VTAM	Netman	Windows NT 4.0
JES2	CA-7, CA-11)	VPS	Remedy	Novell 4.11
TSOE	VFTS	VMCF	E-mail	Microsoft Office 97

PROFESSIONAL EXPERIENCE

NATIONAL GROCERY COMPANY, Austin, Texas (1989 - Present)

Rapidly advanced from entry-level associate in store setting to I/O Operator to Computer Operator to Senior Computer Operator in MIS-Operations Department of major grocery chain encompassing 140 stores.

Senior Computer Operator – MIS-Operations Department (1998-Present)

▪ Promoted and assumed greater and supervisory responsibility of MIS computer operations.
▪ Operate console; run production flows and batches of all output generated by 140 stores (tags, payroll, payroll checks, sales and progress reports, end-user reports, price books, bulletins).
▪ Manage Help Desk operations and offer technical solutions to end-users as needed.

Computer Operator – MIS-Operations Department (1995-1998)

I/O Operator (1992-1995)

Produce Associate / Bakery Associate / Checker / Stocker / Sacker (1989-1992)

▪ ▪ ▪

Key credentials are included as part of the name, in large type. Work experience is listed only minimally, so that more attention can be given to technical experience qualifications.

PAUL R. SCHROEDER

1254 N. Maricopa Avenue
Scottsdale, AZ 85257

Home: (602) 555-7632
e-mail: itmanager@tdi.com

QUALIFICATIONS SUMMARY

Information Systems Manager – Network Analyst

Over 15 years of IT experience, with over 7 years in network design and management. Creative troubleshooter with a record of implementing cost-effective solutions to expensive problems. Bachelor of Science in Technical Management.

Certification

- MCSE (Microsoft Certified Systems Engineer)
- MCP
- MCP + I
- A+

Systems Proficiency

- Extensive knowledge of Windows 95 & 98, Windows NT 4, MS Office, MS Exchange (Server & Client), IIS, DOS, and PC-NFS.

- Solid knowledge of modern LAN/WAN architecture, LAN Media distribution, and troubleshooting. Proven network design excellence including NT domain design and high-capacity Internet connections. Developed WAN solutions to support explosive growth during acquisitions and mergers.

- Proficient with TCP/IP implementation including DHCP, DNS, WINS, PPP.

- Experienced with Cisco Routers, Bay Networks (Concentrators, ASN-Routers, Hubs, Backbone and Workgroup Switches), HP and Xylogics Terminal Servers, Livingston and DIGI Portservers, HP Netservers, DSU/CSUs, and WinFrame remote access servers.

EXPERIENCE

MICROTECH CORP.
Network / Systems Manager

Tempe, Arizona
12/96-Present

(Manufacturer of medical equipment; 800 employees; rapid growth from $40M-$100M in 1998.)

Design, implement, and manage all aspects of corporate LAN/WAN, e-mail system, and several NT Servers. Streamline corporate acquisitions and consolidations with IT solutions. Supervise IT support staff of 14. Create corporate-wide connectivity solutions.

- Replaced a troublesome 2-server Novell network with a robust Windows NT system employing TCP/IP, switching, routing, terminal servers, portservers, firewalls, dedicated PPP T-1s, CCIS T-1s, and MS-Exchange.

- Implemented and managed corporate telcom system spanning 2 cities and including a formidable voice mail and IVR system supporting the nation's largest dedicated sales force in the medical industry.

Continued . . .

This well-written resume follows our preferred combination format of presenting professional experience: a brief paragraph describing scope and responsibilities, followed by easily distinguishable accomplishments set off by bullets.

Paul R. Schroeder   Résumé/2

Experience, Microtech (Continued)

- Managed IT transition during corporate relocation to a new 100,000-square-foot facility. Managed network design, vendor selection, and cutover coordination with telephone carriers.

- Coordinated remote site linking and WAN connection supporting rapid growth during 3 corporate acquisitions.

INTERNATIONAL CIRCUITS CORPORATION   Phoenix, Arizona
Information Systems Engineer (Promoted from IS Technician)   6/93-12/96

(High-volume circuit board manufacturer; $100M, 1014 employees.)

Managed and optimized the company-wide computer network (300 nodes). Supervised the maintenance, repair, and periodic upgrade of all company PCs (230) and printers. Provided highest-level software troubleshooting and support.

Ensured the reliable operation of all communications systems, including the 220-station phone system (PBX), Voice Mail, Auto-Attendant, all WAN/Hi-Cap connections to the Internet; the KRONOS clock system and its integration with the company's payroll system; the company-wide paging system, and modem/fax lines.

- Redesigned, expanded, and optimized the existing network. Segmented network for maximum efficiency.

- Slashed repair costs an estimated $40,000 annually and reduced downtime by handling 100% of repairs in-house.

- Standardized all company computer equipment while planning for future growth, upgrades, and maintenance.

- Supervised 2 technical support employees. Trained Communication Technician and Help Desk employees.

ARMCO   Phoenix, Arizona
Electronics Technician   1/85-6/93

(Manufactures and repairs computers, peripherals, and phase conversion equipment.)

Had sole responsibility for all manufacturing and repair aspects of the business. Built IBM-compatible systems and peripherals, and repaired both PC and Macintosh systems. Custom-built phase conversion equipment and repaired alarm systems and phone systems. Handled customer relations, including customer service and support for all of the above functions. Supervised 2 part-time employees.

EDUCATION

DEVRY INSTITUTE OF TECHNOLOGY   Phoenix, Arizona
Bachelor of Science in Technical Management   October, 1998
- Magna Cum Laude, Dean's List, President's List

Certification:
MCP & MCP +I (12/98), MCSE (12/98), A+ (5/98)

CHAPTER 8

Resumes for Web, Internet, and E-Commerce Professionals

- Web Designers
- Web Graphic Artists
- Web Applications Developers
- Webmasters
- Internet Sales and Marketing Professionals
- E-Business Managers
- E-Commerce/Internet Executives

**Quality Computer
Graphics &
Web Site Design**

HTML/DHTML

Document Layout/
Construction

Web Design Principles

Page Set-up

Scanning/Photo
Manipulation

Image Optimization

WYSIWYG Editors

Text & Font
Management

Forms/Tables/Frames

Color Theory

Original Sketches

Auto Tracing of
Drawings

Client-Server Concepts

Cross-Browser Issues

Portfolio of samples:

**http://www.avisto/
rob/portfolio/**

Robert Berlane

561 Thompson Street ▪ Boston, MA 02116 ▪ (617) 876-3215 ▪ rob@aol.com

COMPUTER GRAPHICS/WEB DESIGNER

Highly self-motivated and goal-oriented professional committed to pursuing a long-term career in computer graphics and Web design. Offer a 14-year track record demonstrating strong analytical and problem-solving skills, computer proficiency, and ability to follow through with projects from inception to completion.

Qualifications Summary

- Certified in computer graphics and Web design through an intensive 350-classroom-hour program.

- In-depth experience applying graphic design principles to produce innovative and tasteful print documents and Web sites.

- Intrinsic creative talent and lifelong interest in photography; offer a keen eye for quality design and document/Web site layout.

- Fluent in the MS Windows 95/98/NT operating environments. Proven ability to quickly learn and apply new technologies.

- Completed high-impact graphic and Web design projects including menus, newsletters, logos, postcards, CD covers, stationery, retail packaging, and a 50-page Web site.

- Advanced training and experience in the application and usage of QuarkXpress 4.0, Adobe PhotoShop 5.0, Adobe Illustrator 8.0, and Microsoft FrontPage 2000.

- Exceptionally well organized; strong work ethic and willingness to work hard to achieve employer objectives.

Education & Training

CERTIFICATE IN COMPUTER GRAPHICS/WEB DESIGN, Jan. 2001
American College of Technology, Boston, MA

BACHELOR OF SCIENCE, Cum Laude, Chemistry, May 1986
Dominican University, River Forest, IL

Employment

Medical Technologist, Boston General Hospital, Boston, MA, 1986 - Present

Collect, process, and analyze more than 2300 patient samples daily in the chemistry laboratory of this large metropolitan hospital. Interface extensively with physicians and other medical professionals. Test, troubleshoot, and perform QA protocols on sophisticated instrumentation.

This great-looking resume would attract attention even if the individual didn't have strong qualifications! The technical summary in the left column is an effective way to highlight key technical skills. Note the reference to his online portfolio—a wonderful selling strategy for a Web designer.

LYDIA MOSBACH

lydiamosbach@mindspring.com

3596 Bogart Avenue
Columbus, Ohio 43240
(614) 766-9844

ENTRY–LEVEL WEB DESIGNER

Visionary, creative professional qualified by 5 years of academic and professional achievements in web site production and project management. Combined expertise in graphic design and technical editing with exceptional ability to conceptualize and bring project to full fruition.

QUALIFICATION HIGHLIGHTS

- Cutting-edge technical knowledge of HTML programming and desktop publishing software.
- Extensive graphic layout, design, production and marketing experience.
- Demonstrated experience in promotion strategies.
- Proven record of effectively managing multiple tasks without compromise to quality.
- Innovative, creative and enthusiastic in approaching projects.
- Recognized for strong work ethic, integrity and commitment to success.

EDUCATIONAL ACHIEVEMENTS

Master of Arts, December, 2000
University of Reading – Reading, England

Visiting Scholar, 1999
Summer Program in Archaeology, 1998
American Academy in Rome – Rome, Italy

Internationaler Ferienkurs, 1998
Universität Heidelberg – Heidelberg, Germany

Bachelor of Arts, Art, 1997
Mount Holyoke College, South Hadley, Massachusetts

SELECTED PROJECT HIGHLIGHTS

The Parthenet: Internet Resources for Students of Art History – Conceived in 1995 to assist students in online research. Contains numerous sources of information about art history. Award-winning site highly used and listed in academic Internet guides worldwide. (1998 to Present) www.mtholyoke.edu/parthenet.html

Digital site emulation at Kenchreai, the Eastern port of Corinth – Studied the applications of technology in the field and created a multimedia web site. Manipulated plans into 3D animated sequences of the site's building phases. (1997-1999)

Consultant to the Matrix Project at Yale University and Mount Holyoke College – Worked with team of medieval scholars to create an online database of medieval women's religious communities in Western Europe. (1996 to 1998)

The Travels of Mac and Cheese – Developed as a spoof on the deification of Kraft Macaroni and Cheese. Site involved "reenactment" of box of Mac and Cheese traveling around Europe and photographing journey for the website. (1996 to 1997) www.mtholyoke.edu/mandcc/mandc.html

This new graduate has a solid portfolio of interesting projects that are highlighted on the resume. Her strong academic credentials take center stage on page 1.

LYDIA MOSBACH

lydiamosbach@mindspring.com

Resume, Page Two of Two
(614) 766-9844

Matrix: Resources for the Study of Women's Religious Communities – Developed site's original design, graphics, layout and database format for presentation at national conference. (1996 to 1997) matrix.bc.edu (Can be viewed in present form at Boston University.)

Hildegard and Clare Resource Center – Identified need and developed site concerning medieval religious women. Provides resources and links for in-depth study of Hildegard of Bingen (Germany) and Clare of Markyate (England). (1996 to 1997) www.mtholyoke.edu/medieval/resource.html

Mount Holyoke College History Department – Commissioned by the History Department to develop their informational web page, which is now maintained by department secretary. (1996 to 1997) www.mtholyoke.edu/acad/hist

Birgitta the Wonder Beetle – Original site narrating the travels and tribulations of Birgitta the Wonder Beetle; provided travelogue, insights and links to new VW Beetle enthusiast sites. (1995 to 1996) lydiamosbach.mindspring.com/Birgitta.html.

EXPERIENCE

Online Editor and Member – The Journal of the Women's College Art Coalition (1995 to 1997)
- Published online edition of The Journal, an undergraduate scholarly journal concerning women's issues in the fine arts. Designed and maintained web sites.
- Generated publicity and outreach programs to 83 other women's colleges in the nation.

Intern, The Development Office – Mount Holyoke College (1994 to 1997)
- Orchestrated fundraising efforts for the Alumnae Fund of the College. Managed large-scale phone-a-thons; organized callers and donation recordkeeping.
- Developed incentive strategies and events to encourage and maintain caller morale.

Intern – Columbus Museum of Art – Columbus, Ohio (Summer 1995)
- Internship in Registrar's Office. Catalogued prints and works on paper as part of a full museum inventory and installation of the permanent collection. Researched works to be deaccessioned.

TECHNICAL KNOWLEDGE

Proficient in many Remote Sensing, GPS, GIS, CAD and GeoPhysics Applications.
Data processing, database development and related archaeological field uses, both Mac and PC.
Networking, hardware/software maintenance, repair and troubleshooting.

Internet – Netscape, Explorer, Telenet, FTP

Graphics/Drafting/Authoring – PhotoShop, Quark, CorelDraw!, PageMaker, AutoCAD, Pagemill

Basics/Database – MS Office, FileMakerPro, 4th Dimension, MS Access, ProCite, FileWorks, Excel

Equipment – Scanners, CD-RW, digitizers, plotters, slide scanners

Languages – HTML 4, dHTML, Java, UNIX

JERRI BAXTER

555 Ryan Circle
Colander, IA 50236

(515) 585-3156
jerri_baxter@mailcity.com

AREAS OF EXPERTISE

WEB DESIGN • DATABASE DESIGN • DATABASE MANAGEMENT

Professional Profile

Creative team player who works well with both technical and business staff. Extensive work with design, development, testing, launching, and post-launch maintenance of applications. Good technical skills and excellent people skills proven by team management and strong leadership.

Technical Skills

Software: Oracle, MySQL, MS Office
Hardware: Unix, PC, and Macintosh system administration
Languages: Programming in Perl, SQL, C++, COBOL, HTML
Operating Systems: Windows 95, Windows NT, Linux, UNIX, Mac OS

Employment History

Senior Application Developer, Web Design, Inc., Ames, IA   1999 – 2001
Designed and developed web-based, database-driven applications. Applications were written in Perl using the Perl DBI module to connect to either MySQL or Oracle databases under Linux.

Accomplishments:
- Designed contracting system for client while working as team leader; spun off similar application using the same code base.
- Developed centerpiece that all applications now use for user information.
- Wrote large application critical to company's success while under adverse conditions.
- Interacted with business units on product design and client requirements.
- Produced timeline; created, tested, implemented, and maintained various applications and their databases.
- Created numerous internal tools for data management as needed.
- Implemented user registration – original layout of the common database used across all applications today.

System Administrator/Lab Manager, Innovative Design Lab, ISU, Des Moines, IA   1996 – 1998
System Administrator for 36 UNIX-based HPs running HP-UX, 40 Macintoshes, 10 PCs running Windows 95, and 20 Windows NT computers used daily in class labs.

Accomplishments:
- Interviewed, hired, trained, and supervised nine lab monitors.
- Set up and maintained servers for the network.
- Installed and maintained plotters, printers, and other equipment.
- Provided computer support for the College of Engineering by maintaining class labs.
- Replaced file servers and upgraded computers.

Education

Bachelor of Science, Iowa State University, Des Moines, IA, 1999
Management Information Systems/Finance

There's nothing "fancy" about this resume, but its clean format and subtle design features make it extremely attractive. Something as simple as using a different font for the name gives it a unique appearance.

LISA M. FITZGERALD
2431 Watt Street, Tucson, AZ 85719 • 520-688-3880 • fitz@msn.com

WEB DEVELOPER

PROFESSIONAL PROFILE

INNOVATIVE WEB DEVELOPER with hands-on experience combining solid understanding of HTML, VB Scripting and web browser capability across multiple platforms. Excellent knowledge of constraints involved in online media design. Highly creative and equally skilled in back-end complex programming such as Active Server Pages (ASP) as well as graphical design concepts. Able to manage web site development processes from architectural and functional design concept, including page creation authoring, through successful completion. Able to implement site server strategies and multimedia fundamentals. Dynamic dedicated professional with outstanding communication skills, able to focus on customer service and company vision. Core technical skills include:

Highly proficient writing HTML in Notepad

Active Server Pages, VB Scripting, and Java Scripting

Web Editors: Home Site, Hot Metal Pro

Software: PhotoShop, Corel Photo Paint, Paint Shop Pro, Lview, Access, Visio

PROFESSIONAL DEVELOPMENT

Logic and Analysis for Programmers	**Quantitative Communication**
Programming 1 (in C)	**Systems Design and Analysis**
Digital Computer Techniques	**Advanced Systems Management**

PROFESSIONAL EXPERIENCE

Graphic Web Solutions, Tucson, AZ   1998-present
WEB SITE DEVELOPER, MANAGER
- ❑ Design, develop and implement new web interfaces, graphics and layouts.
- ❑ Create, manage and maintain company web sites.
- ❑ Direct all phases of business operation including strategic planning, financial management, client acquisition/retention, and marketing.

Internet Marketing Solutions, Inc., Phoenix, AZ   1994-1998
WEB SPECIALIST
- ❑ Developed web sites for company intranet, including Competitive Intelligence Web Site for Marketing and Image Catalog.
- ❑ Provided technical support to associations designing sites; created and implemented web forms using ASP.
- ❑ Created file structure on company server to assist other departments with web site design and permissions.
- ❑ Implemented file structure on production server and uploaded changed files for employees.
- ❑ Initiated design and publication of online Café menus resulting in financial savings by eliminating hard copies.

ADMINISTRATIVE ASSISTANT TO DIRECTOR   1992-1994
- ❑ Supported Director of Information Systems; managed schedule and updated calendar.
- ❑ Coordinated all phases of company events, including Golf Scramble, Company Picnic, Summer Bowling League.

PORTFOLIO OF WEB DESIGN

- ❑ www.executivefinalcopy.com
- ❑ www.kinterlanddogs.com
- ❑ www.networksinc.com
- (Full portfolio presented upon request)

EDUCATION

- ❑ **Web Development Certificate**, University of Phoenix — 1999 — Curriculum included 230 hours of study.
- ❑ University of Maryland — 30 credits applicable to **AA in Business Administration**

To support her strong professional qualifications, this designer provides a portfolio of three sites where interested employers can view her work immediately.

PAUL L. RODRIGUEZ

156 Small Circle Road
Raleigh, North Carolina 27613
(919) 899-5689
rodriguez2213@mindspring.com

OBJECTIVE

To obtain a multi-task **graphic design, web design** or related **production-oriented position** within a corporate structure as part of a design team.

SUMMARY OF QUALIFICATIONS

❑ Define priorities, develop strategies, organize, develop and work in a team environment and as a liaison to personnel to determine graphic design, promotions, graphic illustration and composition, art direction and graphics/design needs.

❑ Able to put into place technical project goals to produce presentation graphics, customize promotions and advertisements, special-design pieces and develop major/minor projects.

❑ Currently serve in art director and graphic designer role with strong project management and production direction experience during collegiate training for WUAG and UNCG.

❑ Excellent planning and consulting skills developed from extensive work with sales department, customers and team members on a variety of challenging projects.

❑ Skill base includes:
  — Consultative Design/Commercial Design
  — Development/Major Projects and Minor Accounts
  — Project Leadership/Supervision
  — Multimedia Strengths (strong film, photography, print, radio production, animation, and multimedia (RealAudio) experience)
  — Production Leader (experience includes creating and editing copy and audio for PSAs and other team-based communications projects)
  — Personnel Supervision/Training/Development
  — Customer Interface and Requirements
  — Productivity Improvement
  — Public Relations/Communications

❑ Keen understanding of technology and a unique combination of skills that permits strategic analysis while pinpointing opportunities.

TECHNICAL SKILLS OVERVIEW

TECHNICAL SKILLS (INTEREST AND FOCUS) ON WINDOWS AND MAC:

❑ **Presentation/Graphics:** HTML, Flash 4.0, Quark Xpress, Adobe Illustrator and Photoshop, Corel Draw, Corel Photo/Paint, Macromedia Freehand and Fontographer, Transmac, Multi-Ad Creator.

❑ **Networking/Database:** experience working in a networking environment utilizing Win 95/98 server with PC workstations; Microsoft Office package (for Macintosh and PC), WordPerfect.

EDUCATION

UNIVERSITY OF NORTH CAROLINA at CHAPEL HILL, Chapel Hill, NC
Bachelor of Arts in Communications with a Concentration in Cinema/Broadcasting

This individual, looking for advancement, gives a broad overview of his qualifications on page 1, followed by detailed experience highlights on page 2.

PAUL L. RODRIGUEZ

Page 2

PROFESSIONAL EXPERIENCE

ZINGO GRAPHICS, Research Triangle Park, NC
Art Director; Graphic Designer/Illustrator, 1996 - Present

- In this multi-task creative and management position, lead development of custom design images. Modify existing images and graphics to exceed client needs. Work in consultative role with sales department personnel to ensure execution of creative, promotional-based strategies for clients.

- Produced multiple projects and spearheaded emerging design projects for IBM Corporation, Cisco Systems, NIEHS and others.

- Hired, trained, developed and managed Art Department staff in all aspects of design and design procedures.

- Responsible for HTML; developed creative graphics for web publication.

- Analyze and modify existing images while communicating with various clients on the design and screen printing processes. Utilize extensive hands-on knowledge of the process of screen printing and incorporating design techniques to produce desired finished effect.

- Obtain information sheets from marketing managers and sales; analyze specifications and operate various graphics programs, including CorelDraw, Adobe PhotoShop, Corel Photo Paint and Adobe Illustrator for PC compatibles.

- Work closely with computer operations and IT aspects of position to ensure obtainment of the newest, best applications to increase cross-platform capabilities and networking.

- Obtain photography from existing photographs; schedule photo shoots. Utilize PhotoShop, Freehand and Illustrator to design text, graphics and photography for packaging. Send digital files to printer, make changes and execute final procedures.

OTHER WORK EXPERIENCE

KINKO'S, Durham, NC
Document Specialist

GREENLAND, INC., Chapel Hill, NC
Landscape Specialist

TECHSOURCE ASSOCIATES, RTP, NC
Information Specialist

Further information and references available upon request.

Richard Samson
125 13th Avenue North — St. Paul, MN 55101 — 651.555.2321 — rsamson@bell.com

KEY HIRING ASSETS
- Expert in building virtual communities on the Internet toward commerce, education, non-profit, government, and consumer goals. Reputation as technology "Dear Abby" for a broad-based online community.
- Exceptional ability to communicate technical information to end users. Provide end-user training and ongoing support in network, e-mail, Internet/Web, various Windows applications.
- Offer a unique, valuable perspective gained from longevity in the field coupled with an inner drive and love for information technology, keeping me on the cutting edge.

INFORMATION TECHNOLOGY COMPETENCIES
- ☑ **Novel NetWare Certified Engineer**
- ☑ **Microsoft Certified Systems Engineer:** Design, install, maintain, troubleshoot, and repair computer systems and peripherals. Supervise in the process of configuration, assembly, and testing of systems. Provide training for technicians and non-technical users. Evaluate new products. Provide customized solutions to fit customers' requirements. Extensive Web Design experience. Knowledge of numerous technologies, network topologies, and protocols. Experienced in building / rebuilding computers and related equipment from scratch.
- ☑ **Programming Languages:** UNIX. LINUX. CGI / PERL. HTML. DHTML. JavaScript. C.
- ☑ **Intranets / Systems Administration & Support:** Telecommunications & Phone Systems. E-mail. Workstations. Terminals. Windows NT Network. Fileservers. Search Engines.
- ☑ **Applications:** Net Objects Fusion. Netscape. Netscape Mail. TCP/IP. IE Microsoft. PaintShop Pro. Adobe Acrobat. Internet Explorer. Cute-ftp. Ws-ftp. Demicron Java Applet Configurator. Pegasus Mail. Majority of software programs on the market.
- ☑ **Operating Systems:** LINUX. Win 95-98. NT. Win Beta 2000.

CAREER PATH
Chief Webmaster — ST. CHARLES UNIVERSITY – St. Paul, MN   1999 – present
- Develop and manage the SCU website. Create an environment that encourages the development of SCU's site. Educated campus to increase the number of active web "content providers." Use systems technology wherever possible to automatically develop and deliver content to the site. Partner with campus and unit webmasters to create a "look and feel" for the site. **Recipient of the "Webmaster Award," an Internet award recognizing unique and useful content, exceptional graphic design / layout, and clear and simple navigation.**

Network Support Technician / Help Desk Specialist — FOOD MARKET, INC. – Minneapolis, MN 1992 – 1999
- Provided technical support for large grocery distribution chain whose clients included Cub Food stores in 18 states. Came on board during very dysfunctional period for company's IT services. Consulted with external / internal users to facilitate entry and retrieval of information for distribution, shipping, receiving, inventory, accounting, and personnel. **Delivered IT functions $5,000 under budget and 2 months early.**

Network Technician — ELLINGSON TECHNOLOGY – St. Paul, MN   1989 – 1992
- Provided network support for manufacturer of flexible circuits and suspensions for hard disk assembly. Set up and maintained network: hardware, switches, routers, and peripherals. Coded products shipped and received. Tracked logistical processes of chemical inventory for EPA, HAZMAT, etc. **Reduced costs 35% by implementing previously unused software to allow migration of manual to computerized tracking.**

IBM AS/400 Support Administrator — BONNIEVILLE NUTRITION – Minneapolis, Park, MN 1982 – 1989
- Supported AS/400 Unix-based systems for large (1,500 employees) manufacturer of food and pharmaceutical products whose customers included Merck and ADM. Set up HR database. Supported all aspects of warehousing and distribution operations. Supervised staff of 3.

This is one of the resume writer's favorites in the computer field. It has many special fonts and an attention-getting graphic.

John Joseph Derry

176 Woodhaven Drive, Eatontown, NJ 07724 · (732) 927-5555 · JJDer@bol.com

Web Applications Management
E-Commerce · B2B · Project Management

KEY QUALIFICATIONS

✓ **Technical Strengths:** Up-to-date, diverse training in e-Business Management coupled with years of experience in analytical, technical process engineering profession.

✓ **Project Coordination and Teamwork:** Highly productive in team environments as both member and team leader. Efficient in handling multiple project priorities.

✓ **Communication:** Able to communicate technical information in an easily understandable way. Recognized for relationship-building with team members and clients. An effective listener.

✓ **Personal Attributes:** Innovative problem-solver. Committed to goal achievement. Dependable.

EDUCATION

☑ Cybersoft Internet Professional – CIP 1, Cybersoft, Inc., Woodbridge, NJ
August, 2000 — **Certified e-Business Architect, e-Business for Managers**
December, 1999 — **Certified Cybersoft Communications 1000** including Fundamentals of Networking, Database, Web Development, Web Design, Multimedia, and Internet Business

☑ Bachelor of Science, Industrial Engineering, Connecticut Institute of Technology

TECHNICAL SKILLS

e-Commerce: e-Business and B2B Infrastructures and Consumer Payment Protocols
Applications: ERP, e-Procurement, Selling Chain Management, Customer Relationship Management
Software Tools: MS Word, HTML, FrontPage 2000
Operating Systems: Windows 98, Windows 95

PROFESSIONAL EXPERIENCE

1995-1999 — ENGINEERING SYSTEMS, INC., Astro Space Division, Eatontown, NJ
Manufacturing Engineer, Production Engineering Department

Provided assembly documentation and engineering floor support throughout all phases of production flow, including fabrication, assembly, and test operations, for the manufacture of diverse satellite products contracted by major government clients (USSA and the U.S. Air Force).

ACCOMPLISHMENTS

- Promoted to Team Leader for the introduction of new equipment and upgrades. Performed research and analysis of new equipment for cost effectiveness and quality. Tested in production mode. Full authority to sign off fully tested equipment to production line engineer.

- Investigated and introduced a new solvent, as well as new manufacturing equipment, that improved recycle characteristics and cut hazardous emissions into the atmosphere by 40%.

- Collaborated with 60-person design engineering team to ensure that designs were producible in the manufacturing environment. Provided cost-effective manufacturing recommendations.

- Trained 8 entry-level engineers in 4-month period to prepare efficient, labor-effective work plans for a multi-line production floor in an 80,000-square-foot facility.

- Reduced cycle time by 30% through the development of assembly and test tolling.

Notable on this resume are the checkmark bullets and the strong emphasis on career accomplishments.

Jennifer C. Wallach

73 Barbizon Lane • Woodstock, VT 05412
802.885.1111 • jcwallach@hotmail.com

Qualifications Summary

- Highly motivated and accomplished **Web Page Developer/Technical Communications Professional** with strong project management and implementation abilities; resourceful design and research/documentation specialist.
- Innovative and creative initiative-taker with demonstrated expertise in all facets of web page design, desktop publishing, and computer/Internet technologies; flexible and adaptable in positively responding to changing organizational needs.
- Effective problem-assessment and problem-solving abilities; expert communications and editorial skills.
- Highly proficient with the following web development and graphic tools/skills: HTML, Java Script, DHTML, and XML; Microsoft FrontPage and Office Suite, Adobe PageMaker and Photoshop, QuarkXPress, and CorelDraw.

Professional Experience

3/97–Present   ARGON INTELLIGENCE GROUP, INC. (AIG) • Barnard, VT
Web Page Developer
- Broad range of creative/technical responsibilities includes development and ongoing product management for corporate web site as well as sites for major clients; maintain corporate internets, intranet, and extranet with key responsibility for creation of product pages.
- Corporate/client project scope entails maintaining excellent customer relationships, managing and executing monthly updates, and coordinating/supervising contract designers.
- Successfully initiated, developed, and documented interface designs for company's first completely online HTML help system for retail systems product; implementation yielded substantial cost savings over paper production as well as enabled more timely releases/updates.
- Graphic Designer for corporate marketing materials; design/author user manuals for ancillary retail systems products; provide technical consulting on as-needed basis across all disciplines.

1995–96   DOBSON COMMUNICATION CORPORATION • South Woodstock, VT
Marketing/Public Relations Intern
- Managed production of three monthly newsletters; oversight responsibility included story idea selection (collaborating with market coordinators), story assignments/editing, liaison to ad agency regarding layout requirements and art specifications, and prepress approval of final product.
- Developed and wrote internal as well as external communications including news releases, feature stories, and promotional feature pieces.
- Implemented wide range of creative design assignments from conducting a web page competitive analysis and implementing a company recycling program to producing a competitive event for employees of eight branch stores and executing a customer essay contest.

Education   NEW HAMPSHIRE COLLEGE • Manchester, NH
Bachelor of Arts Degree — Journalism/Public Relations (1996)
- Officer, Public Relations Student Society of America (1994–96)
- Member, Phi Beta Lambda (Professional Business Leaders)

Continuing development includes attendance at professional seminars/conferences and meetings complemented by subscriptions to professional journals.

Affiliations   **PUBLIC RELATIONS SOCIETY OF AMERICA**
- Webmaster/Newsletter Editor
HTML WRITERS GUILD
SOCIETY OF TECHNICAL COMMUNICATION

This individual transferred her writing, marketing, and PR skills to a career as a Web page developer. Most of her resume focuses on communications strengths and the value she's brought to her employers.

BRETT WAGNER
bwagner@execpc.com

14326 North Lake Drive
Bayside, Wisconsin 53402

Office (414) 347-5634
Residence (262) 242-9455

SALES AND SALES MANAGEMENT

E-Commerce / E-Procurement / ASP / Infrastructure & Management Consulting

Dynamic and motivated sales and management professional with 10 years' experience marketing technology products/services to high-growth, emerging, mature, and competitive enterprises. Outstanding presentation, negotiation, and closing skills. Demonstrated expertise in:

- Client Relationship Management
- Key Accounts/National Accounts
- Competitive Market Share
- Goal Attainment/Revenue Growth
- New Accounts/Prospecting
- New Product Positioning/Launch

PROFESSIONAL EXPERIENCE

Information Technology Consulting, Inc., Milwaukee, Wisconsin   1999 to Present
(Nationwide technology service provider to Fortune 500 & middle-market organizations.)

REGIONAL MANAGER with full P&L responsibility for aggressively establishing state of Wisconsin territory in the sale of e-business and infrastructure resources to major manufacturers and service organizations. Consult with executive-level personnel, including CEOs and VPs of Marketing & IT, on solutions for Internet sales, project management, systems integration, application development, enterprise systems management, and application service provision.

- Exceeded sales quota objectives for 1999 and 2000.
- Forged strong alliances with local technology vendors including Clarify, PeopleSoft, SAP, Oracle, and Tivoli. Developed opportunities to make joint presentations to key accounts.

Fortune 500 Information Services, Milwaukee, Wisconsin   1989 to 1996 / 1998 to 1999

RELATIONSHIP MANAGER with primary responsibility to consult with major U.S. corporations on the purchase/lease of business information and software for strategic decision-making and planning. Conduct in-depth analysis of current needs and draft proposals. Negotiate and administer service agreements and coordinate contract fulfillment/installation.

- Named Regional New Business Associate of the Year in 1995 and Regional Representative of the Year in 1993. Received awards in 1990, 1991, 1993, and 1995 for account retention, revenue growth, and sales performance.
- Achieved consistent annual production growth of 18%-20%.

Eastern Healthcare Products Company, Mansfield, Massachusetts   1996 to 1998

ACCOUNT REPRESENTATIVE recruited to sell medical supplies to long-term care facilities, durable medical equipment suppliers, home health agencies, and physician clinics throughout the Upper Midwest. Actively pursued new business, qualified needs, and conducted hands-on demonstration/in-service sessions for key accounts.

- Assumed full responsibility for $4.9 million in revenues and acquired $250,000 of new business in the first 12 months. Preserved several accounts on the brink of switching suppliers.
- Launched 6 new products successfully.

EDUCATION

BBA (Bachelor of Business Administration) in Marketing, University of Wisconsin—Milwaukee

Here's another individual who started in a nontechnology career and successfully transitioned his skills to the world of e-commerce.

Michael R. Jensen

111 East 11th Street
New York, New York 11111
(212) 222-2222
mrj@eternalspring.com

Internet Services - Sales - Consulting Services

Service-oriented **Sales professional** offering considerable experience in **Internet consulting** and **broadband data technology**. Consistent producer, at ease dealing with high-level executives and IT professionals. Highly focused individual who enjoys working in a team environment and working toward shared goals and objectives. Areas of expertise and strengths encompass:

◆ **Account Development**	◆ **Presentation Skills**	◆ **Account Management**
◆ **Relationship Building**	◆ **Needs Analysis**	◆ **Problem Resolution**
◆ **Creating Strategic Alliances**	◆ **Negotiations / Closing**	◆ **Training & Supervision**

Professional Experience

GBX CORPORATION, New York, New York   1999 - Present
Internet Consultant
- Generated $100,000 recurring revenue, year-to-date, in the marketing of data centers, T1 lines, web hosting services, co-location, and high-speed broadband data technology.
- Targeted, and successfully established relationships with, major firms including Infoseek, Sports Illustrated, The Venator Group, Advanstar Communications, Elite Model Management, Infinity Interactive, 9Net Avenue, E-liance, Big Foot.com, Razor Fish, NetMix, Indignet, Star Diamond Group, Edgar Online, and Screaming Media.
- **Ranked #4 in sales** within the President's Club.
- Successfully created valuable strategic alliances by offering profit-sharing programs and special marketing agreements to various ISPs, web developers, consultants, and telecom specialists.

MERRILL LYNCH, New York, New York   1995 - 1999
Senior Sales Representative
- **Cultivated $50 million in assets** and produced in excess of $400,000 in gross commissions annually.
- Raised capital for two Internet start-up companies that currently trade publicly.
- Consulted extensively with clients, assessing needs and providing investment guidance and recommendations.
- Provided guidance, training, and support to incoming account executives.

AT&T, New York, New York   1992 - 1995
Senior Sales Representative
- **Achieved 150% of quota** all eight quarters with company.
- Targeted key accounts in lower Manhattan and provided consultative services on the use of high-end business equipment and telecommunications equipment.

Education, Training & Skills

SYRACUSE UNIVERSITY, Syracuse, New York
Bachelor of Arts - Marketing / Economics & Political Science (double major)   1992

- PSS (Professional Selling Skills) Training
- Achieve Global (sponsored by Time Mirror)
- Well versed in various Internet technologies. Knowledge of Word and Excel

This is a straightforward sales resume for a gentleman who made a career change a few years back, leaning toward Internet and information technology. He wishes to continue within Internet services, and this is emphasized on the resume.

Bernd Hieber

c/o Hermann – Koehl – Str.11
89231 NEV - VLM
Germany
Telephone from USA 0113-366-635-5278
Telephone from Europe +33-666-355-278
Email career@abc.org
Online Résumé Portfolio http://www.abc.org/career/print.html

E-Business Specialist / Business Development Strategist / Marketing Executive
Creating & Driving Winning E-Business Strategies for the New Economy

Dynamic planning expert offering fresh insight and a passion for innovation; proven record of contribution to high-profile international business. Powerful strategist able to map creative budgeting, resource planning, and business development, empowering organizations with the tools, technologies, and strategies to bridge the digital business gap.

Respected leader, able to build team cohesion and inspire individuals to strive toward ever-higher levels of achievement. Exceptional relationship and management skills; relate and interface easily at the top executive levels. Complete, in-depth understanding of Internet tools, trends, and business models. Solid background and qualifications in all core business functions – finance, marketing, sales, and operations.

AREAS OF EXPERTISE

- Budget Planning / Management
- Resource Management
- Personnel Training / Supervision
- Team / Group Leadership

Strategic Planning
Organizational Planning / Analysis
Presentations / Public Speaking
Multilingual; speak 3 languages

HIGHLIGHTS OF PROFESSIONAL ACHIEVEMENT

Inventoried existing budgetary controls, reinventing goals, strategies, and models to meet the demands of the new digital economy. Achieved increased competitiveness, heightened market valuation, and revenue gains.

Formatted strategies and action plans that have exceeded IPO and shareholder requirements for financial planning and reporting.

Facilitated negotiations and consensus for selection / integration of numerous development plans in company budgets.

Identified opportunities to accelerate monthly financial reporting, resulting in substantial extension of management's response options.

Pioneered and promoted award-winning Total Customer Satisfaction Project, increasing competitiveness through 8% cost reduction in packaging, 17% in storage, and 23% in shipping. Recruited to present model in final round of Motorola's worldwide project presentation competition in Toronto, Canada.

Designed and built creative Internet portal for the high-growth organization abc.org; credited with national awards and recognized by international health-care professionals as an expert in e-business marketing.

Noticed for developing highly complex and effective projecting tools for sales, costs, orders, and manpower planning requirements. Integrated marketing, product, and resource plans in budget models, now being employed as corporate-wide standard.

The resume for this internationally experienced professional is full of achievements, key words, training, and other professional credentials. It's highly readable due to excellent organization, a clean typeface

Confidential Résumé of Bernd Hieber   Page 2

PROFESSIONAL EXPERIENCE

Arrington Global Travel Distribution – Sophia-Antipolis, France, 1996 – Present

Senior Officer, E-Commerce Division

Senior consultant managing all Internet commerce initiatives. Direct long-term planning, budgeting, forecasting, and analysis for online sales and marketing activities in an increasingly competitive global marketplace. Provide reporting support for mergers, joint ventures, and partnership agreements. Coordinate and consolidate all company e-commerce functions including 17 divisions, 62 departments, 158 cost centers, and 185 projects. Lead, motivate, train, and coach team comprising talented cost control officers who produce standard and ad-hoc analysis reporting as input for crucial executive management decisions.

Motorola Multiservice Networks – Crawley, United Kingdom and Darmstadt, Germany, 1984 – 1996

International Financial Assistant

International financial specialist with collaborative responsibility for the reorganization, centralization, and relocation of administration, manufacturing, and customer support for Europe, Middle East, and Africa Markets (EMEA). Key role in implementation of new tools and management systems in finance and operations. Creative participation in innovation of centralized stock and shipment management.

EDUCATION AND SPECIAL TRAINING

M.B.A., Business and Marketing
University of Tuebingen, Germany
Degree awarded 1995

Business and Marketing Studies
St. Olaf College, Minnesota, USA
1990 – 1991

Business and Marketing Studies
University of Tuebingen, Germany
Degree awarded 1990

Effective Presentation Training – Motorola University
Working as a Team / Six Sigma – Motorola University
Working Smarter - Leadership Development Ltd.
Six Steps to Best Quality – Motorola University
Trans-Cultural Competence – Motorola University

PROFESSIONAL AFFILIATIONS

Member, International Sales and Marketing Executives
Member, Internet Marketing Association
St. Olaf Career Advising Network

PUBLICATIONS

Standards, Certification, and Accreditation in the European Union 1994, VDE Verlag, Berlin, Germany

Author / Coauthor of 7 scientific and non-scientific articles. Complete list of titles can be found at
www.abc.org/career/publications.html

Supporting documentation, additional information, and references available on request.
View complete online Résumé Portfolio at http://www.abc.org/career/english.html

(Arial), and effective use of horizontal lines and type enhancements. Note the reference to a complete online resume portfolio.

ROBERT ROSSTINE

Home: (407) 987-6543
Mobile: (407) 654-9685

robross@takeout.com

17 Glenn Falls Drive
Orlando, Florida 32700

Electronic Commerce / New Business Development / Sales & Marketing Management Executive

Results-oriented Management Executive with ten years of experience leading successful start-up, turnaround, and high growth companies. Consistently successful in identifying and capitalizing upon market opportunities to drive revenue and profit growth. Strong Internet, clicks-and-bricks experience. Speak conversational Japanese and Spanish. Areas of expertise include:

- Strategic / Tactical Business Planning
- Partnership / Alliance Development
- Capital / Fund-raising
- Supply Network Development

- P&L Management
- Software Engineering / Development
- Staff Development / Management
- Investment Qualification Requirements

Recognized for E-commerce Expertise by The Orlando Sentinel (October, 1999),
INC Magazine (September, 1998), and Small Business Opportunities (October, 1999).

PROFESSIONAL EXPERIENCE

FastServe.com, Inc., formerly TakeOut.com, Inc., Dallas, Texas   May 1999 to Present
A take-out food delivery operation serving over 37 major markets in the U.S. and Europe.

Director, New Market Development – FastServe.com, Inc. (May 2000 to Present)

Led the launch of an e-commerce business (TakeOut.com) specializing in a one-hour order delivery operation and grew it to an $800,000 operation within first year. Sold to FastServe.com, assisted in ownership transition, and currently manage new market development.

- Engineered integration of TakeOut.com's software and data into FastServe.com's Delivery Magic within two weeks.
- Assisted in integration of all internal and external operating systems, Internet marketing programs, customer tracking systems, menu guide production, and recruitment strategies.
- Conducted due diligence studies and identified new markets for penetration to meet FastServe.com's business development goals.
- Lead development of restaurant partnerships, order fulfillment/call center operations, menu guide development and production, and staff recruitment.

President/CEO – TakeOut.com, Inc., Orlando, Florida (June 1999 to May 2000)

Built a clicks-and-bricks Internet company based on a newly developed unproven software program and the development of contracts with over 95 bricks-and-mortar companies.

- Conducted due diligence studies, established company direction, developed strategic business plans, created a marketing program, instituted operating infrastructures, and recruited a management team and staff of 35.
- Raised $250,000 in operating seed capital and pioneered the start-up of an online based one-hour restaurant takeout and delivery service.
- Engineered solutions and worked closely with software programmers to build the nation's first web-based restaurant delivery software that was redundant, efficient, effective, and technically sound.
- Overcame customer resistance to web ordering through development of an online order entry system and averaged 35% of sales via the Internet, slashing labor costs and errors.
- Opened for business on August 2, 1999, and recorded over $2,300 in sales in first week. Tracking $800,000 sales for year 2000 with over 30,000 unique online customers.

Highlighting accomplishments and starting off with a strong summary and essential key words, this resume is a powerful introduction for an e-commerce executive.

ROBERT ROSSTINE

Page 2

PROFESSIONAL EXPERIENCE (Continued)

Delivery By Taxi, Inc., Herndon, Virginia

February 1998 to May 1999

Corporate Manager

Recruited to turn around a failing restaurant delivery business with 128 franchisees that had declined from generating $80 million to under $50 million annually. Challenged to identify problems and implement solutions within one of three corporate stores, document outcomes, build SOPs, and distribute manuals to corporate offices and franchisees.

- Developed a corporate marketing program and improved the quality of existing business unit marketing materials.
- Implemented new operating management and accounting procedures.
- Instituted database mailing programs used by all corporate stores and spearheaded a series of software improvements.
- Delivered over 90% revenue increases within six months for two of the corporate stores and a 20% increase for the third store.

Themed Diner, Maitland, Florida

January 1995 to December 1997

District Manager

Hired to manage six privately owned and operated restaurants during a rapid growth period. Developed into a national chain with 26 locations.

- Managed the recruitment, staffing, and training initiatives for a 220-employee operation.
- Built several tracking and food control systems.

Catering & Gourmet Gifts, Inc., Orlando, Florida

July 1991 to December 1993

Owner

Launched catering facility and upscale retail gourmet gift store and marketed a mail-order catalog.

- Achieved profitability after only 10 months.
- Produced $500,000 in sales after only two years; expanded to three locations within three years.
- Managed a catering kitchen, retail store, mail-order warehouse, and 23 employees and drivers.

EARLIER CAREER included General Management positions within the restaurant and retail industries.

EDUCATION / TECHNICAL TRAINING

Wright State University, Dayton, Ohio – Business Finance Concentration

RETS Technical College, Dayton, Ohio – Hotel and Restaurant Management

PROFESSIONAL DEVELOPMENT

Sales and Marketing Technologies Seminar, S&M Tech, Orlando, Florida, September 1999
(Workshops included Search Engines, Effective Marketing, Redundancy, Advanced Technology)

Restaurant Delivery Service Association, Las Vegas, Nevada, May 1998
Marketing, Operational Industry Standards, New Technology Workshops

Internet Seminar, Nothing But Net, Orlando, Florida, April 1998
(Workshops included Web Page Sales, Internet Business History, Networking & Partnership Building)

COMPUTER SKILLS

Operating/Network Systems: MS Windows 3.1/97/98, NT, DOS
Software: MS Office 97, Works, PowerPoint, PC Anywhere, QuickBooks, Quicken, Peachtree
Technical Skills: Installation, maintenance, and management of networked systems

KEITH L. SMITH

keith@estores.com
(510) 542-4567

661 Orchard Road
Berkeley, California 94707

INTERNET TECHNOLOGIES ENTREPRENEUR
E-commerce / Software Development / Online Merchandising

Creative, results-driven executive with *proven track record in building profitable start-up ventures*, developing strategic partnerships, and driving revenue/profit growth in electronic commerce and retailing. *Decisive, visionary leadership; expert at identifying and capturing Internet market opportunities, creating value and convenience in Internet technologies, and inexpensively acquiring specialty market customers.* Combines expertise in strategic planning, P&L management, marketing, and business development with ingenuity in advanced technology infrastructure and business systems.

Participative leadership style; able to build motivation, consensus, and cooperation with cross-functional teams in fast-paced environments. Effectively manage all facets of project life-cycle development, from initial feasibility and market analysis through specification, development, quality review, and implementation.

*Strategic Planning ✦ Marketing Management ✦ Strategic Financial Management
Budget Administration ✦ Risk Analysis ✦ Customer Relationship Management
Service Design / Delivery ✦ Scientific Marketing ✦ Data Mining ✦ Customer Profiling
Internet Media Buying ✦ Advertising ✦ Internet Direct Marketing ✦ Venture Funding
Software Design/Development Management ✦ Business Development*

PROFESSIONAL EXPERIENCE

FOUNDER, PRESIDENT AND CEO
I-Commerce, Provo, UT

1995 – 1998

Challenge: Lead start-up venture from concept through development and market launch to market leadership. *Capitalize on innovative product and service ideas* to competitively position business, build partnerships, and grow revenues.

Craft marketing strategy, distribution methods, and packaging. Acquire business-to-business and business-to-consumer relationships online.

Action: Founded company to create e-commerce sites for specialty retailers, but quickly *identified opportunity* to build unique software tool allowing merchants to manage site content — ShopSite.

Integrated *viral marketing strategies* to promote ShopSite. *Eliminated product distribution costs* by offering Internet downloads for authorized users. Purchased cooperative advertising to pool online marketing dollars and resources.

Surveyed merchants to assess needs and rate system effectiveness. *Optimized online marketing strategies*, analyzing cost per sale per message per market venue.

This resume, and the one that follows, was created as part of a financing package for a start-up e-commerce company seeking venture capital. Note the effective use of the CAR strategy in describing key accomplishments.

KEITH L. SMITH   Page Two

FOUNDER, PRESIDENT AND CEO, I-Commerce, continued

Action: **Recruited talented, high-level managers** from leading technology companies. Instituted disciplined software development practices, including code management, version control, and documentation techniques.

Forged strategic alliances with key partners, including Microsoft, Adobe, Verio, and Mindspring.

Results:
- ShopSite user base has grown to over 35,000, making it the **most widely used small business e-commerce software worldwide**.

- **Pioneered method for protecting software from piracy**, enabling I-Central to attract and forge alliances with hundreds of ISP distribution partners.

- Raised $1 million in venture capital. **Delivered 400% return for investors** in an average of 9 months.

- Utilized **disciplined budget strategies** to stretch resources and grow operations on thin cash. Never missed a payroll. Devised internal accounting system for order management, sales, and billing.

- **Sold company for $11 million in May 1998 to Open Market** (NASDAQ: OMKT).

GENERAL MANAGER
Electronics Education International, Irvine, CA   1993 – 1994

Challenge: Lead aggressive business turnaround for designer, manufacturer, and distributor of educational kits and software for electronics training. Drive revenue and profit improvement for company with slow 10% annual sales growth.

Action: Streamlined operations and business practices to **achieve profit goals with only half of previous inventory and staffing levels.** Redesigned inventory and accounting processes to optimize inventory levels and reduce costs. Competitively positioned company against larger business ventures.

Results:
- **Doubled revenues in first year**.
- **Increased profits more than 80%** through innovative marketing strategies, internal efficiency planning, and revitalized business processes.

EDUCATION

B.S., Corporate Finance *(cum laude graduate),* NEW YORK UNIVERSITY, New York, NY, 1993

JAMES CARTWRIGHT

james@estores.com
Business: (801) 542-4567 x102   Cellular: (801) 529-9978

1213 East 500 South
Salt Lake City, Utah 84102

CORPORATE FINANCE AND MANAGEMENT PROFESSIONAL
Start-up Ventures / E-commerce / Specialty Market E-Tailing

Versatile professional with strong track record of building successful start-up organizations focused on Internet technologies and online merchandising. Combine multi-function experience in internal financial management, marketing/sales, and human resources with functional expertise in e-commerce architecture, systems integration, and project management.

Take-charge manager with solid analysis, planning, and organization abilities. Flexible and focused with exceptional problem-solving capability. Efficiently and effectively prioritize a broad range of responsibilities to consistently meet tight deadlines and achieve performance objectives. Articulate and effective communicator; work well with individuals on all levels.

VALUE OFFERED

Financial / Business Management: Financial Planning and Analysis, Budget Administration, Forecasts, P&L Management, Financial Statements, Cost Control, Performance Improvement, Acquisitions, Strategic Partnerships, ROI.

Project Management: Technology Needs Assessment, Cost / Benefit Analysis, Staffing, Team Building and Coordination, Resource Management, Alpha and Beta Testing, Schedule Parameters, Presentation Design Review, R&D.

Marketing / Sales Ability: Internet Marketing Strategies, Online Media Planning / Buying / Analysis, Affiliate Market Linking Strategies, Search Engine Optimization, Product Sourcing, Market Assessment, Business Development, Competitive Market Positioning, Market Development, Relationship Management.

Technical Expertise: Business / Marketing / Technical Liaison, Cross-Functional Technology Teams, User Training and Support, Systems Development Methodology, Systems Functionality, Systems Architecture, Technology Integration.

PROFESSIONAL EXPERIENCE

INTERNET MEDIA, INC, Boston, Massachusetts   1998-1999
Interactive advertising agency, offering website promotions, brand awareness, creative development, PR, and media strategy / buying / analysis. Now with 7 offices nationwide, generating $10-20 million annually. Sold partnership interest in 1999.

Cofounder / Controller
Established new company with business partner of ICentral. Coordinated business planning and market development strategies. Personally directed financial planning, accounting, payroll, taxes, consolidated financial reporting, investor relationships, and administrative affairs.

- Contributed to team that designed, developed, and managed the implementation of adOctane, a proprietary *media planning, buying, and analysis* tool.

- Assisted in development of *business identity* and *marketing communications strategy*. Instituted and administered *financial/accounting systems and payroll*.

This individual is the financial brains behind the e-commerce company he started with Mr. Smith (see resume 73). The Value Offered section is particularly effective in detailing the breadth of his expertise.

JAMES CARTWRIGHT

PROFESSIONAL EXPERIENCE

I-COMMERCE, INC, Provo, Utah   1995-1998
Start-up Internet software company specializing in e-commerce solutions for small to medium Internet retailers. Developed ShopSite, the most widely used small business e-commerce software worldwide. Sold to Open Market in 1998.

Cofounder / Controller
Directed *corporate finance/accounting and operations functions* from sales and collections to procurement and accounts payable. Completed monthly statistical and financial reports; managed budgeting, forecasting, cash flow, audits, reconciliations, tax preparation, insurance benefits, and 401(k) administration. Oversaw all management aspects of HR activities.

Provided marketing/sales and technical support, including *project management* and *customer service/education*. Assisted with *systems architecture* from functional perspective.

- Participated in development of *unique business model and product positioning* that grew ShopSite user base from start-up to 5000+ merchants.
- Oversaw design and implementation of *proprietary billing/order processing and sales force automation systems*. Integrated product pricing, release, and platform updates in system. Implemented and monitored sales policies, controls, and commissions structures.
- *Advanced company's profit performance* through strategic planning, financial forecasting, internal/external reporting, financial analysis, cash management, tax planning, and business plan development. Streamlined and enhanced corporate budgeting process.
- Served as sole point of contact for KPMG assessment of ICentral's accounting/tax systems, ensuring compliance with GAAP and IRS regulations.
- *Managed investor and banking relationships*, including budgeting, forecasts, statement preparations, and documentation for due diligence/acquisition.
- *Negotiated contracts* for capital equipment financing, merchant services, and vendor relationships.

ELECTRONIC EDUCATION INTERNATIONAL, Irvine, California   1992-1995
Designer, manufacturer, and distributor of educational kits and software for electronics training.

Assistant Manager
Marketed specialty electronics kits and software through catalog/telephone sales and trade shows. Supported financial, administrative, order fulfillment, and distribution functions.

- Developed broad knowledge of specialty retailing and business-to-business operations, marketing, and sales.

EDUCATION

CORPORATE FINANCE degree program, 1 semester to complete
University of Utah, Salt Lake City, Utah, GPA 3.8

CHAPTER 9

Resumes for Project Managers and Technology Consultants

- Technology Project Managers
- IT, IS, and MIS Project Managers
- Telecommunications Technology Managers
- Technology Leaders
- Technology Industry Consultants

Charles Farrow

27 Central Avenue, Toms River, NJ 08754
(732) 929-5555 Home • (732) 929-8888 Mobile • cfarrow@ole.com

Project Management
IT Systems Installation and Technology Integration

Results-driven leader with information systems installation and integration experience. Work closely with end-users during the design, development, and training stages. Expert in full-cycle project planning and implementation. Skilled in applications analysis and back-office operations. Demonstrated business acumen and ability to meet fiscal and deadline commitments. Core competencies include:

✓ Strategic Business Planning	✓ Reengineering	✓ Project Management
✓ Interdepartmental Coordination	✓ Change Management	✓ Resource Management
✓ Management & Administration	✓ Technology Transfer	✓ Client Relations

Energetic and decisive business leader able to merge disparate personnel into team-centered project teams. Demonstrated team-building, relationship-building, and communications skills.

PROFESSIONAL EXPERIENCE

CCS Systems (software vendor/ASP to Fortune 500 companies), Toms River, NJ   1990-2001

Director (1994-2001), **Training Director** (1990-1994)
Managed multimillion-dollar IT projects for large-scale corporate home office applications. Fully responsible for project P&L. Clients included Westney, Cal-Mart, James, Home Store, Jill Jones, D-Mart, and River Royal. Maintained direct and ongoing client contact to ensure smooth operations.

Accomplishments

☑ Achieved productivity gains of up to 50% through the development and implementation of projects on time, on spec, and on budget. Consistently met or exceeded performance criteria.

☑ Vital member of steering committee that identified user needs and developed customized solutions for more than 150 clients. Personable, direct approach contributed to client loyalty.

☑ Led projects through entire project development cycle to develop application-specific systems capable of meeting current and long-range corporate information management requirements. Produced and managed deliverables through formal project plans.

☑ Matrix-managed 20-member cross-functional team (hardware, software, quality control, technical support, and training), assigning team responsibilities and overseeing tasks and timelines. Often called upon to use personal judgment, diplomacy, and analytical sense to troubleshoot problems.

☑ Pioneered innovative team building and cross-functional project management techniques to expedite workflow, simplify processes, and reduce operating costs.

☑ Designed and implemented user setup, end-user training materials, and testing procedures.

River Royal (Division of Royal, Inc.), New York, NY   1983-1990
Divisional Planner (1987-1990) Promoted from Planner and Senior Planner (1983-1987)

EDUCATION

B.S., Marketing, 1981: McGill University, Ontario, Canada

COMPUTER SKILLS

Windows 98, Microsoft Office 2000, Word, Excel, PowerPoint, Access, Outlook, Internet

With all his professional experience at one company, this individual was able to construct a concise, one-page resume that effectively highlights his project accomplishments.

RESUME 76: CINDY KRAFT, CPRW, CCM; VALRICO, FL

SCOTT G. RUSSELL

504-583-2222   sgr@gte.net

4483 Margeurite Avenue, New Orleans, LA 70112

PROJECT MANAGER skilled in developing and implementing successful automated management methodologies with minimal business interruption. Consistently successful in delivering cost reductions and improved operational efficiencies. Exceptional leadership, analytical, and communication capabilities. Project management expertise includes . . .

Internal IS Productivity Management	Y2K Compliance
Corporate IS and User Training	Disaster Planning and Recovery
Network Management	Network-based EDI
Corporate IS Help Desk	Data and Internet Security / Firewall
COLD Storage	Remote Telecommunications Support
Data/Voice over ATM	Business Intelligence
Optical Storage	Bar Coding for Warehouse Inventory

TECHNICAL SKILLS

Hardware

Telecommunications (ATM, ISDN, Frame Relay, T-1)
Network Hardware (Cisco, Verilink, Compaq, Dell)
Telephone Switches (Nortel and Lucent)
Remote Access (Citrix and Cisco)
PictureTel Videoconferencing
Cisco Routers and Switches
Midrange (DEC, IBM)

Operating Systems

Novell 3.12 ♦ Novell 4.1x ♦ Novell Netware ♦ Windows NT ♦ Windows 95 ♦ Windows 3.1

Applications
Microsoft Office ♦ Lotus SmartSuite

SELECTED CAREER HIGHLIGHTS

♦ Designed the LAN for a furniture store with offices throughout the United States. Developed the project methodology and technology budget, negotiated with vendors, executed the sourcing and purchases, and managed implementation of an integrated network, accounting system, and dynamic inventory application. **Result: Transformed a manual inventory process that took up to 7 months to complete and lost customers due to inefficient ordering and delivering processes into an efficient operation that provided instantaneous inventory information and substantially improved customer satisfaction.**

♦ Managed the implementation of a common accounting system for a printing company with 23 offices nationwide. Researched the required equipment and software and made recommendations to the owner. Directed the network, intranet, EDI, e-commerce, reporting system, and email installations. **Result: Significantly increased operating efficiency and provided easy access to reports.**

♦ Challenged to network a Fortune 50 company with 9 separate mining sites. Developed the 5-year conversion methodology and budget, researched existing and necessary infrastructure, negotiated with telecommunications vendors, directed sourcing and purchases, and developed standards documentation. **Result: Senior management can automatically monitor, and instantly review, mining production numbers from each individual site.**

Lightly shaded gray boxes set off section headings, and the remainder of the resume is well balanced and includes plenty of white space for excellent readability.

SCOTT G. RUSSELL

Page 2

PROFESSIONAL EXPERIENCE

Project Management Consultant, 1999 to Present
VALUE COMMUNICATIONS, New Orleans, Louisiana

Direct project management from proposal, budgeting and technical planning through installation and diagnostic testing.

Manager, Information Services, 1998
CYPRESS SOLUTIONS, INC., New Orleans, Louisiana

Hired to direct the 2-year conversion from a mainframe to a midrange platform. Reviewed existing infrastructure and developed the project methodology. Authored network, O/S and infrastructure standards. Negotiated with and qualified vendors. Ensured Y2K compliance. Spearheaded the formation of a steering committee to keep the company informed and involved. Developed and implemented a staff training program.

Information Systems Administrator, 1988 to 1997
WILSON MILLER COMPANY, Greenburg, South Carolina

Recruited to manage the company's 5-year major system upgrade. Reported directly to the CFO. Selected as the only IS on the 13-member re-engineering team. Developed the project methodology and presented recommendations to senior management. Compiled a comprehensive document addressing standards, policies and procedures, timelines and task assignments.

TRAINING

Novell Netware 3.12 Courses
Advanced Administration Courses, Novell Netware 4.11 Administrator
Microsoft Windows 95 Advanced Level Administration
Advanced Communications Course, Lucent Technologies
Certified Software Manager, Software Publishers Association
Information and Computer Security, National Security Agency
Project Management for Technology Courses, American Management Association

---

EDUCATION

Bachelor of Arts, Economics
Penn State University, Harrisburg, Pennsylvania

Vijay Rahman

31050 Oaks of Maine Road
Burlington, North Carolina 27215

387-287-5160
vr428@aol.com

TELECOMMUNICATIONS

NETWORK ANALYSIS · PLANNING · PROJECT MANAGEMENT

SKILLS SUMMARY

Technical:
ATM network end-to-end architect
Passport, DWDM transport and DMS switching product expert
Technical and business solutions provider

Management:
Matrix/multi-project manager
Budget development, control and accountability specialist
Critical path and end objective team leader

Interpersonal:
Mentor, coach and advisor for cross-functional groups
Customer service specialist
Relationship builder with internal and external key people

Communications:
Effective negotiator
Perceptive listener, problem solver, contingency examiner
Concise instructor and demonstrator of new products and procedures

Computer:
PC and Mac; Windows and Mac operating systems
MS Word and Visio
MS Project, MicroPlanner, Excel, PowerPoint

PROFESSIONAL EXPERIENCE

MOON RIVER COMMUNICATIONS   1999 to Present
**Communications provider of Incumbent Local Exchange Carrier, Internet Service, Competitive Local
Exchange Carrier and Long-Distance service.**

Project Manager
Network Analysis and Planning Department
- Design and implement revenue-generating ATM network for voice and data services.
- Utilize Passport ATM switch, OPTera DWDM Transport, ATM Edge and DMS500.
- Accomplished bringing network into "succession" readiness.

Note that the Skills Summary in this resume starts off with technical skills but also includes other important but less definable qualifications.

Vijay Rahman, page 2

NORTHERN TELECOM (NORTEL)   1984 to 1999
$18 billion industry employing 80,000 worldwide, designing, building and delivering communications and Internet Protocol networks for Internet service providers, local, long-distance, cellular and PCS communications.

Achievements

➤ 1995 President's Award for Commitment to Customer Satisfaction and Company Success (one of six selected from among 10,000 Nortel employees).

➤ Fourteen years of exceptional performance reviews and increasing responsibility.

Technical Project Manager — Team Leader (1993 to 1999)

- Facilitated development and delivery of the Spectrum product and software with training, documentation, installation, customer engineering, manufacturing and physical packaging for IXC and LEC markets.
- Led team with integrated design and delivery for Extended Application Computing Module (XA-Core) deployment team.
- Secured $250 million contract as a result of team building and project management of Operations Deployment of AccessNode for MCI Metro.
- Managed and held to favorable figures a $2.2 million R&D budget and a $15 million capital budget.

Operations Test Engineering (1984 to 1992)

- Identified and oversaw capital and program requirements for repair of Nortel products
- Interfaced with Pacific Bell for no-fault-found study on field returns
- Primed for test issue resolution of Japan's NTT direct inspections
- Developed system test processes and Packlevel test programs

EDUCATION

Bachelor of Science in Electronics Engineering Technology, 1983
North Dakota Institute of Technology, graduated with honors

Continuing Education

Kepner-Tregoe Problem Solving and Decision Making	Sonet Technical Overview
S/DMS AccessNode Overview	ISDN Technical Intro
FrameMaker 5.5	Access Line Protocols
Finance for the Non-Financial Manager	Presentation Excellence
Negotiating to Yes	Project Management
Time Management	Leadership Communications
OPTera OC192/Connect X AMP & P	OPTera LongHaul

PATRICK WOOLEY, CPA

76 Everett Drive, Red Bank, NJ 07701
(732) 219-5555 • pwooley@net.com

FINANCIAL INFORMATION SYSTEMS
Project Management • SAP Design & Implementation

✓ A data-savvy financial professional with combined qualifications in finance and accounting (CPA and financial analyst), as well as in financial information systems and project management.

✓ An analytical thinker who understands complex details as well as the broader business implications. Data integration expertise areas include ERP modules FI, CO, and SL.

✓ Successful in utilizing technology to improve operational efficiency, reduce costs, and meet reliability goals.

✓ Energized by challenges, steep learning curves, and high-pressure deadlines. Solid team leader with strong training skills.

RECENT PROFESSIONAL EXPERIENCE

Drug Empire, Inc., Red Bank, NJ   1998–present
Team Member, Global Implementation
SAP Consultant (hired temp-to-perm)

Recruited to assist in global multinational SAP implementation for a Fortune 500 pharmaceutical company. World-class financial system incorporating a shared service center structure and approach.

Primary focus: European rollout of SAP system, implementing new functionality into a live productive system. Project manager and chief architect of Euro currency conversion project: Security, Systems Testing, and Training. Manage virtual, cross-functional team of 20.

- Oversee risk-inherent retroactive conversion transforming financial data from European national currencies into new Euro currency. Configured and tested SAP solution, meeting Euro currency conversion requirements.

- Key player in SAP design process including custom module development to fit client needs. Wrote functional specifications; conducted testing, integrated configuration, and on-site production support for global system foreign currency revaluation processes, European tax (VAT), and statutory requirements.

- Documented, tested, and managed user authorizations for general accounting security profiles in 10,000-user base system.

- Key team role in 4 major implementations: UK/Ireland, France, Italy/Germany, and Spain/Belgium/Netherlands, as well as concurrent domestic implementations at major client companies.

- Developed and refined end-to-end project management skills. Recognized by management with 3 President's Awards for successful implementations / rollouts.

- Effectively conduct knowledge transfer activities (SAP processes and SAP system functionality) for project team members and domestic and international end-users and super-users.

Finance

Financial Analysis
General Accounting
Budgeting
Forecasting
Consolidations
Financial Reporting
SEC Reporting
Risk Management
Auditing
Currency Exchanges
Fixed Asset Management

Information Technology

Project Management
SAP Solutions
Data Analysis
Systems Design
Systems Configuration
Systems Development
Systems Testing
FI Functionality
VAT Functionality
Applications Development
Resource Utilization
Systems Implementation
Month End Close Process

Knowledge Transfer

End-User Training
Project Team Development
Small Groups, One-on-One
Coaching
Mentoring
Team Building

Business Expertise

Problem-Solving
Communications
Team Leadership
Client Relations
Quality Management
Planning & Organization

The information-packed left column shows a good way to hit lots of high points without distracting from the traditional resume format.

PATRICK WOOLEY,
CPA

(732) 219-5555 • pwooley@net.com
Page 2

**PROFESSIONAL
EXPERIENCE**
continued

Smith Domestics, Inc., Farmingdale, NJ   1995-1998
Supervisor of Financial Analysis

- Overall responsibility for consolidations, financial statement preparation, internal reporting, and SEC reporting. Prepared consolidated federal and state tax return and all local income and sales/use tax returns.
- Oversaw $3M international risk management program. Administered policy renewals, claims, audits, and billing.
- Maintained fixed asset records for $50M in property, plant, and equipment and tracked all capital projects.
- Coordinated smooth licensing process for a New York holding company with an outside accounting firm.

Financial Data Systems, Inc., Woodbridge, NJ   1992-1995
**Supervisor of Financial Reporting & Analysis
Financial Analyst**

- Maintained general ledger and coordinated monthly closings, consolidating parent company and 6 foreign subsidiaries.
- Corporate liaison to foreign subsidiaries in accounting issue.
- Prepared timely financial statements, as well as monthly and quarterly management reports.
- Tracked stock options and grants, including outstanding shares and calculating earnings per share.

Jenkins, Sotheby & Smythe, Pennsbury, PA   previously
Davidson & White, Harrisburg, PA
Senior Accountant / Staff Accountant

EDUCATION

Graduate, Unix/C Development Training Program   1998
Computer Institute of New Jersey, Woodbridge, NJ

Bachelor of Science, Business Administration   1982
South University, Harrisburg, PA

Seminars: Security and Authorizations in SAP/R3, FI Financial Management, CO, SL, ABAP 4 Workbench, SAP and the Euro

ASSOCIATIONS

American SAP Users Group (ASUG)
American Institute of Certified Public Accountants
New Jersey Institute of Certified Public Accountants

TECHNOLOGY

Software: SAP/R3, ABAP 4 Workbench, Unix, Shell Programming, Visual Basic 4.0, PowerBuilder 4.0, Oracle, Windows NT, SQL, MS Word, MS Excel, WordPerfect for Windows, Lotus 1-2-3, Windows 98, DOS 6.2, Lawson G/L

Hardware: IBM Pentium-Based PC and Apple Macintosh

Abby Randolph

5 Timber Lane • Somerset, NJ 08873 • 732-555-1212 • arandolph@yahoo.com

IT PROFESSIONAL - PROJECT MANAGEMENT AND BUSINESS ANALYSIS
Consumer marketing, provisioning, customer fulfillment and database marketing

In-depth expertise in all aspects of business application lifecycles including project management, analysis, design, programming, training and strategic systems planning. Adept in both large and small applications across mainframe and client-server architectures. Highly skilled large-scale project manager able to work with clients to identify their business requirements and translate them to IT.

KEY ACCOMPLISHMENTS

- Achieved $5M in cost reductions through development and implementation of project plans to continue development of releases and in response to audits in projects of $100K - $1M.
- Provided IT support to ensure accurate processing of 28 million orders, 72 million fulfillments and 335 million promotional responses annually.
- Increased joint fulfillment volumes from 3 to 22 percent, saving $1M per month in fulfillment costs.
- Reduced expense on external vendors by $5M annually.
- Directed system enhancements to support the ordering, enrollment, provisioning and fulfillment of 100+ new marketing offers annually.
- Significantly improved provisioning and fulfillment processes to increase timeliness and reduce costs.
- Produced 27 percent reduction in software defects.
- Significantly reduced run times and costs associated with various applications.
- Developed long-term system plans and championed use of IT for competitive advantage.
- Developed a methodology for converting from a strategic to a tactical plan.

PROFESSIONAL EXPERIENCE

Telecommunications Technology, Inc.   1970 - June, 1998
Engaged in key leadership roles that contributed consistent value-added expertise, significant cost reductions and growth with increasing responsibilities and continuous professional development during this period.

District Manager, Consumer Communications Services – CIO   1995 - June, 1998
Led a team of 70+ IT professionals in the development, operation and maintenance of the Residence Market Management System - critical to the company's provisioning of long distance service. Responsible for order provisioning, marketing program fulfillments and promotional history maintenance for 100+ million customers.
- Supported 100+ marketing offers to strengthen company's position in long distance annually.
- Reduced list generation cycle times by 60 percent.
- Initiated 30+ enhancements to improve provisioning process.
- Implemented significant system enhancements to maintain consumer account information integrity.
- Implemented enhancements that extended the system's joint fulfillment process to other bundled offers.
- Utilized innovative approaches to contain costs of enhancements.
- Significantly improved client satisfaction and employee morale through frequent and open communication, strong teamwork and recognition.

District Manager   1993 - 1994
Managed the relationship between the CIO and the Wireless, Personal Number and Consumer Enterprise organizations to ensure support of client initiatives. Responsible for systems engineering, LAN/Server services, strategic systems planning, financial management and executive support.
- Completed a long-term marketing systems architecture.
- Instrumental in enabling a move of applications from mainframe to client-server platform.

Note the brief summary underneath the most recent position description. It gives a thumbnail summary of this candidate's activities and accomplishments at the company.

Abby Randolph

732-555-1212 • Page Two

District Manager   1990 - 1993

Led the development and operation of various marketing and product management systems. Supported 100+ IT professionals and championed IT support at the executive product round table.

- Led a cross-functional team initiative that resulted in a major redesign of the ability to household 150M consumers 50 percent faster.
- Led a number of data-mining initiatives to acquire and retain customers.

District Manager   1988 - 1990

Spearheaded efforts to form a stronger relationship between consumer marketing executives and IT. Implemented four projects identified by the Consumer Marketing Systems Plan, including early implementation of a client-server application.

- Led a groundbreaking effort to utilize IT for competitive advantage.
- Optimized capability of an advertising system for storage of images and transmittal to agencies.

Executive Assistant to the VP of Data Processing and Corporate Telecommunications   1987 - 1988

Responsible for speech and external customer meeting preparation, conference planning, commitment reviews and employee communication as part of a leadership development assignment.

Staff Manager   1985 - 1987

Responsible for development and marketing of a systems planning process to build enterprise-wide systems plans.

- Managed project to develop a systems tool to support the strategic systems planning process.
- Marketed application of the systems planning process across all organizations.
- Developed tactical planning methods to successfully translate strategic systems plans into projects.

Manager   1980 - 1985

Led various teams of six to eight IT professionals that specialized in systems analysis, design services and methods.

- Established and managed a team that spearheaded prototyping and Joint Application Design (JAD) services to engage users in the developing requirements.
- Marketed services interdepartmentally, successfully completing 15 - 20 prototypes and JAD workshops annually.

Manager   1978 - 1980

Managed a team of 10 - 12 IT professionals responsible for payroll system development. Managed a team responsible for database design consultation, training material development and manual publication.

Member of Programming Staff   1970 - 1978

Responsible for various programming positions in system development, technical support and training. Project leader for inventory management and general decision support systems. Developed and delivered three courses.

EDUCATION
BA – Mathematics – Douglass College – 1970

EXECUTIVE EDUCATION
Advanced Management Program for Telecommunications – University of Southern California
Leadership Development Program – University of Maryland

CERTIFICATIONS
Joint Application Design (JAD)
Project Management (In Progress) – Stevens Institute of Technology

PUBLICATIONS
How to Solicit User Requirements – Communications Monthly – June, 1990

Duane Schneider
duaneschneider@mixcom.com

2231 West Kendall Avenue
Glendale, Wisconsin 53209-1429

Office (414) 271-8717
Residence (414) 287-3468

TECHNICAL PROFILE

A dedicated SYSTEMS PROFESSIONAL/PROJECT MANAGER with 20+ years of technology development and management experience. Strong technical background in multi-language, multi-platform programming and systems design with expertise in project coordination, determination of scope and priority, project implementation, and training/development of IT staff. Proficient time-management skills; able to implement projects on schedule and within budget.

Languages:	COBOL, COBOL/VSE, VSE JCL, SQL, BAL, Dylakor, Visual Basic, C, C++
Operating Systems:	OS/400, VSE/ESA, DOS, Windows NT/95/98
Software:	CICS, DB2, VSAM, Project Management Tools, Easytrieve, ICCF
Platforms:	AS/400, IBM 370/390, IBM ES/9000, PCs & Compatibles
Networks:	Novell

SYSTEMS APPLICATION DEVELOPMENT/PROJECT MANAGEMENT EXPERIENCE

- Billing/Invoicing
- Order Processing
- Order Entry
- Returned Goods
- Sales Management
- Customer Service
- General Ledger
- Accounts Payable
- Accounts Receivable
- Purchasing
- Warehouse
- Inventory Control
- Shipping and Receiving
- Distribution

PROFESSIONAL EXPERIENCE

IT CONSULTING CORPORATION, Milwaukee, WI   1997 to Present
(A world leader in the implementation of professional systems solutions with annual revenues of $2 billion.)

PROJECT MANAGER
Consult with local businesses and lead project teams in major systems conversions and Y2K efforts. Assist executive-level management in defining project boundaries and formulating budgetary guidelines/price estimates. Develop project plans and schedule; hire staff. Coordinate programmer/analysts' efforts. Manage time frames and budgets.

Accomplishments
- Completed all projects within contracted periods.
- Coordinated a staff of 6 in a project to validate 10+ million lines of code in C/C++, Easytrieve, MS-Visual Basic, Java, & HTML. Completed project in 6 months.
- Led a team of 4 in 2 separate projects to convert source code at a remote financial clearinghouse. Converted JCL, BAL, Easytrieve, and COBOL code (over 500,000 lines). All work completed on time and within price estimates.
- Led 7 teams of 5 analysts in a client/server standardization and Y2K compliance effort for a large health care provider. Project involved 2500+ client workstations with 300 servers and 300+ applications to test. Completed project prior to Y2K with no downtime to client.
- Reviewed clients' systems to improve business operations, capitalize on new technology opportunities, and support user needs.

As a project manager with extensive systems experience, this individual wanted to include both technical qualifications and project highlights right up front. His resume shows a good way to present a great deal of information in a readable format. Key words are used effectively.

DUANE SCHNEIDER RÉSUMÉ – PAGE 2 OF 2

PROFESSIONAL EXPERIENCE (Continued)

HOSPITALITY SUPPLIES INC., Elmhurst, IL   1983 to 1997
(Leading catalog & Internet distributor to the hospitality industry with over 37,000 products.)

MANAGER—INFORMATION SYSTEMS (1986 to 1997)
Managed IT department and grew it to 34 employees. Converted from a dedicated mainframe environment to a distributed environment including mainframe, midrange, and PCs. Established job descriptions and evaluated subordinates' performance. Prioritized service requests from user departments. Ensured all coding, testing, documentation, and security conformed to high standards.

Accomplishments
- Coordinated the purchase and installation of AS/400 system. Instituted procedures to allow system to operate at 99.5% availability.
- Redesigned order-processing system to allow for shipments from multiple distribution centers.
- Established a help desk. Chose software, selected personnel, and ran training sessions. Instituted problem solving procedures and prioritization protocol. Implemented metrics to categorize incoming calls and identify categories with high call counts so corrective action could be taken.
- Designed system (COBOL and CICS) to streamline backordered merchandise shipping. Interfaced PC-based receiving system with mainframe-based order processing system.
- Led a team of programmer/analysts in the installation, data population, and customization of third-party sales management program.
- Developed a return merchandise system (COBOL and CICS) with callable modules interfacing with accounting applications to adjust customer balances, issue refunds, and generate credit memos.
- Implemented strategy and procedures to migrate from a VSAM database to a DB2 relational database. Developed and modified COBOL programs incorporating SQL commands.

MANAGER—PROGRAMMING AND OPERATIONS (1983 to 1986)
Recruited and trained programming and operational personnel. Defined functional project requirements and supervised 10 programmer/analysts. Coordinated schedules and supervised staff of 5 operators.

Accomplishments
- Led a team of programmer/analysts in 18-month project to modify and expand product master file. Modified all affected systems to accommodate expanded file.
- Wrote more than 100 programs (COBOL, batch, and online) that interfaced with every business system within company.

MIDWEST TECHNOLOGIES, Chicago, IL   1981 to 1983
(Consulting and contract service organization.)

PROGRAMMER/PROJECT LEADER
Identified, analyzed, and solved corporate systems issues for contracted clients. Designed, developed, and implemented reporting applications (CICS & BASIC) for financial and operational reporting.

EDUCATION

MBA PROGRAM, Marquette University, Milwaukee, WI: Anticipated graduation 2002
BS (BACHELOR OF SCIENCE), University of Wisconsin, Madison, WI
VISUAL BASIC CERTIFICATION COURSE: Currently enrolled to obtain Microsoft certification
CERTIFICATE COURSES, RPG Consulting, Milwaukee, WI: **FileAid Batch, Expediter Plus, QA Director**
UNDERGRADUATE COMPUTER SCIENCE COURSES (30 CREDITS), Hartright College, Urbana, IL:
   Programming and Systems Analysis Coursework

BEVERLY L. BUCKMAN

99 Tempest Drive
Chicago, Illinois 60643

(312) 999-9999
BuckmanBL456@hotmail.com

TEAM LEADER / PROJECT MANAGER / DEPARTMENT MANAGER

High-performance **Information Technology** professional with excellent analytical, communication, and interpersonal skills. Diverse technical experience derived from rapid learning and effective application of cutting-edge technologies. Team leader with fine-tuned multi-tasking capabilities, used to motivate, train, and mentor people at all levels of technical expertise. Creative problem-solver who accurately assesses technical situational challenges and successfully transforms ideas into appropriate workable solutions.

PROFESSIONAL EXPERIENCE

PHARM LABS, Chicago, Illinois   3/97 to 9/00
Formerly ABC Medical, Inc., US headquarters of $450 million global pharmaceutical company

Senior Technical Analyst (permanent position following consulting assignment)

Reported to Information Technology Manager on all development and maintenance of facility computing technology and infrastructure. Supervised user migration to Windows 95 desktop and Lotus Notes messaging through designing and implementing complete remote-access dial-in system for field-based users. Led successful campaign to identify and solve all Y2K system-related problems in a timely fashion with minimal impact to business operations. Initiated virus protection for company computing systems.

- Appointed Project Manager to successfully relocate US headquarters by focusing efforts on reducing and eliminating business dependence on outside service. Conceived, designed, and executed new computing infrastructure, plus decommissioned and transitioned all computing services impacted by the move.
- Oversaw local implementation of international IT networking and infrastructure initiatives by guiding team in analyzing, developing, and establishing global networking and application standards.
- Managed multiple IT team projects by coordinating internal and external resources to complete assignments.
- Instituted data backup strategy and system consisting of site power protection, offsite data storage, and disaster recovery plans to effectively protect business from data and computing services loss.

BASE ELEMENTS CORPORATION, Chicago, Illinois   8/89 to 3/97

Project Engineer

Created and implemented company-wide computing services and infrastructure for 50-user environment. Conceived, designed, developed, and implemented real-time PC-based, as well as dedicated, data-capture and playback hardware. Devised and generated software for delivery of real-time DOS and Windows-based signal acquisition/analysis software in PC environment.

- Built and set up company-wide LAN consisting of 10 NetWare servers and 50 clients running DOS, Windows 3.x, Windows 95, Windows NT. Provided network file, print, backup, and database services.
- Relocated computing infrastructure to new corporate headquarters, completing process on schedule and within budget.
- Managed outsourcing of networking infrastructure installation in new facilities.

UNIVERSITY OF IOWA, Iowa City, Iowa   9/88 to 5/92

Adjunct Instructor

Taught general physics: Prepared lecture material and conducted lab demonstrations.

Continued on page 2

An extensive Professional Skills Summary is placed on page 2 so as not to overwhelm the resume. The experience summary clearly distinguishes accomplishments from job responsibilities through a combination paragraph/bullet format.

Page 2, Resume of Beverly L. Buckman   (312) 999-9999

CENTER COMMUNICATIONS, Iowa City, Iowa   10/84 to 11/88

Senior Technical Associate (promoted from Research Technician)

Served as computing architecture team member under lead Ph.D. researcher working on Visual Speech Recognition system, image processing hardware, and software. Conceived, mapped out, and tested custom 1.25 micron two-level metal CMOS IC, with use of switch and circuit-level simulation, plus design-rule checking. Drafted, developed, and debugged software in C language under UNIX. Aided in design, building, and troubleshooting of analog and digital hardware, signal processing, and software.

PROFESSIONAL SKILLS SUMMARY

NETWORK & TELECOMMUNICATIONS

Networking Operating Systems: Novell NetWare 3.x, 4.x, 5.x; Windows NT 3.x, 4.x, 2000 Server and Workstation
Network Protocols and Infrastructure: IP and IPX on Ethernet, Shiva Remote Access Servers, Cisco Routers and Switches, T1, ISDN, Frame Relay
Network Services: DNS, WINS, DHCP, Proxy Server, IIS, Check Point Firewall, Network Printing
Network Administration: Network Monitor, Network Administration Tools
Telecommunications: POTS, Telco voice and data provisioning, Dial-on-Demand, and Point-to-Point services
Network Basics: Network wiring methods and computing infrastructure

SOFTWARE & APPLICATIONS

Languages: C, Visual C++, Pascal, Fortran, Visual Basic, Macro Assembler, Assembly (various), APL
Development: Software Development Kits, Compilers, Assemblers, Version control, Make utilities, Debugging and Code checking tools
Databases: Oracle, SQL, MS Access
Applications: MS Office Suite, E-mail/GroupWare
CAD: P-CAD, AutoCAD, Visio
Project Management: MS Project

COMPUTER OPERATING SYSTEMS & PLATFORMS

Operating Systems: MS-DOS; Windows 3.x, 95, 98, NT 3.x, NT 4.x, NT 2000; UNIX
Platforms: IBM PC/AT, HP 9000, VAX Family, Sun Workstation
Processors: Intel 80x86, Motorola 6800 and 68000

TECHNICAL & DESIGN

Troubleshoot, configure, and repair personal computers, servers, and computing equipment. Design, manufacture, troubleshoot, and repair all types of analog and digital circuits. Utilize analog, digital, and specialized test equipment. Maintain current knowledge of computers, software, and electronics by independent study and practical application. Experienced with schematic capture, PCB layout, design rule checking, bill of materials, analog and digital logic design, and prototyping techniques.

EDUCATION

ELECTRICAL ENGINEERING

Bachelor of Science in Electrical Engineering, University of Iowa, Iowa City, Iowa, 1986
Electrical Engineering coursework, Coe College, Cedar Rapids, Iowa, 1982 to 1983

CONTINUING PROFESSIONAL DEVELOPMENT (Global Knowledge, Chicago, Illinois)

Advanced Cisco Router Configuration, 11/99
Introduction to Cisco Router Configuration, 2/99

BRIAN D. DE BOER

123 Pheasant Court
Liberty, Missouri 64068
816-555-5555 • bdeboer@aol.com

CAREER PROFILE

Telecommunications professional with 20+ years' experience in Project Management/Design, Sales/Service and Purchasing/Billing. Indispensable in financial turnaround of major telecommunications company's cabling business from negative revenues to **million-dollar-per-year profits**. Concurrent responsibilities in sales force instruction and collaboration with track record of motivating others to act upon technical and customer-related initiatives. History of strategic technology deployment to streamline processes, slash expenses and drive profits. Highly communicative in relating and monitoring expectations.

Computer skills: MS Word, Excel, Exchange and Explorer; ABC Technologies DOSS 5, WACSA, FSAC-SS, WirePro, HTML; familiar with SAP. Honest, with a high level of integrity and proven work ethic.

- ➢ **Project Management**
- ➢ **Purchasing / Inventory Management**
- ➢ **Contractor Management**
- ➢ **Sales and Marketing / Presentations**
- ➢ **Custom Wiring / Cable Contracting**
- ➢ **Customer Relationship Management**

CAREER ACHIEVEMENTS

Project Management
- Spearheaded ground-up construction of a large contractor database (40+ contractors) over four states. **Results:**
  - ➢ **95% contractor-membership** in the ABC Technologies authorized service program.
  - ➢ **35% climb** in company's **cabling margin,** primarily through analysis/reduction of expenditures.
- Boosted sales force productivity by training team on key customer questions and methods to identify sales opportunities. **Result: 50% increase in new business lead generation.**
- Streamlined job bid turnaround time from one week to 2-3 days by maximizing technology utilization.
- **Slashed** accounts receivable **paperwork** approximately eight hours weekly by successfully implementing direct billing method.
- Successfully **engineered a contract** with a major **17-location account**, culminating in accountability as national account contact for all Systimax cabling. **Results:**
  - ➢ Upgraded all production/box plants nationwide.
  - ➢ Project-managed all locations and sourced nationwide to attain a single point of contact.
  - ➢ Delivered finished product that exceeded client expectations and increased future business.
- Nominated by account executives (based on outstanding accomplishments) to attend first XYZ Communications Elite meeting.
- **Increased profit** margin 25+%; tagged by ABC Technologies to present success strategies (on generating a profitable cabling business) at wiring conference.

Sales
- **Exceeded sales quota 175%,** two years (Millionaires Club).
- **Achieved 150% of sales** quota, two years (Superachievers Club).
- Recruited to ABC Technologies Network Systems National Task Force that originated a pricing structure for Global Emerging Market organization.

Continued...

Here is a primarily functional format, showcasing achievements under key subheadings and placing details of work experience on page 2.

BRIAN D. DE BOER
816-555-5555 • bdeboer@aol.com
Page Two

CAREER PROGRESSION

Steady telecommunications career progression (each change a desk-to-desk business transfer). Initiated career with National Communications and presently perform project management at XYZ Communications — each transition generated from company / divisional "spin-offs" (mergers, acquisitions, purchases, etc.).

XYZ COMMUNICATIONS (ACQUIRED A DIVISION OF ABC TECHNOLOGIES), Olathe, Kansas, 2000-Present
Regional Wiring Coordinator • Contractor Manager • Provisioning Coordinator
Charged with supervising 40 contractors in four states. Project-plan and execute custom cabling jobs from order to installation to billing to customer satisfaction. Participate in design meetings at customer sites. Negotiate with suppliers for optimum material prices and continually streamline processes/procedures resulting in declining expenses and climbing profits. Accountable for purchasing and inventory management.

ABC TECHNOLOGIES (ACQUIRED A DIVISION OF MIDWEST TELEPHONE), Olathe, Kansas, 1996-2000
Provisioning Coordinator • Contract Manager • Wire Design Specialist / Account Executive
Similar to prior Account Executive position at Midwest Telephone.

MIDWEST TELEPHONE (A SPIN-OFF FROM NATIONAL COMMUNICATIONS), Lenexa, Kansas, 1984-1996
Account Executive • Systems Technician
Consistently exceeded sales quotas, earning placement in Millionaires and Superachievers clubs. Originated a profitable cabling business from ground up to 40 contractors in four states by effectively networking, accruing leads, generating proposals and closing sales.

NATIONAL COMMUNICATIONS, Lenexa, Kansas, 1970-1983
System Technician • Repair Technician • Installer

COMMUNICATIONS EDUCATION / KNOWLEDGE

Bachelor of Science in Telecommunications, University of Missouri, Columbia, Missouri

- ➤ Graduate, **ABC Technologies Career Path Program,** 1999
- ➤ **Certifications:** Panduit, Mohawk, Bertek, Belden and ABC Technologies Fiber Optics, ABC Technologies Systimax Certification in Installation, Sales and Design/Engineering
- ➤ **Training:** New Bridge on Basic LAN environments, Bay Networks and AT&T Pardyne DSU/CSU
- ➤ **Installation/Repair:** System 75/G3, Merlin and Partner; Dimension PBX 100, 400 & 600 Installation and Repair of Tier 1/Tier 2 Levels
- ➤ **Call Center Applications:** UCD & DGC Groups
- ➤ **Other:** All Comkey Products; All Other AT&T vintage PBX Switches; Unix Language; Basic/Advanced Electronics

PROFESSIONAL AFFILIATION

- ➤ **Member,** BICSI, 1995-Present

RESUME 83: ARNOLD G. BOLDT, CPRW; ROCHESTER, NY

Juan Dominguez

3 Rose Lane
Utica, New York 14617
315-767-9089 (Home) / 315-456-0989 (Office)
E-mail: jdomingu@yahoo.com

SUMMARY

IT Professional with demonstrated project management and systems implementation capabilities. Excellent ability to assess user needs, establish project specifications, evaluate hardware/software solutions, and supervise installations. Strong hands-on experience with a variety of hardware platforms and software applications, including networking, peripherals, and database management. Experience troubleshooting system problems, providing user training and help desk support, and serving as Systems Administrator for network and database applications.

TECHNICAL PROFICIENCIES

PC Workstations	UNIX System Administration	Windows 98 / 95 / NT
AS/400 Systems	Oracle System Administration	Office Suites (MS / Corel)
Peripherals	Novell 5.0 / 4.1	Access databases
Networks / Telecommunications	Lotus Notes	Project 98
	HTML	

PROFESSIONAL EXPERIENCE

NORTHSIDE CORRECTIONAL FACILITY; Rome, New York (1996-Present)
Information Services Business Analyst   **1998 – Present**

- Direct IT implementation projects related to new facilities, relocation of offices, and upgrade of information systems for department with over 1,100 employees.
- Manage projects from concept through launch, including developing systems specifications, overseeing vendor and contractor activities, and validating system prior to handover to end-users.
- Confer with management team to assess needs and establish scope of projects.
- Coordinate activities with Tri-County Information Systems (TCIS) to review competitive bidding process and provide bidders with project walk-throughs.
- Function as System Administrator of Sun Solaris UNIX and Oracle Database in support of Jail Management System (JMS). Administer MoRIS system for Sheriff Police Bureau.

Major Projects:

Spearheading project to automate various departmental forms in an effort to reduce large volumes of paperwork. Evaluate potential hardware and software solutions for compatibility with existing platforms and for desired functionality.

Defined user and department needs and recommended software solution to provide Sheriff's Quartermaster with improved operating efficiency and enhanced customer satisfaction.

Managed the installation and setup of 200+ user data network for the Tri-County Jail and Northside Correctional Facility. Developed specifications, participated in vendor selection, and monitored vendor compliance with contractual commitments.

Coordinated the installation, training of personnel, and "go-live" launch of MoRIS system for Sheriff's Zone Offices throughout the county.

Established interfaces between MoRIS / JMS and outside agencies, including DCJS, NYSPIN, and Rome Police Department, to facilitate sharing of information among agencies.

Managed the relocation of offices for 80 people, including general layout, network and telecommunications cabling, and installation of PC workstations. Supervised contractor activities.

The clean appearance of this typeface makes the italic type very readable. Note how "major projects" are highlighted for this IT project-management professional.

Juan Dominguez   Résumé – Page Two

PROFESSIONAL EXPERIENCE (continued)

NORTHSIDE CORRECTIONAL FACILITY (continued)
Systems Support Technician   1996 – 1998
- Coordinated equipment acquisition and installation for AS/400 terminals and IBM Token Ring workstations.
- Scheduled installation, relocation, and repair of computer equipment.
- Managed inventory of departmental hardware and software.
- Installed, configured, and troubleshot LAN hardware and software.
- Assisted with installation and management of a Novell 4.1 LAN serving department's A-Zone facility.
- Supported data communications for Sheriff's Department.

UTICA DEPARTMENT OF TRANSPORTATION; Utica, New York (1993-1996)
Assistant Project Manager   1995 – 1996
- Served on Project Team that designed, installed, and supported automated system for gathering data from road sensors throughout a seven-county region.
- Defined departmental needs for the region and recommended appropriate technology solutions.

Network Administrator   1993 – 1995
- Installed and configured LAN hardware and software supporting 25 locations in seven counties.
- Served on statewide Regional Automation Technical Support Committee.

PORTICO LABORATORIES; Baton Rouge, Louisiana
Technical Support Manager & Communications Specialist   1983 – 1993
- CNA Certified (1989); WangNet Certified (1985).
- Defined user needs and recommended solutions.
- Planned and managed implementation of integrated manufacturing shop floor management application.
- Supervised and scheduled over 20 system consultants.
- Supported sales activities through technical support.
- Managed Help Desk activities.

EDUCATION

ST. BONAVENTURE UNIVERSITY; St. Bonaventure, New York
Certificate in Project Management

ST. BONAVENTURE UNIVERSITY; St. Bonaventure, New York
Bachelor of Science, Computer Science *(In Process)*

References Available Upon Request

LEE CARRION

58172 Georgia Hwy. 736 ◆ Townsend, Georgia 31714

Home: 816-937-7270
E-mail: lcarrion@stechu.tec.ga.us

Cell: 816-937-1141
Pager: 1-800-591-7371, pin# 691 5379

VISIONARY TECHNOLOGY LEADER

**Project Management ◆ Research & Development ◆ Strategic Planning & Analysis ◆ IT Consulting
Team Leadership ◆ Product Development ◆ Staff Training**

Focused, dedicated and highly motivated professional offering 10 years of solid contributions and blended background in technology management and accounting. Exceptional dedication to growing with cutting-edge technologies and seeking to achieve beyond expectations in every endeavor. Motivational leader and communicator, capable of building cohesion and project engagement across all levels of staff, management, vendors and customers.

Proven expertise in lifecycle project management from conception to completion, driving process improvements at all levels with forward-thinking, strategic-planning attitude to surpass expectations and goals. Accomplished trainer, developing online classes and delivering diversified training to more than 600 professionals. Strong belief in training and education as path to success and positive change.

Areas of Strength & Expertise:

- Technology Management
- Networking & Infrastructures
- Change Management
- Virtual Team Leadership
- Customer Service

- Strategic Planning
- Technology Training
- Security Policies
- Regulatory Issues
- Evaluation & Testing

- New Product Development
- Budgeting
- Team Building
- Media, Firewalls & Servers
- Hardware & Software

TECHNICAL SKILLS

Highly skilled in troubleshooting, resource capitalization, documentation, policies and procedures and new technology launch. Fully fluent in:

Software: Windows NT 4.0 & Windows 2000 Advance Server, Exchange 5.5, MS Office 2000, Macromedia, Peachtree, Checkpoint Firewall-1, CISCO Basic Routing, Virus Application

Hardware: Routers, Servers, PCs, Media

PROFESSIONAL EXPERIENCE

Southeast Technical Institute 1998-Present

TECHNOLOGY SPECIALIST

Drive new technologies, coordinating networks in multiple locations. Manage media, firewall, servers and computer labs. Direct projects through virtual teams; supervise and train Information Technology staff. Provide internal customer service, computer troubleshooting for instructors and executive personnel, and external customer service, supporting and training local business community on software and hardware. Collaborate with campus executives and staff to track project progress and ensure fulfillment of IT goals. Develop budgets.

Achievement Highlights:

- Cultivated campus network to support 400-500 students, setting up labs, servers, firewall, routers and Internet access. Designed media labeling for patch panels, implemented policies and procedures, instituted test centers, ordered all technical supplies and trained IT staff.

The headline and subheading that lead off the resume demonstrate an effective placement of key words, further supplemented by the "areas of strength" at the end of the profile.

LEE CARRION · Page 2

PROFESSIONAL EXPERIENCE continued (Southeast Technical Institute)

♦ Initiated numerous technology and process improvement measures including scanning forms for campus-wide accessibility, implementing fax online, designing online short-cut learning, planning for phone locations and number schemes and preparing for pending installation of Exchange 5.5.

♦ Achieved savings of more than $100,000 through effectively managing extensive Y2K project, devising plan to integrate 1,000 new PCs, operating systems, software upgrades and drivers.

♦ Consolidated numerous operating systems to single Windows 2000 Advance Server/Professional 2000, facilitating tech support efforts.

♦ Converted main campus from Token Ring to Ethernet, networking labs to accommodate 600 PCs and peripherals.

♦ Selected PC for fullest utilization of computerized lab resources; feature removable drives enabling instructors to have drive information related only to class being taught.

Atlanta Sports Therapies   1994-1998

ACCOUNTANT

Trained and supported companies on planning and setting up accounting software, maintained spreadsheets, performed audits on equipment, and set goals to decrease debt ratios, constantly updating on accounting regulations and technology improvements. Managed purchases, sales and rental of property, coordination of international trips. Created 3D images for presentations and maintained digital camera images and scanned images on PC.

Charlois, Shepard, Pruyn & Black, CPA Firm   1990-1994

JUNIOR ACCOUNTANT

Supported clients in accounting, training clients and staff on accounting software, ensuring proper use of software, planning budgets and managing accounting books for several companies. Maintained complex spreadsheets, coordinated loan application forecasts and projections, completed tax returns, performed audit procedures on non-profit organizations and supervised bookkeepers.

EDUCATION & TRAINING

Bachelor's in Accounting – Valdosta State University
Associate's in Business Administration – Abraham Baldwin College

Professional Development:
Extensive **Technical Training** including NetWorld Interop Conference, Windows NT 4.0, Windows Advance Server 2000, TCP/IP, Exchange 5.5, CISCO Basic Routing, Checkpoint Firewall-1, MS Office 2000, NetMeeting, DOS 6.2, Basic Oracle – Introduction Class, Basic Linux – Introduction Class, Mastering the Secrets of VPNs, Voice over IP, Accounting Creative Solutions, Peachtree, QuickBooks Pro.

Management Training including Over the Top Zig Ziglar, Becoming a Team Leader, Business & Personnel Management, Dale Carnegie How to Handle Difficult People, How to be a Supervisor in a Competitive World.

Pending Certifications &Training in MCSE 2000 & CCNA.

PROFESSIONAL AFFILIATIONS / PRESENTATIONS

Member: CPA Association, Chamber of Commerce, Toast Masters, Kiwanis.

Presentations: Technology Mission – 1997, Becoming a Leader – 1996, Telephone Techniques – 1995

CLIFFORD BLAIR

207 Middle Avenue ■ Fort Lee, New Jersey 07024 ■ (201) 265-2359
cblair@optonline.com

SENIOR SYSTEMS CONSULTANT ■ IT ARCHITECT

- Information technology, disaster recovery, and systems professional with comprehensive experience in the development of leading-edge external business support through IT security and asset management projects within the Enterprise Resource Planning software arena.

- Proven impeccable and dedicated customer support, with a foundation of personal initiative, persistence, and desire to meet technical and business challenges presented by a rapidly changing industry.

TECHNICAL ENVIRONMENTS

<u>Operating Systems</u>: MVS ■ CMS ■ UNIX ■ Windows 95/98/NT 3.51 ■ OS/2 ■ DOS
<u>Programming Languages</u>: COBOL ■ PL/1 ■ SQL/SQR ■ SAS ■ MARK IV ■ Query/Crystal
<u>Database Management Systems</u>: Oracle ■ Sybase ■ Informix ■ IMS

PROFESSIONAL EXPERIENCE

<u>COMPUTER SERVICES</u> • New York, NY   **9/96 to Present**
(Division of Renaissance Worldwide, Inc. • Consulting Services • 500 Consultants)
Senior Consultant
  Senior consultant, leading technical consultation, design and programming to meet clients' IT needs; specifically, PeopleSoft, HRMS and Payroll applications. Supervise two to four developers.

Consulting Assignments:
Suffolk County • 1/00 to Present
  Developed a custom absence-tracking process. Formulated medical enrollment interfaces and Time Interfaces to paysheets. Provided DBA support to project team.

Nassau County • 9/98 to 1/00
  Pioneered a custom leave accrual and decrementation process. Programmed institution's 403(b) plan, benefit provider interfaces, and SQL scripting supporting data conversion.

ING Barings • 8/98 to 9/98
  Facilitated data conversion and programming for conversion validation.

Long Island Savings Bank • 8/97 to 6/98
Technical Lead
  Performed as technical lead, providing support during Interactive Design/Prototyping™ sessions. Coordinated set-up of Unix/Sybase database server. Installed PeopleSoft HRMS 6.0. Converted data from existing PC-based HR and ADP payroll systems, writing interfaces and performing on-line modifications.

Siemens Electric Inc. • 7/97
Technical Consultant
  Installed tax updates and post-production support as technical consultant.

Teradyne Inc. • 5/97 to 8/97
Technical Consultant
  Provided post-production support of the PeopleSoft HR/Payroll system. Wrote/modified benefits and payroll interfaces.

Note how this candidate's consulting assignments are clearly defined, showing the breadth of his experience.

CLIFFORD BLAIR

- Page Two -

ISI Mars Inc. • 1/97 to 5/97
Technical Consultant
Developed interfacing strategy, conversion, data clean-up and on-line modifications.

AFC Enterprises Inc. • 9/96 to 1/97
Technical Developer
Assisted in the development of a major interface from POS data entry systems to PeopleSoft. Wrote interfaces to 401(k) and additional benefits record keepers. Supported payroll during parallel testing.

LONG ISLAND LIGHTING CO. • Hicksville, NY   **1986 to 1996**
HR Systems Analyst
Performed technology and programming support and developed data models and procedures for converting a training administration system to PeopleSoft. Administered data security using a Resource Access Control Facility. Served as LAN administrator.
~ *Converted LAN to Windows NT. Streamlined procedures by automating COBRA compliance.*
~ *Coordinated conversion of Employee/Pension/Salary Administration Systems to DB2 Database.*
~ *Developed and implemented PC-based HRIS, replacing manual files.*
~ *Participated in a task force to design a flex benefits plan, and a process reengineering task force established to evaluate and streamline current procedures.*
~ *Researched and selected a new HRIS/Payroll package.*

INNOVATION ASSOCIATES • Endicott, NY   **1986**
Computer Programmer / IBM Federal Systems Division
Maintained programming and support to Plant Maintenance Control System using PL/I and IMS DB-DC. Improved maintenance by translating all reports from GIS to SAS.

NEW YORK STATE ELECTRIC & GAS • Binghamton, NY   **1985**
Systems Analyst Intern
Supported computer functions for Generation Department. Expanded PC database using RBASE 5000. Developed reports using SAS. Prepared long-term plan for computer resources.

EDUCATION

State University of New York at Binghamton, Binghamton, NY
Master of Business Administration in Management Information Systems (MIS), 1985

University of Rochester, Rochester, NY
Bachelor of Arts in Political Science, 1980

MEMBERSHIPS/ASSOCIATIONS

International Association for Human Resources Information Management (IHRIM)
Institute of Electrical & Electronics Engineers (IEEE) Computer Society Member

TECHNICAL EDUCATION

Introduction to HR & Benefits ▪ Benefits Administration ▪ PeopleSoft Security ▪ Payroll 6.0
PeopleTools I & II/7.5 Delta ▪ Building PeopleSoft Pension Upgrade & Data Management
Business Process Design

FRANK ELLIOTT

50512 Jetson Boulevard — Los Angeles, California 90033

310 821-4758
Pager: 310 236-8173

INFORMATION TECHNOLOGIES / VOICE AND DATA COMMUNICATIONS
DATA CENTER OPERATIONS / SYSTEMS PROGRAMMER
SOFTWARE DEVELOPER / INVENTOR

Creative and results-driven expert in the design, development, and delivery of cost-effective, high-performance technology solutions to meet challenging business and multimedia demands. Extensive qualifications in all facets of project life cycle development from initial feasibility analysis and conceptual design through documentation, implementation, user training, quality review, and enhancement. Solid technical and musical training; strong customer service skills. Effective communicator with developers and senior management. Extensive knowledge of video/audio recorders and enhanced CD. Worked with over 60 Fortune 500 companies. Basic conversational Spanish.

Experience applicable to diverse industries, markets, and opportunities.

PATENTS

U.S. Patent 4,520,710	Drum and Cymbals Pedals Assembly
U.S. Patent 4,640,176	Quick Disconnect Retainer for a Detachable Drumstick Head
U.S. Patent 4,640,177	Drumsticks or Mallets with Para-Hemispheroidal Heads and Their Assembly

SYSTEMS

— Heavy design and programming experience with

Windows	OOP	Visual Basic
Solaris	HTML	FORTRAN
UNIX	Java	Turbo PASCAL
DOS	C++, C	COBOL

and various scripting languages such as Shell, Batch, and JPL, as well as major application packages (e.g. Microsoft Excel, Word, PowerPoint, Project, Access, and several others).
— Telecommunications, modems, packet switching equipment, major LAN software (e.g. NT, Sun workstations, controllers, interfaces).
— Various typesetting and graphics packages (e.g. FileMaker Pro, X-Press, PageMaker, PhotoShop, Draw, HP Graphics, AutoCAD, and many others).

PROFESSIONAL EXPERIENCE

ACTIONLENGTH TECHNOLOGIES, INC., Pasadena, CA   2000 - 2001
Consultant

Led a user-interface portion of a state-of-the-art global banking software project through R&D cycle to develop application-specific systems capable of meeting current and long-range information management requirements. Participated in cross-functional project teams and team meetings. Performed task- and task-flow analysis on customer transactions to identify core components and patterns of use, as well as needs assessment on customer's transaction suite to identify natural functionality clusters.

Assisted in the development of sophisticated GUI across multiple delivery platforms, with a high degree of interactivity utilizing multimedia. Researched and analyzed the project to be completed and collaborated with developers to render this global ATM product more flexible and user-friendly. Acted as liaison with 8 translators and assisted them in resolving unforeseen difficulties.

This individual's impressive patents are highlighted on page 1 of the resume. A brief footnote to the summary section "sells" his experience to different industries.

FRANK ELLIOTT   Page 2

ELFI PRODUCTIONS, Los Angeles, CA   1999
Consultant
> Designed lighting system and assisted in construction of production office for Elfi Productions' commercial rehearsal studio.

CREATIVE COMMUNICATIONS, INC., Hollywood, CA   1998 - 1999
Data Manager
> Managed data entry personnel and rightsized large database operation. Implemented improved backup system and procedures. Entailed extensive debugging and multiple software and hardware revisions/changes and close working relationship with senior management. Trained staff in use of GUI.

ROTOR AMERICA, INC., Los Angeles, CA   1998
Software Developer (contract project)
> Designed, proved, and delivered ahead of schedule a new electronic newsletter, a management tutorial/preview, and phased-rollout options, using MS Excel 5.0 and Visual Basic. **Recognized by Microsoft** for using innovative and useful techniques.

SYSTEMS WORLDWIDE, San Gabriel, CA   1997
MIS Assistant Director (temporary)
> Appointed to handle 100 networked stations. Repaired printers and trained users. Managed successful disaster recovery of approximately 400 MB of critical, highly valuable data on damaged SCSI-based writable optical disk.

CAPITAL PROJECTS, Los Angeles, CA   1995 - 1997
Budget Analyst
> Prepared capital improvement budgets (ranging from $10,000 to $240M) and related proposals and charts for presentation to various state and federal agencies. Streamlined computer processes for project initiation. Consulted with managing architects on utilization of office systems and simple yet cost-effective improvements. Improved invoice payment method and relationships with key departments. Simultaneously took on full workload of transferred co-worker. Gained exposure to advanced use of AutoCAD and 3-D rendering programs by experts at UCLA.

Consultant (Self-employed)   1993 - 1995
> Miscellaneous projects, including broadcast equipment repair and audio and video production. Also hosted and co-hosted radio programs on two 100,000-watt FM stations, served as announcer and producer on numerous radio spots, and directed 30-minute video.

Specialist with Kelly Services, Kansas City, MO   Prior to 1993
President, Canton Incorporated, Kansas City, MO
> Established and operated business primarily involved in R&D and manufacturing of percussion musical instrument products, including all phases of product design, line and contracted operations and marketing strategies. **3 U.S. Patents awarded** for revolutionary percussion actuator products.

EDUCATION
> Courses in Music, Computer Science, Math, and Phonetics, University of Missouri, Kansas City. Completed 12-module AT&T course in C programming language.

STEVEN I. SACHS

2110 Valley Lane ~ Newton, TX 77479 ~ (281) 855-4252 ~ stevsachs@techtrak.com

Career Goal:
LEAD DEVELOPER / TECHNICAL ANALYST / SENIOR CONSULTANT

SUMMARY

A dedicated **Information Technology Professional** with experience as an IT consultant, website developer, programmer analyst, and test analyst working with clients in a variety of industries. Effective leadership and client relations skills combined with extensive technical expertise (especially Internet-related). Proven ability to quickly learn and apply new technologies and translate client requirements into valid technical solutions. An effective communicator with clients and team members, easily interfacing between the technical and non-technical. Willing to take on any task and well-respected by peers, clients and management.

TECHNICAL SKILLS

Operating Systems: **Windows 95/98/NT, UNIX (HP-UX)**

Languages: **C++, Visual Basic 5.0, COBOL, HTML, JavaScript, Perl, Assembler, UNIX ksh, Powerscript**

Development Tools: **Borland C++, Visual C++, MicroFocus COBOL Workbench, ColdFusion Studio, Spectra WebTop and COAPI, PowerBuilder 6.5, S-Designer, SPIM Assembler Simulator**

Special Technologies: **SQL, Oracle, Microsoft SQL Server, Allaire ColdFusion 4.5, Allaire Spectra, Rational RequisitePro, Visual SourceSafe Administration, Arena Simulation Modeling**

Special expertise in Internet technologies

PROFESSIONAL EXPERIENCE

WOW CONSULTING – Newton, TX   1999 to Present
(A $7 billion global information technology consulting firm)

Consultant

Work with cross-functional project teams consulting on technology projects for client companies in a variety of industries. Meet with client representatives and research existing IT strategies to determine requirements and identify opportunities for improvement. Create logical database design, write programs, create test plans, and execute test scripts. Conduct code reviews of junior developers and administer source code control for development teams. Serve as technical resource for Internet-related technologies. Organize documentation for client review and obtain client sign-off on deliverables. Train end users on new applications. Manage junior developers and subcontractors and train junior developers in programming, ColdFusion, and Spectra, as well as in client relations techniques.

Worked on 5 projects and project phases to date, delivering excellent results to each client company and maintaining a track record of client satisfaction, follow-on work sold, and assignment completion on time and under budget.

Selected Accomplishments:
- Instrumental in securing one of company's first multimillion-dollar custom development Internet projects.
- Received unsolicited *Team Delivery* award from a satisfied client for a project completed under extreme deadline pressures.
- Received several company awards, including *Peer Respect Award, Unsung Hero Award* and *WOW Values Award.*

This resume leads off with a Career Goal (or objective) to clearly identify the candidate's goals at this point in his career.

Steven I. Sachs ~ Page 2

WOW CONSULTING *(continued)*

Project Highlights:

- Developed a Knowledge Management prototype of a web-based knowledge management system for an oilfield services firm. Presentation of the prototype won a $5 million contract. First release of the software will allow over 200 engineers to interact with one another through a Request Tracking system. Final release will have an audience of over 12,000 and will include content managers.

- Ensured Year 2000 compliance of 5 systems for a financial services firm as Test Analyst. Project phase came in $20,000 under budget, and follow-on work was sold to client.

- For a surgical instrument manufacturer, created 2 PowerBuilder applications that increased productivity of the human resources and engineering departments. Converted 3 DCL scripts to UNIX korn shell scripts. Project phase was completed under budget and accounted for approximately $40,000 of the project baseline. Follow-on work was sold to client.

- Implemented an upgrade of a benefits and payroll package that affected the payroll and benefits delivery for 13,000 employees of a business forms manufacturer. Analyzed 1300 custom-built components and made modifications where necessary.

- Wrote Perl scripts with multipart error-checking routines, allowing over 500,000 users of an online brokerage firm to perform complex stock option ordering strategies.

TEAM ALPHA CONSULTING GROUP – Oxford, TX   1995 to 1999
(Independent contracting group providing website development services for businesses)

Lead Internet Developer

Directed up to 3 developers creating dynamically generated Internet websites for businesses. Served as point of contact for clients to determine requirements and resolve problems. Designed and coded HTML and ColdFusion, wrote Perl scripts, established standards and graphically manipulated images.

Projects:

- Created prototype for an Internet-based hotel room reservation system for a conference center. Determined and converted detailed requirements into a logical database and application design. Wrote all scripts in the reservations module. The prototype allowed for increased flexibility of room assignments and checkout, as well as a Year 2000 solution.

- Developed a website for a data warehousing consulting firm. Wrote all HTML, created graphics, and set scope.

NATIONAL INSURANCE COMPANY – Colbo, TX   1994 to 1995
Programmer / Analyst (Internship)

Member of data conversion team that wrote data cleansing and validation programs for a new system that affected 3 million policyholders upon implementation. Accessed validation/data-cleansing software to validate customer addresses and standardize name format.

- Wrote 7 COBOL programs to perform data cleansing and conversion. Programs were written to allow concurrent use in order to improve performance.

EDUCATION & TRAINING

UNIVERSITY OF HOUSTON – Houston, TX
Bachelor of Science, Applied Science ~ Major: Systems Analysis (1995)

Specialized training: Advanced ColdFusion Development

CHAPTER 10

Resumes for Technology Industry Managers and Executives

- IT, IS, and MIS Managers
- Technology Operations Managers and Executives
- CIOs, Vice Presidents, and Directors of Technology
- Telecommunications Industry Executives
- Technology Industry Management Executives

MARILYN KOCINSKI

606 Limetree Drive, Morrisonville, NY 12962 ~ (518) 643-3782 ~ E-mail: mk321@gateway.net

INFORMATION TECHNOLOGIES MANAGEMENT

QUICK PROFILE:

Creative and results-driven expert in the design, development and delivery of cost-effective, high-performance technology solutions. Client oriented; an accomplished leader and entrepreneur capable of building motivated and productive teams. Extensive qualifications in all facets of project life-cycle development, from initial feasibility analysis and conceptual design through documentation, implementation, user training, quality review and enhancement. Experience is balanced and spans a wide spectrum of industries, e.g. electronics, telecommunications, manufacturing, health care, insurance, law enforcement, transportation and distribution. Excellent verbal and written communications skills.

- **LANGUAGES:** Cobol, Algol, Pascal, Simula, RPG, Fortran II, Fortran IV, 370 Assembler, PDP-11 assembler, VAX assembler, 8086 assembler, C, C ++, Basic, Visual Basic, Progress, Informix, Dibol, DBL synergy, Power Builder, Web Speed

- **DATABASES:** Progress, Oracle, Informix, Ingress, DB2, SQL Server

- **OPERATING SYSTEMS:** EXEC 8, OS/MVS, RSTS, VMS, AIX, Unix, HP UX, SCO Unix, CTIX, Windows NT, Windows 95/98, OS/400

- **MISCELLANEOUS:** Visual Basic for Applications, Outlook, Word, Power Builder Data Architect, YACC, LEX, MTS, MQ

BUSINESS BACKGROUND:

1981-Present   Adams & Cross, Inc., Schenectady, NY
Technical Director — Information Technology

Led this organization (a systems solution provider) through a series of upgrades to capitalize on emerging technologies and application enhancements. Concurrently serve as CEO. Established key business relationships with various upper-level managers, technical and financial officers, and in their behalf, have conceived and implemented numerous mission-critical systems and services, examples of which are cited below:

➢ 1999-2001: Built version 8.2 of MGA Master installed at Ameraset Assurance Co., Urban Underwriters (Robert Plan), and Material Damage Corp.

➢ Directed the re-engineering of a ticketing system for scalability and performance for Lasergate Systems. Installed at American Skiing Corp., Biltmore Estate, and Regal Cinemas game facilities.

Design allowed Lasergate to take small peer-to-peer network-based application and re-engineer to a high-transaction-volume system that allows American Skiing to function effectively. ($1.5 million project)

Note how something as simple as a distinctive font used for the name, combined with a wide horizontal rule, makes this resume stand out. Results of each project and position are highlighted in bold, underlined text.

continued   Adams & Cross, Inc.
Technical Director — Information Technology

➢ **1997-1999:** Progressive Insurance — Using Automation Resources MGA Master, built a usage-based auto insurance policy-writing and accounting system. System uses GPS and cellular technology to rate based on time and position risk. Information is then gathered from the insured vehicle and compiled into a bill. System also provides statistical reporting based on a mixture of traditional property insurance and usage-based insurance.

Significantly, Internal I/S quoted $10 million and 5-year project duration. We did it in 1 ½ years and for just under $1 million.

➢ **1990-1996:** Brooke Corporation — Using Automation Resources Agency Master, constructed large WAN-based agency cluster resulting in a client/server system with UNIX-based databases and NT-based databases to handle insurance agency policy management, accounting, and imaging.

The benefit gained by Brooke was a system allowing them to readily acquire 60 agencies throughout Kansas, Colorado, and Nebraska, thus building one of the first agency clusters.

➢ **1993:** MGA Master — Instrumental in the design and construction of a complete policy-writing system with integrated imaging and workflow management for a paperless office. System also had integrated MVR and CLUE lookup. Installed at Connecticut Specialty.

System allowed MGA to sell and service over $20 million in premiums (PIP and PD) with fewer than 20 people.

➢ **1992-1994:** Nokia — Designed, built, and delivered a quality control tracking system for Nokia's Telecommunications Division.

➢ Installed an accounting system for the company's US operations.

➢ Designed and built a customs export control system to track purchase of electronic components.

The benefit to this client is that it allowed them to more effectively manage and control all parts installed in their computer and telecommunications equipment.

➢ **1983-1988:** Shands Hospital (University of Florida), University of North Carolina, Atomic Energy of Canada — Designed, built, and delivered a computer-controlled imaging system to assist physicians in locating tumors. Designed and built a system to control radiation therapy machines used to treat tumors.

This was significant, as it allowed users to design new therapies for patients with cancers in the head and neck areas. With the new system, patients could be treated with greater dignity, not having to be marked with a grid in ink.

1976-1981   Wingate & Associates (a Digital OEM retailer)
Vice President

EDUCATION:

■ Case Institute of Technology, Cleveland, OH: BS Physics, 1979
Honors:
■ Awarded Dayton C. Miller Prize for thesis.
■ State of Ohio Awards: 1st place Earth Science, Honorable Mention, Chemistry
■ Recipient of the National Science Foundation Scholarship to Georgia Tech

MARILYN KOCINSKI — **Page 2**

RICHARD C. TOBER

147 Windsor Drive, Rossford, Ohio 43460
419-666-6224   rctmismaster@aol.com

MIS Management

Results-driven **MIS DIRECTOR** with project management expertise overseeing information system functions, computer operations, and systems programming. Maintain excellent rapport with senior management team to analyze computer system and plant needs, submit recommendations and proposals, and develop plans for systems development, operations, installation and implementation while maintaining system integrity. Skilled at empowering end-users and translating technical information in non-technical terms to achieve quality and maintain efficiency. Excellent project / process leadership skills and proven ability to lead organizational change.

Project Management ~ Systems Integration ~ Process Improvement ~ Quality Assurance
Strategic Planning ~ End-User Training ~ Procedures Development ~ Troubleshooting
Relationship Management ~ Facilitation / Presentation ~ Budget Management / Analysis

TECHNICAL OVERVIEW: IBM AS/400 Model 500 RISC   Printer Languages: QMS, RJS, ZPLII
Languages: RPG400, CL, AS/400 Query, VB   Barcode Languages: Intermec IRL, EZ Builder

CAREER HISTORY

DIRECTOR OF MIS   **CSX PRODUCTS – Walbridge, OH**   **1979 – Present**

Recruited to CSX Products in 1979 as Manager of Data Processing and promoted to Director of MIS in 1990. CSX Products is a multifaceted company that produces wrap products used in the construction, automotive and packaging industries. Randall Corporation in Monroe, Louisiana, recently purchased CSX.

High-profile position reporting directly to Vice President of Finance. Accountable for development and maintenance of operations and procedures for information processing at all CSX facilities. Assess needs to develop new information processing systems and improve existing program designs. Successfully interfaced corporate offices and off-site locations to align strategies and achieve goals. Provide training and assistance to end-users to ensure peak levels of performance. Lead Process Improvement Teams to improve accounting and cost accounting systems. Facilitator for plant-wide process improvement programs. Responsible for 2 direct reports and 80 end-users at 4 remote sites.

Took over IS department in 1979 with existing IBM System 3 that ran all applications in batch environment. In 1982 converted to IBM System 38, enabling CSX to shift all applications online, giving users control and eliminating data entry. Converted to AS/400 Model B30 in 1990; currently using Model 500 RISC. Major applications include order entry, shipment posting, bill of lading, invoicing, A/R, A/P, G/L, hourly payroll, production / inventory, print plate tracking system, and bar-coded product identification tags.

<u>SELECTED HIGHLIGHTS AND ACCOMPLISHMENTS:</u>
- Played leadership role in driving information systems through acquisition process.
- Spearheaded conversion from IBM System 3 to IBM System 38 in 6 weeks, achieving reduction in annual hardware lease cost of $60K and leading to $40K reduction in personnel costs.
- Relocated CSX AS/400 data center and had remote sites operational in two hours. Entire process, including local users, completed over weekend for business operation on Monday.
- Guided conversion from batch to online processing, transforming most applications. Reduced order entry time from 3- to 4-day cycle to *immediate* and invoicing from 3-4 days to day of shipment, saving substantial time and significantly decreasing chance of error.
- Developed and implemented physical inventory system that reduced inventory process from 3-day, handwritten, manual input procedure with plant downtime of 2 days to 1-day process utilizing Intermec Trackker 2420 ANTARES portable scanners and uploading data to AS/400.

EDUCATION

<u>B.S., INFORMATION SYSTEMS</u>: University of Toledo, Toledo, Ohio
<u>ADDITIONAL TRAINING:</u>   Situational Leadership   Qual Pro Coursework: Process Improvement, Design of Experiment
Visual RPG Seminar   DMC Coursework: RPG 400, Database Design, Control Language

This is a concise presentation of an accomplished career. It's easy to pick out the key words and significant accomplishments.

JAVIER M. SOLERO

753 Bidwell Street, Arlington, VA 22201
Home: (703) 555-5555 • Email: SOLERO@abc.com

SYSTEMS IMPLEMENTATION / PROJECT & OPERATIONS MANAGEMENT / CUSTOMER SUPPORT

Results-driven professional with 15 years' experience in project management, systems implementation and product support. Excellent problem-solving skills and strong orientation in customer satisfaction. Experienced in streamlining operations and processes to increase productivity, quality and efficiency. Unique combination of educational background, strong interpersonal skills, leadership and management experience within global and technology-driven industries. Proven ability to manage project from planning through execution and completion. Expertise includes:

- Engineering Management
- Systems Analysis and Implementation
- Project and Operations Management

- Customer Service and Problem Solving
- Supply Chain Management
- Operations Research and Decision Making

Background includes international travel and exposure to different cultures. Multilingual with fluency in Spanish and Arabic. Possess a Doctorate degree in management.

PROFESSIONAL EXPERIENCE

Alpha Omega Company, Reston, Virginia   1996 – Present
GLOBAL CUSTOMER SUPPORT MANAGER   1998 – Present

Manage the customer relations, resource planning, team management and reporting for the support department. Establish support procedures for internal, interdepartmental and customer relations.

- Improved employee satisfaction and morale and reduced turnover by re-engineering the department and establishing a training and coaching program.
- Increased customer satisfaction by 400% and reduced open calls by over 470% by developing a new customer service program and building a high-caliber support team.
- Achieved a global help desk strategy that enables the department to run 24/7, overcoming cultural issues, communication problems and adverse situations.

PROJECT COORDINATOR — Major Account Project   1997 – 1998

Served as key person in coordinating and supporting Warehouse Management System implementations at customer's multiple sites; acted as focal point for maintaining and solving global issues that affect multiple sites; coordinated the design, development and testing of new functionalities and software changes; and organized, planned and managed major software upgrades for all customer sites.

- Reversed customer's unsatisfactory view of Alpha Omega into complete satisfaction, with plans to implement system into all sites worldwide; client now provides recommendations to Alpha Omega's new customers.

PROJECT IMPLEMENTATION MANAGER — Canadian Account Project   1996 – 1997

Managed the overall project implementation for a Warehouse Management System package, including project scheduling, resource management and contract compliance; prepared customized training plan and materials; conducted operational review to validate requirements and system enhancements; and scheduled and oversaw hardware, network and software installation.

- Saved the contract and resolved critical issues by overcoming language and business culture barriers, identifying translation problems of original proposal and authoring and gaining approval on an Implementation Requirements Document that better defined system specifications.
- Delivered a system that improved productivity and provided more control over inventory.

This candidate's strong technical experience is supplemented by college-level teaching experience and advanced academic credentials.

JAVIER M. SOLERO   **Page 2**

DEF Software Development, Silver Spring, Maryland   1993 – 1996
SYSTEMS ENGINEER / PROJECT MANAGER

Managed full development cycle of a computer-based learning system. Researched and evaluated existing computer-based application; developed needs assessment and requirements of computer-based learning systems; defined system objectives and criteria; composed tests and evaluation methodologies to measure system validity.

- Received accolades from students and teachers for improving math learning through systematic approach that combined drill and practice, open-ended discovery and work-based learning.

Energy Analysts, Inc., Washington, D.C.   1992 – 1993
SYSTEM ENGINEER / OPERATIONS MANAGER

Managed all aspects of the operational procedures of the company, including resource allocation, budgeting and project tracking; developed recommendations and analyses based on customers' needs and requirements.

- Created and implemented a multitude of computer programs for energy analysis.
- Turned project delivery times from consistently past due to 10-15 days before deadlines by instituting a new production and quality control system and automating all routine aspects of company operations.
- Developed an easy-to-use reference documenting all operations and administrative procedures of the company.

TEACHING EXPERIENCE

The George Washington University   1990 – 1994
INSTRUCTOR: Taught two graduate-level courses.

International Technical School, Beirut, Lebanon   1982 – 1984
TEACHER: Taught business mathematics; developed class syllabus; created and graded exams and case studies; chose textbook and class materials. Participated in defining mission and overall policies of the school.

EDUCATION

The George Washington University, Washington, D.C.

- **DOCTOR OF SCIENCE:** Artificial Intelligence / Human Factors; Minor in Operations Research
- **MASTER OF ENGINEERING:** Engineering Management

International University, Beirut, Lebanon

- **BACHELOR OF ENGINEERING:** Civil Engineering

COMPUTER SKILLS

➢ Open VMS	➢ N-See Tutor (Authoring systems)	➢ Dynamo
➢ Unix	➢ Lantastic (Networking System)	➢ M1
➢ Windows	➢ Microcyclone (Simulation Modeling)	➢ VP Expert
➢ DOS	➢ Freelance 2.0	➢ Excel 5.0
➢ SQL plus	➢ Autosketch 3.0	➢ Access 1.0
➢ Visual Basic 3.0	➢ MS Project 1.0	➢ Action 3.0
➢ Tool Book	➢ Expert Choice (Expert System Shell)	
➢ Authorware 2.0	➢ Lindo (Cost/Benefit Analysis)	

NORMAN STEVENS

6701 Murietta Ave. ◆ Valley Glen, CA 91405
(818) 994-6655 ◆ Fax (818) 994-6620 ◆ NS5555@aol.com

IS / MIS MANAGEMENT ◆ TECHNOLOGY DEVELOPMENT
*Voice & Data Communications / Integration ◆ Information Technology
Project / Budget Management ◆ Strategic Planning*

Expert in the design, development and delivery of technology and communication solutions to meet challenging business demands. Extensive qualifications in all facets of projects from initial feasibility analysis and conceptual design through implementation, training and enhancement. Excellent organizational, budget management, leadership, team building, negotiation and project management qualifications.

Certified in Lucent, Octel, NEC & Northern Products

PROFESSIONAL EXPERIENCE

FOODCORP INTERNATIONAL, Valley Glen, CA ◆ 1992 to Present
Achieved fast-track promotion through positions of increasing responsibility for multi-billion-dollar international company with 30,000 employees worldwide.

Manager of Telecommunications — 1997 to Present
Technology Executive responsible for management of $15 million department budget. Fully accountable for overall strategy for telecommunications technology acquisition and integration, vendor selection and negotiation, usage forecasting, workload planning, project budgeting and administration. Plan and direct implementation of emerging telecommunications solutions at all FoodCorp domestic locations consisting of 125 facilities. Provide direction regarding telecommunications technology to FoodCorp affiliates throughout U.S. Lead cross-functional project teams; supervise technical and administrative staff with 20 direct reports. Fully accountable for department's strategic vision and leadership.

Representative achievements include:
◆ Directed $40 million annual MCI Network conversion at 200 locations within six months, saving company $15 million over a three-year period.
◆ Designed and managed implementation of network utilizing Lucent and Octel at more than 100 locations in 12 months, realizing annual cost savings of $1 million.
◆ Served as Technical Project Director for $12 million consolidation of East Coast Headquarters with West Coast location.
◆ Facilitated move of corporate headquarters, involving 3,000 employees, over a 4-day weekend.
◆ Implemented videoconferencing technology at more than 60 sites.
◆ Built a 4-digit dialing network for FoodCorp locations within a four-month period.

Assistant Manager of Telecommunications — 1993-1997
Management Trainee/Intern — 1992-1993

EDUCATION

B.S. in Political Science ◆ UNIVERSITY OF CALIFORNIA, Berkeley, CA

Professional Development/Continuing Education: Various American Management Association Workshops and Courses; BCR Technical/Technical Management Courses

Detailing only one professional position in his resume, this individual includes "representative achievements" that imply he could certainly add to this list. His one-page resume makes a strong statement.

Robert Sandoval

5555 East 55th Street
Brooklyn, New York 55555
(718) 555-5555

Management ▪ Technical Architecture ▪ Global

Collaborative manager with over 23 years' experience in the development and implementation of mainframe and distributed applications. Recognized for skill at evaluating, recommending and selecting information technology. Areas of expertise and accomplishment encompass:

- Start-up Operations
- Project Management
- Critical Production Support

- Strategic Planning
- Needs Assessment
- Design Validation

- Database Administration
- E-Commerce Solutions
- Vendor Relations

Professional Experience

Argabrite Financial Brokerage, New York, New York   1990-Present

Vice President / Manager — Corporate Systems Technology Services (1999-Present)

Selected to oversee the start-up of the Corporate Systems Technical Architecture Group and develop a three-year Technology Plan. Collaborate with partners to understand business requirements and identify technological solutions to business problems. Provide technology vision and direction, evaluate and research emerging technology as well as validate technical architecture alternatives. Furnish high level of service to clients in the delivery of technical architecture services. Build key vendor relationships to enhance support, influence product direction and exploit functionality.

Serve as member of the Enterprise Applications Technology Governance Committee that evaluates and selects standard software products for application development. Manage **strategic initiatives** in three key areas of the organization: Financial Systems, Global Human Resources and Office of the General Counsel.

Financial Systems:

- Develop and maintain plans, formulate strategy, coordinate project activities and review status of critical deliverables.
- Oversee the evaluation, planning, and selection of the hardware to support the Oracle Financials 11.0 release upgrade. Identify hardware and network requirements for infrastructure testing. Schedule vendor evaluations and research Oracle's Network Computing Architecture.
- Direct performance stress test, evaluating network and hardware resource utilization from strategic locations, network predictive modeling and hardware capacity planning. Evaluate intelligent storage devices for scaleable, cross-platform data sharing.
- Participate on the Books and Records technical evaluation team to review FTI application architecture and recommend technical architecture, as well as on the E-Commerce team to evaluate and implement the Ariba/E-Commerce solution with Oracle Financials applications.

Global Human Resources:

- Evaluate global technical architecture and recommend deployment strategy. Perform design validation and determine requirements for network performance test to evaluate the global architecture for scalability, availability and performance.
- Coordinate network upgrades, outstanding requests and related network issues. Evaluate ETL and OLAP tools for data mart implementation and define the global architecture.
- Formulated data strategy with project team and collaborated with project planning team. Direct global network redundancy and business resumption testing.

Office of General Counsel:

- Assist the project team with web architecture alternatives, content management and text search tools, and document management software evaluation.

Vice President / Manager — Private Client Information Management (1995-1999)

Directed distributed and mainframe database administrators (DBAs) providing database support services to facilitate database development and implementation. Oversaw data integration, high-priority issue resolution, business and technical planning, allocation and management of resources and status reporting. Created and managed work plans, technical solutions and documentation and developed database management services. Managed critical production support for over 80 distributed and 15 mainframe databases.

"Mr. Sandoval was looking for a senior technology position within a global environment. His resume is designed to highlight his leadership and start-up skills, along with his technical competencies."

Robert Sandoval

5555 East 55th Street
Brooklyn, New York 55555
(718) 555-5555
Résumé - Page Two

Professional Experience (continued...)

Financial Systems Strategy:

- Standardized and consolidated the firm's General Ledger and SubLedger applications using Oracle Financials ERP applications.
- Directed team of DBAs to manage all database changes; establish, configure and maintain the application and database environments; define and implement database and application migration procedures; and formulate the change management process and procedures.
- Established off-site standby database disaster environment; implemented Neonet messaging software to synchronize data across platforms; and completed benchmark testing of web reporting application.

Corporate Library Electronic Archiving & Retrieval:

- Coordinated selection and design of database to store historic statements on optical disk storage. Oversaw database design, tuning and implementation.

Additional projects included database evaluation, selection and production database implementation for the Human Resource Data Mart, and database support of the Peoplesoft database implementation for Global Human Resource Information Processing.

Vice President / Manager — Enterprise Information Management & Technology (1990-1995)

Managed group of database administrators (DBAs) providing database support to Global Systems & Technology. Provided all aspects of database management services. Implemented mainframe database disaster recovery process for business resumption, Distributed Relational Database Architecture (DRDA) data sharing, and database system software installations and upgrades. Initiated distributed database support and negotiated distributed database support services with clients.

Technical Skills

Hardware:	Sun, Sequent, IBM, Amdahl, Hitachi, DEC, Compaq
Software:	DBMS: Oracle, Oracle Express, DB2, IDMS, ADABAS, SQL/DS
Operating Systems:	Solaris, SunOS, MVS, Windows NT, Windows 98
Front Ends:	PowerBuilder, Developer/2000, Visual Basic
Web:	Oracle WebServer, Netscape, IIS
Languages:	Java, C, C++, PL/SQL, Pro*C, COBOL, CICS
Network:	SQL*NET, Net8
Protocols:	TCP/IP, SPX/IPX, ODBC, DRDA
Middleware:	Neonet, Shadow Direct, MDI Gateway
Case Tools:	IEW, ADW, PowerDesigner
ERP:	Oracle Financials General Ledger, Accounts Payables, Purchase Orders, Fixed Assets, Project Accounting, Peoplesoft Human Resources
System Management:	Enterprise Manager, Patrol, Autosys, PVCS, NetDeploy
Data Warehouse / ETL:	Informatica
OLAP:	Impromptu, Powerplay

Education

Pace University, New York, New York
Currently pursuing **M.B.A.** in **Strategic Management**

Baruch College, New York, New York
B.A. in **Finance**, June 1988

JASON ANDREW YOST

21847 Melissa Drive
Johnstown, Ohio 43229
(614) 363-3110 — JAY@hotmail.com

INFORMATION TECHNOLOGY / PROJECT MANAGEMENT
DATA CENTER OPERATIONS

Talented IT professional qualified by nearly 20 years of visible achievements in leading-edge information management environments focusing on data center management. Merge hands-on leadership style with excellent communication skills to continually drive focused teams to performance excellence within rapidly changing industry. Proven record in streamlining operations, increasing productivity and leading projects to full fruition.

Develop and implement effective client solutions; expertise in system design, development and planning. Possess extensive hands-on experience and strong organizational skills to provide changes in procedures/policy with no loss to customer service; strengths in identifying problems and correcting emergency situations.

CORE MANAGEMENT STRENGTHS

- Productivity Improvement
- Strategic Planning
- Application Management & Development
- Quality Control

- Technical Support
- Client Relations
- Staff Development & Leadership
- Technology Needs Analysis
- Project Development & Management

CAREER PROGRESSION

HARLEY GLOBAL SERVICES – Columbus, Ohio   1992 to Present
Technical Services Customer Support Manager

- Recruited to lead team of 93 data center operations / support groups for the Bank One Account. Define all strategic planning and change management processes for multi-billion-dollar data center. Develop all service level agreements with client and establish formal problem and procedures processes.
- Oversee all data center operations, Production Assurance, SE27/P1 (Priority One Help Desk) and Online Support (ATM Connectivity and Connectivity Management).
- Project manager for data center moves, production enhancement and development of teams to improve personnel morale and productivity.
- Instrumental in implementing strategic tape strategy for midrange services using STK 9740 tape and VCC.
- Deliver production deadlines with SLA standards for all batch processing and on-line availability with no penalties accrued in last 12 months.
- Orchestrated strategic plan to implement replacement tape strategy for current Silo technology using combination of IBM VTS and STK9490 for mainframe services.
- Contracted third-party organization to accommodate Bank One needs, resulting in significant cost savings to Bank One and improved profitability to Harley.

With big, bold headings and a clear focus on career progression, this resume effectively showcases the professional background of a senior IT manager.

JASON ANDREW YOST

21847 Melissa Drive
Johnstown, Ohio 43229
(614) 363-3110— JAY@hotmail.net

BANK OF HOPE CORPORATION – Columbus, Ohio   1980 to 1992
Vice President, Data Center Operations Ohio
(Ascended quickly through ranks from computer operator to Vice President)

- Challenged to direct efforts of team of 82 data center operations personnel and support groups. Oversaw evaluation, selection and implementation of extensive automation software products, which boosted productivity and reduced costs.
- Program Manager for the evaluation and implementation from multiple vendors of midrange systems solution for console consolidation and tape backup consolidation.
- Directed selection of replacement product for CA7 Scheduler from multiple vendors resulting in the implementation of Zeke / Zebb for batch job scheduling and JCL execution.
- Project Manager for replacement of IBM CPUs/Dasd resulting in swapping out 11 terabytes of IBM disk with EMC2 disk and 3 IBM CPUs with Hitachi CPUs in 4 months.
- Credited with consistently maintaining impressive 99.8 percent production delivery rate 24 hours a day, 7 days a week.
- Implemented new cost center for midrange processing reducing mainframe run rates; key player in creation of change review process.
- Managed remote location (Phoenix) lights-out processing; moved Data Centers, Dayton to Indianapolis and Indianapolis to Columbus; directed replacement of all Columbus / Phoenix Data Center scheduling systems.
- Project manager for implementation of SWAT team resulting in batch run time savings and deletion of unnecessary production job execution.
- Fostered staff training, development and growth; employee turnover percentage never greater than 6 percent during management career.

Previous assignments include:
Assistant Vice President, Data Center Operations
Senior Data Processing Officer
Data Processing Officer
Data Center Manager
Shift Manager DCO
Shift Supervisor DCO

TECHNICAL SKILLS

- MVS, Jes2, Sysplex, O/S 390 Operating Systems
- CA7, Zeke, Zebb, VCI Scheduler Packages
- Remote mirrored DASD, EMC2, IBM
- IBM, HDS, some UNIX, HP, Tandem
- STK Silo (all), IBM VTS, 6250 3490/E, 3480 tape hardware

PROFESSIONAL DEVELOPMENT

- IBM Management Training... Team Building... Career Development... Time Management
- Leadership Development... LDP II... Leading Strategic Change... Omegamon
- Columbus Paraprofessional Institute – Computer Programming

THERESA BARTON

555 West Drive • Kellerton, Iowa 50133 • (515) 745-5108 • theressabarton@aol.com

---

INFORMATION TECHNOLOGY SENIOR MANAGER
Relationship Management / Team Building / Business Strategies

Innovative IT senior manager with more than 15 years of successful experience in building cross-functional Information Technology teams and gaining competitive market advantages through vision and leadership. Strong technical qualifications with impressive performance in strategic planning and organizational expansion. Excel in budgeting, technical staffing, technology development, infrastructures, and product commercialization for large and small company structures. Highly effective interpersonal and communication style.

Leadership, Management, and Business Expertise

- Strategic Alliances, Joint Ventures, and Corporate Partnerships
- New Product Design, Engineering, Funding, and Commercialization
- Financial Planning / Analysis, Budgeting, and Cost Management
- Quality, Reliability, Performance, and Productivity Improvement
- Training, Team Building, and Competitive Benchmarking

Demonstrated Technology Experience

- Extranet, Intranet, E-commerce, and WAN 1
- HTML, C++, XML, COM, and SQL Server 7.0
- N-tier Client/Server-Based Internet Technology

- Delivery of Products in ASP Mode
- Web-based Enterprise-level Reporting
- Healthcare Information Technology

TECHNOLOGY & LEADERSHIP EXPERIENCE

Vice President—Product Development, SHS.com, Kellerton, Iowa   1997-2000
Direct extranet, intranet, e-commerce, and Wide Area Networking system architecture design to ensure optimum integration and information access for this 3-year-old startup company serving long-term healthcare industry. Oversee all software development strategies and QA activities.

- As General Manager, led due diligence with potential clients for web-based product. Guided n-tier, client/server-based Internet technology presented in Internet Explorer using HTML, C++, COM, and SQL Server 7.0 used in enterprise-level reporting.
- Built teams and aggressively restored failing IT projects that were inconsistent with senior management objectives. Redefined project objectives, transformed key technology positions, accelerated product development cycle, and eliminated cost overruns. Resulted in dramatic market share turnaround.
- Engineered processes, amplified leadership, and provided direction for key internal groups—Legacy System, Product Management, and Product Development.
- Guided architectural design of cutting-edge technological approaches including browser-based presentation using XML, COM, and basic e-commerce structures.
- Forged strong account relationships to fully respond to customer needs.
- Set strategy for design and development of assisted living product, pharmacy-to-nursing home (B to B), and medical supply purchasing integration.
- Managed multi-million-dollar budgets and staff of more than 60.

This resume shows clear career progression and effectively uses key words under two relevant subheadings in the summary section.

THERESA BARTON

Page Two

Director of Subsidiary Systems, MIS Department ························ 1995-1997
American Healthcare Group, Inc., Des Moines, Iowa
Directed MIS operations for 14 companies in US, Canada, Europe, and Australia for one of largest long-term care providers in US. Directed business computing needs of entire operation.

❑ Expanded MIS subsidiary department staffing from 1 to 15 persons.
❑ Provided leadership and framework to actively identify IT needs of each company and respond to most critical issues.
❑ Formed strong allegiances with senior management of all operating companies including rehab, medical supplies, home healthcare, pharmacy, and nursing homes.
❑ Led 15 managers and analysts in results-based, focused projects.

Director of Information Systems, Iowa Dental, Des Moines, Iowa ········ 1994-1995
Directed delivery of software and hardware services for claims processing and risk underwriting for this $19 million company and managed $500,000 IT budget.

❑ Defined methodology for client/server approach for three core business computing environments.
❑ Eliminated costly manual processes in both claims processing and underwriting.
❑ Contributed nationally to Delta network as member of Deltanet Coordinating Committee.

Senior Account Manager, Cooper, Kareem, Darhma, Inc., Davenport, Iowa ···· 1993-1994
Managed accounts for one of nation's largest claims processing companies targeting managed care segment of healthcare. Assisted marketing with product shows and prospect follow-up.

❑ Championed innovative solutions to managed care claims processing needs of company's largest client.
❑ Teamed with staff to identify critical aspects of transition from mainframe to RS6000-based system.

Manager, Medical Information System, Chicago, Illinois ················ 1988-1991
Managed Hospital Information System for largest HMO in region. Accelerated and executed plans for network refinement, application development, and operations management. Tactfully managed complex interpersonal relationships with hospital departments and senior management.

❑ Spearheaded move to desktop PCs, business-unit integration, and cross-communication of company's mainframes, resulting in $1 million savings.

TECHNOLOGY CONSULTING

Executive Director, Computer Works, Inc., Kansas City, Missouri ····· (concurrent) 1983-1993
Challenged to provide analysis, design, and programming services to US corporations. Introduced PC-based solutions during formative years of industry. Expanded business contract negotiations, including sub-contractors for Apple Computer, Merrill Lynch, Nordstrom's Department Stores, and Aladdin Software.

❑ Developed creative approaches for EDI relationships with suppliers.
❑ Created update to securities application.
❑ Designed database referential integrity software for Microsoft software market.

EDUCATION

MS, Information Science, 1997   University of California, Los Angeles, California
BA, Anthropology, 1980   University of California, Los Angeles, California

THOMAS C. BURRELL, MCSE, CNE, CCNA

5687 Brookstone Drive
Chicago, IL 60601
Phone: (555) 786-8083 ▪ Email: tom@burrellhome.com

INFORMATION SYSTEMS DIRECTOR / NETWORK SERVICES MANAGER
Proven Technical & Management Expertise in a Career Spanning 15+ Years

Technically sophisticated and business-savvy management professional with a pioneering career reflecting strong leadership qualifications coupled with "hands-on" IS and networking expertise. Maintain focus on achieving bottom-line results while formulating and implementing advanced technology and business solutions to meet a diversity of needs. Superior record of delivering simultaneous large-scale, mission-critical projects on time and under budget. Team-based management style and excellent interpersonal/communication skills.

IT Strategic Planning / Business Solutions / Team Leadership / Budgeting / Project Management
Capital Expenditure Planning / Contract Negotiations / Vendor Relations

Professional Experience

INFORMATION SYSTEMS MANAGER, Avery Clinic Health System, Chicago, IL   **1993 - Present**

Recruited to upgrade and replace obsolete technologies at this world-class health care organization with more than 2000 users in 15 remote locations. Hire, train, develop, and lead a 20-person technical team. Manage a $2 million capital budget and $1.2 million operating budget. Scope of position is expansive and includes departmental direction and full design, installation, engineering, implementation, support, training, administration, and management authority for:

- LAN/WAN Network Services
- 24x7 Data Center Computer Operations
- Applications Systems
- Web/Internet Design & Operations

- PC Desktop Systems
- UNIX Systems Administration
- Database Administration
- Help Desk Operations

Spearheaded transition from outdated organization-wide and departmental technologies to highly functional, streamlined, and cost-effective client-server technologies and business solutions that have dramatically improved efficiency, decreased expenses, and optimized data integrity and safety.

Key Projects & Achievements:

- Directed design and installation of the complete $8 million LAN/WAN infrastructure. Utilized state-of-the-art technologies to provide network connectivity of disparate Mainframe, AS/400, UNIX, Windows NT, Novell, and PC systems.
- Completed, in just 8 months — 22 months ahead of schedule — a complex $15 million project forecasted to take 2.5 years and involving replacement of more than 30 systems.
- Delivered $2 million in cost savings through aggressive negotiation of contracts and pricing on a budgeted $10 million for hardware/software purchases and consulting services.
- Saved more than $1.2 million in technical consulting fees by negotiating complimentary network design services from vendors.
- Performed the work of 3 full-time equivalents, slashing labor expenses substantially by expanding personal responsibility to include UNIX, network, and database administration.
- Decreased inventory, application pricing, and licensing expenses $750K by establishing standardization for applications, PC desktops, and networking systems.
- Defused and resolved long-standing conflicts and department problems; elevated morale and decreased high employee turnover rates, achieving the best retention rate in the company.

The subheading "Key Projects & Achievements" helps to break up what could be an overly dense experience section. Important technical certifications are noted at the very beginning and detailed at the end of the resume.

THOMAS C. BURRELL • Page 2

INFORMATION SYSTEMS MANAGER, 1993 - Present, continued

- Managed from planning through completion a $2.4 million Windows NT workstation and network printer implementation project. Delivered on time and $600K under budget.
- Attained consistent 99% up time by implementing disaster recovery and fault tolerance plans. Instituted the first highly reliable corporate-wide, centralized backup system.
- Championed introduction of Internet/intranet/Web technology, corporate-wide email, shared calendaring, and online meetings. Set up and managed a TCP/IP environment, installed a Novell network, and implemented a data warehouse database.
- Collaborated on numerous management committees including the Systems Application Selection Team; Chair of the Network, Operations, and Security Team; and the Y2K Implementation Team.

NETWORK MANAGER, Stillings, Inc., Akron, OH   **1993**

Managed and delivered, ahead of schedule, a nationwide, $10 million+ network project involving development of a fully redundant credit verification system. Administered a multi-server LAN supporting Novell, UNIX, and Unisys systems, and supported 2000 users in 850 remote sites.

DIRECTOR OF TECHNICAL SERVICES, ProComp U.S.A., Inc., Cleveland, OH   **1990 - 1992**

Built and managed Information Systems, Technical Support, Production, and Repair Departments for this start-up Novell Reseller and PC manufacturing firm. Supervised staff, oversaw computer operations, and managed budgets. Saved $2 million the first year by renegotiating manufacturing contracts and relocating production to reduce costs and improve shipping schedules. Developed and trained a team to provide support to a culturally diverse international customer base.

COMPUTER TECHNICIAN, MTI Systems, Beachwood, OH   **1989 - 1990**
SENIOR SYSTEMS SUPPORT SPECIALIST, A.B. Dick Company, Brecksville, OH   **1985 - 1989**

Education & Credentials

AMERICAN INSTITUTE OF COMPUTER SCIENCE – Chicago, IL
B.S. candidate in Computer Science, completed 3 years of study

TOTAL TECHNICAL INSTITUTE – Chicago, IL
Computer Systems Support Certification – Intensive 2-year program

Technical Certifications:

- **MCSE** – Microsoft Certified Systems Engineer
- **CNE** – Novell Certifed NetWare Engineer
- **CCNA** – Cisco Certified Networking Associate
- **CNA** – Novell Certified NetWare Administrator

Recent Technical Training:

- Cisco Router Programming & Internetworking
- Network Administration for UNIX Systems
- ATM – Asynchronous Transfer Mode
- Windows NT 4.0 Network Administration
- AIX UNIX Advanced System Administration
- Cisco Enterprise Management Solutions

- Bay Networks – TCP/IP, SNMP, FDDI
- EDI – Electronic Data Interchange
- Windows 95 Support
- Windows NT 4.0 Technical Support
- Internet Information Server
- SQL Server 6.5 Database Administration

RENEE S. HARROLD

78 Lakewood Drive
Victoria, NY 06549
Phone: (806) 555-5555 Fax: (806) 555-5555 Email: robert@harrold.com

SENIOR TECHNOLOGY EXECUTIVE
Project Management • Multimedia Communications & Production • MIS Management

Exceptionally creative management executive uniquely qualified for a digital media technical production position by a distinctive blend of hands-on technical, project management, and advertising/communications experience. Offer a background that spans broadcast, radio, and print media; fully fluent and proficient in interactive and Internet technologies and tools.

Proven leader with a strength for identifying talent, building and motivating creative teams that work cooperatively to achieve goals. Highly articulate with excellent interpersonal skills and a sincere passion for blending communications with technology. Capabilities include:

- ♦ Project Planning & Management
- ♦ Work Plans, Budgets & Resource Planning
- ♦ Account Management & Client Relations
- ♦ Department Management
- ♦ Multimedia Communications & Production

- ♦ Interactive / Internet Technologies
- ♦ Information Systems & Networking
- ♦ Technology Needs Analysis & Solutions
- ♦ Conceptual & Creative Design
- ♦ Team Building & Leadership

PROFESSIONAL EXPERIENCE

Investment Group, Inc., Yankee, NY   **1986 - Present**

VICE PRESIDENT OF MIS (1997 - Present)
ASSISTANT VICE PRESIDENT OF IT/CORPORATE COMMUNICATIONS (1992 - 1997)
CORPORATE COMMUNICATIONS OFFICER (1988 - 1992)
ASSOCIATE (1986 - 1988)

Advanced rapidly through a series of increasingly responsible positions with U.S.-based, Japanese-owned investment group. Initially hired to manage market research projects, advanced to plan and execute corporate communications projects, and, in 1992, assumed responsibility for spearheading the introduction of emerging technologies to automate the entire company.

Current scope of responsibility focuses on strategic planning, implementation, and administration of all information systems and technology. Lead technical staff members, manage budgets, select and oversee vendors, define business requirements, and produce deliverables through formal project plans. Manage systems configuration and maintenance, troubleshoot problems, plan and direct upgrades, and test operations to ensure optimum system functionality and availability.

Technical Contributions:

➤ Pioneered the company's computerization from the ground floor; led the installation and integration of a state-of-the-art and highly secure network involving 50+ workstations running on 6 LANs interconnected by V-LAN switching technology.

➤ Defined requirements, then planned and accelerated the implementation of advanced technology solutions, deployed on a calculated timeframe, to meet the short- and long-term needs of the organization.

➤ Orchestrated the introduction of sophisticated applications and multimedia technology to streamline workflow processes, expand presentation capabilities, and keep pace with the competition.

➤ Administered the lifecycle of multiple projects from initial systems/network planning and technology acquisition through installation, training, and operation. Saved hundreds of thousands in consulting fees by managing IS and telecommunication issues in-house.

Note how four positions are grouped together, showing career progression yet not devoting too much space to repetitive position descriptions. The lightly shaded gray box sets off the headline format of the summary.

RENEE S. HARROLD — Page 2

Investment Group, Inc., 1986 - Present, continued

Business Contributions:

➢ Created and produced high-impact multimedia presentations to communicate the value and benefits of individual investment projects to top-level company executives. Tailored presentations to appeal to highly sophisticated, multicultural audiences.

➢ Assembled and directed exceptionally well-qualified project teams from diverse creative disciplines; collaborated with and guided photographers, videographers, copywriters, script writers, graphic designers, and artists to produce innovative presentations and special events.

➢ Performed market research and analyses to determine risks and feasibility of multiple investment projects valued at up to $150 million. Developed and recommended tactical plans to transform vision into achievement.

Broadcast, Print, and Radio Advertising & Production   **1971 - 1985**

DIRECTOR OF ADVERTISING, Schwarzer Advertising Associates, New York, NY (1983 - 1985)
ADVERTISING ACCOUNT EXECUTIVE, Schoppe, New York, NY (1984) / Rainbow Advertising, Brooklyn, NY (1981 - 1983) / Marcus Advertising, Phoenix, AZ (1980 - 1981) / WCHN and WSCZ, Boston, MA (1979 - 1980) / WFDX-TV, WFDX-FM, WKLU, WERS, WQRT, Lehigh Valley, PA (1971 - 1978)
WRITER/PRODUCER, RADIO PROGRAMMING, WPTR, Detroit, MI (1971)

Early career involved a series of progressive creative and account management positions spanning all advertising mediums: multimedia, television, radio, and print. Worked directly with clients to assess complex and often obscure needs; conceptualized and developed advertising campaigns to communicate the desired message in an influential manner.

Achievement Highlights:

➢ Designed, wrote, produced, and launched advertising campaigns that consistently positioned clients with a competitive distinction. Recognized for ability to accurately intuit and interpret clients' desires and produce deliverables that achieved results.

➢ Hand-selected and led creative teams (graphic designers, artists, musicians, talent, cartoonists, animators, videographers, photographers, other freelancers, and third-party creative services) to develop and produce multi-million-dollar advertising campaigns.

➢ Won accolades for the creation, production, and launch of a 4-color fractional-page advertisement that generated the greatest response in the history of the publication. Honored with a featured personal profile recognizing achievements.

➢ Developed and applied a unique style and advertising philosophy that accounted for the nuances of human psychology and utilized innovative, brainy, and sometimes startling techniques to capture attention and influence the target market.

EDUCATION & TRAINING

A.A.S, Broadcast Production, Knapp Junior College, New York, NY, 1971

Continuing education in Marketing Research and Broadcast Production, 1981 - 1983
The School of Visual Arts, New York, NY

TECHNICAL QUALIFICATIONS

Innate technical abilities and interest in emerging technologies and digital communications. Trained and fully versed in all aspects of network design, implementation, installation, and maintenance. Advanced skill in installation, configuration, customization, and troubleshooting of software suites and applications, hardware, and peripherals within Windows environment (3.x, 95, 98, NT 3.5, NT 3.51, NT 4). Proficient with most Web development, multimedia, word processing, spreadsheet, graphic/presentation, and database tools and applications.

RESUME 97: PAULA BRANDT, CPRW; BELLE VERNON, PA

PETRA BRANDT

183 VALLEYVIEW DRIVE, BELLE VERNON, PA 15012 ~ 724.872.9030 ~ petra@home.com

Senior Director, Information Technology

Set Standards in Information Services and End User / Supervisor Training... Improved Customer Satisfaction
Planned, Managed and Rolled Out High-Profile Projects — All On Time, On Budget

~ Cost Control ~ Budgetary ~ Productivity Enhancement ~ Custom Applications Programming ~
Process Automation ~ Program Planning / Evaluation ~ Resource Planning ~ Quality Assurance /
Quality Control (QA / QC) ~ ISO 9001 Certification ~ Marketing Program Development ~ Sales /
Marketing Training ~ User Training ~ Client Connectivity ~ Internal / External Clients ~ Vendor
Selection and Negotiation ~ Multidisciplined Team Leadership ~ Clinical Research ~ Clinical Testing
~ Clinical Trials ~ Health Care, Oil Industry Experience ~

Quality Improvements, Process Automation, Project Management Success

STEWART COMPANY, BELLE VERNON, PA   1996 to Present
Leading US Provider ~ Esoteric and Routine Clinical Testing, Clinical Trials ~ $200MM Division

Senior Director, Information Technology   1998 to Present
$200MM Division ~ 7 Direct Reports, 65 Indirect ~ First Site Y2K-Compliant ~ $13MM Annual Budget Always
Met ~ Boosted Morale ~ Direct Report, Regional Information Technology Director

- **RETAINED STAFF:** Reduced IT employee turnover from 36 percent to less than 7 percent in first year...

- **INITIATED LONG-TERM STRATEGY:** Selected a vendor who authored short-term and long-term LAN
  improvement / expansion strategies — nonexistent prior to my involvement...

- **STANDARDS IN PLACE:** Led 10-person team defining software life cycle development SOPs, secured
  ISO 9001 certification for laboratory with no carry-overs — involved lab staff in design reviews, defined
  time lines and software requirements up-front, and standardized documentation / validation...

- **EXPANDED TRAINING:** First person in IT to conduct team-building workshops — with minimal budget,
  launched a team agreement incorporated as a model for IT that improved customer and staff
  satisfaction... developed sales training in 1 month that streamlined technology and got 500+ IT,
  sales / marketing and business administration decision-makers up to speed seamlessly...

- **IMPROVED QUALITY:** 1 of 8 senior leaders on Quality Management System Steering Committee —
  results improved customer satisfaction and quality...

- **CUT THE EXCESS:** Shaved $60K while negotiating telecommunications, PC support, customer and
  laboratory systems support contracts...

- **OVER / ABOVE:** Adept at translating technical aspects of connectivity options, regularly requested by
  sales / marketing team to detail client non-technical staffs in features...

Director, Customer Systems   1996 to 1998
Staff of 22, 4 Managers ~ $4MM Budget ~ Improved Customer Assistance ~ Reported to Senior IT Director

- **SET COMPANY STANDARD:** Rolled out web-based system generating 90 percent ROI in first year —
  saved $200K+ annually... directed 7-person team who replaced DOS-based systems and created
  mechanism guaranteeing 3-month upgrade at customer site... negotiated $45K savings on original bid...
  product adopted as corporate standard for hospital customer systems... 400+ systems in use today...

- **EXTERNAL CUSTOMER HELPDESK 24 X 7:** Created single point of contact for customer connectivity
  issues, led implementation for round-the-clock technical support...

*Highly relevant results are highlighted at the beginning of each accomplishment statement, making
this a hard-hitting, easily skimmed resume. Note the original heading that replaces the traditional
"Professional Experience" wording.*

PETRA BRANDT – 2 of 2

Director, Information Systems ... STEIN LABS, PITTSBURGH, PA   1991 to 1996
Esoteric Testing Laboratory and Diagnostics Manufacturing Company ~ Staff of 5 ~ Direct Report to CEO ~ Implemented First CPU Interfaces and Customer Connectivity ~ Highly Visible Role with Clients

- **RESUSCITATED CONVERSION:** Because a consultant fell short of expectations, took over project and had it in place in 4 months — managed 2 programmer analysts who converted 2 CPT/UNIX systems into a MUMPS-based system expediting customer processing...

- **COMPETITIVE EDGE:** Brought in customer inquiry / reporting system on time, on budget — created first online access to test criteria and automated patient report printing, keeping Stein "cutting edge"...

- **UNIQUE OFFERINGS:** Led implementation of first bidirectional customer interface (HL-7 and ASTM) and rolled it out with a targeted marketing program... successfully introduced Internet-based database of antibiotic-resistant organisms, enabling end users to upload, track and trend data against entire US...

Project Manager ... HILL ARCHITECTS, PITTSBURGH, PA   1989 to 1991
Software Vendor, Turnkey Distribution Systems ~ Successfully Facilitated DEC System Conversions for Multi-Billion-Dollar, Fortune 500 Clientele ~ All Projects On Time ~ Domestic Locations ~ IS Project Teams, Up to 16 Members

Programmer / Analyst ... THE CANCER CENTER, BELLE VERNON, PA   1987 to 1988
World-Renowned Cancer Research Center ~ Section for Infectious Disease ~ Designed First MUMPS Medical Research Database for Clinical Trials Replacing "3 x 5 Card" Cataloging ~ Wrote Laboratory Tracking System Maximizing Storage while Better Tracking Specimens / Cultures ~ Trained Technicians through Pharmacist, Secretarial and Physician End Users

Programmer ... SIGMA OIL COMPANY, DHAHRAN, SAUDI ARABIA and EL PASO, TX   5 Years
#1 Oil Producer Worldwide ~ Improved Real-Time Electrical Power System Control Efficiency ~ Instrumental in Developing a Purchasing / Traffic System Expediting Shipments to Saudi Arabia

Education

UNIVERSITY OF PITTSBURGH, PITTSBURGH, PA
Bachelor of Science in Business Computer Information Systems

CONTINUING EDUCATION — STEWART COMPANY: Project Management, 1999... Supervisory Skills Certificate Process, 1997... Leading Your Team, 1996... Innovation Process, 1996...

Publications

Brandt, Petra. "Human/Computer Interfaces: A Randomized Trial of Data Entry and Editing Formats," SCAMC Proceedings, The Computer Society of the IEEE, Washington, DC, August, 1989.

Brandt, Petra. "A Database for Clinical Research in Infectious Diseases," Proceedings Quarterly of the MUMPS Users Group, New Orleans, LA, June 1989.

Brandt, Petra. "User-Interface Design: A Study in Data Entry Methods," AAMSI Congress Proceedings, San Francisco, CA, May 1989.

LAWRENCE A. ELBERON
14 Bagota Drive • Neptune, NJ 07753
732-446-2020 • E-mail: laelberon38@aol.com

CHIEF INFORMATION OFFICER

High-powered Information Technology executive with an excellent track record in conceptualizing and directing the development of advanced technology solutions and building and managing IT operations for global organizations. Expertise in:

PC Systems Engineering	E-Commerce and E-Procurement	Technical Staff Retention
WAN and LAN Technologies	Technology Solutions for Internet Start-ups	Troubleshooting / Support
Technical Product Development	P&L Management / Budget Planning	Strategic Partnerships

CAREER HIGHLIGHTS

Acting Chief Information Officer / Director of IT, Richland Corporation, Woodbridge, NJ
(A rapidly-growing sales, marketing, and consulting company providing online / offline sales and marketing services to Fortune 100 companies, including IBM, AT&T, P&G, Hewlett Packard, 3Com, Apple, Johnson & Johnson, and Internet start-ups)

Direct all corporate technology operations for the company's 3 divisions (6 buildings at 4 locations throughout the U.S.), with full P&L accountability. Key advisor to executive staff on strategic planning and direction related to technology products. Total responsibility for technical product development, technical support, and data center operations. Lead a team of 1 director, 3 managers, and 31 technical professionals who provide development and support functions to all 3 areas. Plan and administer budgets.

Continually research and apply technology trends to ensure an efficient state-of-the-art operation and offer clients optimal high-tech solutions. Build Internet start-up companies for clients, from concept to fruition. Develop web-based database applications for clients as a supplement to existing services related to sales, procurement, and fulfillment.

Product Development / Client Services

- Played a key role in delivering $64 million in annual revenues in 1999, through innovative product conceptualization and development, drastically boosting the company's credibility and market presence.

- Achieved high level of visibility among Internet start-ups and large organizations seeking business-to-consumer, business-to-business, and extranet solutions. Developed comprehensive proposals for a broad range of businesses and completed key projects for major companies.

- Initiated and led the company's effort in identifying, customizing, and selling existing applications for clients' use; e.g., designed, built, and supported sales force automation (SFA) tools.

- Evaluated and developed cost-effective strategic partnerships for e-commerce and direct e-mail marketing services, and assessed potential acquisitions.

Internal Technical Operations

- Transformed a loosely structured, marginally performing 3-person IT department into a state-of-the-art unit offering high-quality technical support, networking and infrastructure administration, and business system support for 3 rapidly-growing divisions, including a coast-to-coast 1200-node WAN.

- Totally rebuilt the network, established a formal help desk, and provided internal and client support for 6000 users nationwide; established an effective means of measuring performance against process metrics, and continuously strive for improvement.

- Reengineered entire data center, creating a smoothly operating area that maintains business systems (financial, SFA, messaging, database, and Internet systems) on a 24/7 basis.

- continued -

This is an attractive and well-organized resume for a CIO. Note how accomplishments are broken down into internal and external areas.

LAWRENCE A. ELBERON   **Page Two**

CAREER HIGHLIGHTS (continued)

Manager of Technical Services, T.R. Communications, Princeton, NJ
(A subsidiary of Gantel, Inc., which designs, maintains, and markets satellite broadcast services to major communication organizations worldwide)

Full responsibility for operation and maintenance of a highly sophisticated WAN used to navigate satellites. Closely managed a group of outsourcing vendors who were key to the operation. Regularly explored outsourcing opportunities; developed specifications, reviewed proposals, selected vendors, and managed relationships with outsourcing companies.

- Played a major role in developing and upgrading a broad-spectrum voice and data communications network with 25 locations worldwide.

- Developed a reputation as a technology expert in global networking.

Senior Network Engineer, Crestlane Affiliates, Pomona, NJ
(A private financial institution providing banking and investment consultation services to prestigious clientele)

Designed, maintained, and supported a corporate network accessed by over 1000 employees at 15 branch offices nationwide.

- Succeeded in building and maintaining a highly reliable network designed for zero downtime.

- Integrated contingency planning and disaster recovery planning at component and site levels.

Supervisor of Technical Services, Perlcom, Inc., Fairgate, NJ
(World leaders in the design and production of inflatable safety products for the aviation industry)

Started up and managed the technical department to meet the growing computer needs of the company; assumed full responsibility for all client/server technology. Supervised 3 technicians.

- Integrated a 100 PC-based network, using TCP/IP and SPX/IPX protocols in a UNIX and Novell environment; installed sophisticated client/server applications for companywide networking at 3 facilities.

- Implemented a companywide, state-of-the-art electronic document management system involving database, networking, and applications technology.

EMPLOYMENT HISTORY

Chief Information Officer / Director of IT, Richland Corp., Woodbridge, NJ	1998 – Present
Manager of Technical Services, T.R. Communications, Neptune, NJ	1996 – 1998
Senior Network Engineer, Crestlane Affiliates, Pomona, NJ	1995 – 1996
Supervisor of Technical Services, Perlcom, Inc., Fairgate, NJ	1991 – 1995

EDUCATION / PROFESSIONAL DEVELOPMENT

M.S., Software Engineering (in progress) • Rutgers University, New Brunswick, NJ
B.S., Industrial Engineering, 1990 • Rutgers University, New Brunswick, NJ

Technical Training / Seminars: Novell Certified Network Engineer Training, Business to Business Technology, Business to Consumer Technology, TCP/IP Networks

General Business Training / Seminars: Management / Leadership Skills, Customer Relations Management, Effective Communication Strategies, Negotiating, Dealing with Negative Attitudes, Legal Issues Related to Human Resources

Allison Brown

2345 Marcus Avenue, Apt 611

Phone: 305-123-1234   Miami Beach, FL 33140   Abrown59@aol.com

INFORMATION / TECHNOLOGY/ BUSINESS SYSTEMS EXECUTIVE

Aligning Information Technology with business to create solutions and opportunities that drive change

Dynamic, innovative professional with proven track record designing, developing, and delivering successful **cost-effective, high-performance technology and information systems solutions**. Results-driven, analytical problem-solver with extensive experience in identifying opportunities and developing new business strategies and implementation framework to meet challenging multinational business demands. **MBA, fluent in Spanish**, conversant in French. **Particular areas of expertise** include **strategic planning, staff motivation**, and:

- Financial Services
- Leadership
- Risk Management
- Presentation

- Project Management
- Customer Service
- Systems Administration
- Negotiation

- Internet / Website
- Securities Issuance
- Crisis Management
- Budget / P&L

- Auditing
- Cash Management
- Change Management
- Latin America

Keyword summary: Internet Security, LAN/WAN, Fast Ethernet, contingency/disaster recovery, CRM, RAS, SAS, RDBMS, Sun platform, troubleshoot, UNIX, client/server, data warehouse, OLAP, ORACLE, internal technical operations, desktop support, global integrated financial system, asset management, website development and marketing

PROFESSIONAL EXPERIENCE & SELECTED ACCOMPLISHMENTS

VISA INTERNATIONAL, Miami, FL   **1998-Present**

Vice President, Information Systems, **Latin America & Caribbean Region**

Provide day-to-day leadership and direction in all aspects of technology for a region of VISA known for its innovation and change management. Technology unit supports over 450 users including 5 remote sites in Latin America, and includes project management, consulting, programming and development, infrastructure (LAN/servers), desktop and help desk support. Manage 20 employees and 5-10 consultants.

- Redirected, restructured, and turned around under-performing internal technology division into strong, successful, customer-focused, results-oriented strategic unit.
- Identified problems, provided viable solutions, persuaded senior management to accept proposals, and improved employee morale and involvement, which increased internal customer satisfaction by 55%.
- Initiated, created and spearheaded several large scale, high-profile enterprise projects:
  - Data Warehousing: accessing regional transaction-level data from multiple mainframes.
  - Paperless Office: strategized, planned and implemented pilot to reduce paperflow and storage.
  - Customer Resource Management: evaluated and piloted tools, selected instrument and implemented.
  - Migration from Token Ring LAN to Ethernet: became model for other regions to follow.
- Developed processes, procedures and guidelines for project documentation, process flows, RFPs, pilot programs, hardware and software licenses, and purchases; reduced costs by $500,000.
- Member of several high-profile technical and change management teams working to improve global systems.

FEDERAL FARM CREDIT BANKS FUNDING CORPORATION, Jersey City, NJ   **1987-1998**

Financing and Securities Issuer Division of Farm Credit System, $75 Billion nationwide network of banks/associations

Director and Vice President, **Information Systems & Securities Operations** (1990-1998)

Managed 12 professionals: securities processing analysts, programmer/systems analysts, systems administrators. Recruited to turn around troubled Securities Processing Unit and create a Technology Department.

- Founded and developed high-performing technology group that identified business problems, recommended technical solutions, assessed business/technical risks, worked with users to instill ownership, delivered projects on schedule and at budget.
- Planned and implemented corporation's access to Internet: developed Internet plan, security policy, firewall product; provided Internet training; implemented and maintained Internet connection.

The slogan beneath the headline is an eye-catching, concise, effective summary of this individual's executive philosophy.

ALLISON BROWN   PAGE 2

PROFESSIONAL EXPERIENCE & SELECTED ACCOMPLISHMENTS

FEDERAL FARM CREDIT BANKS FUNDING CORPORATION, Jersey City, NJ
Director and Vice President (1990-1998) (Continued)
- Special Assignment: Built and launched Corporate Website (January-September 1997)
  - Identified and formulated site content and marketing of website; interviewed business units and translated business needs into creative web content; created website layout; established technical parameters and programming standards; worked closely with web programmers, graphic artist, and Internet lawyers.
  - Saved company over $110,000 in project costs.
  - Consulted/advised other FFC banks and outside Board Member corporation on website development.
- Developed interactive financial application which increased productivity by 30%.
- Planned and established corporate disaster "hot" site providing immediate recovery of all critical systems.

Assistant Vice President (1988-1990)
- Formulated and directed long-range plan to change corporate architecture from proprietary minicomputer environment to company-wide client/server model, which reduced support costs by 50%, improved service quality by 75%, increased access to critical information by 100%, and ensured future adaptability.
- Created training program for technical staff to develop account management and consulting skills; reduced project delays by 30% and increased cross-functional awareness.
- Managed major systems projects through entire life cycle, including:
  - Implementation of on-line allocation database handling monthly bond auctions.
  - Origination and design of debt-tracking and payment system that provided on-line historical information on all outstanding fixed-income securities totaling over $63 billion.

Manager (1987-1988)
- Reorganized and redirected problem-ridden operations unit, saving over $200,000.

CITICORP, N.A., Domestic Funding Services (DFS), New York, NY   **1980-1984**
Manager, 1984 — *Assistant Manager*, 1982-1984 — *Management Associate*, 1980-1982
- Managed daily operations for Citicorp and three subsidiaries, serving as liaison between Citicorp traders/Citibank operations and Chief Financial Officer/investors. Managed and trained 10 employees.
- Played a key role in development of new DFS Self-Audit Business Unit, which identified and solved broad range of financial/accounting problems, increasing departmental efficiencies between 50% and 70%.
- Turned around problem-ridden subsidiary, resulting in first acceptable audit in three years.
- Sent to Aruba to start up foreign exchange and cash management unit for overseas subsidiary.
- Managed Citicorp cash management function totaling $2 billion daily.

PROFESSIONAL AFFILIATIONS

Association for Women in Computing (AWC)
National Association for Female Executives (NAFE)
Kellogg Alumni Association

EDUCATION

MBA, Finance & International Economics, **J.L. Kellogg Graduate School of Management**, Northwestern University, 1986
BA, Economics and French, **Fordham University**, 1980

ANTHONY HIGGINS

1345 Lois Lane
Stockton, California 95206

(209) 688-4384
anthony@gotnet.com

CHIEF INFORMATION OFFICER / INFORMATION SERVICES MANAGEMENT

Senior manager with 20+ years' experience in Information Services (IS) Management. Proven track record of increasing operational efficiencies, improving customer service levels, and implementing and maintaining IT initiatives to support successful business processes. Provide vision and dedicated leadership for key technologies, including enterprise systems architecture, networking, desktop and database management systems. Possess strong functional and systems knowledge of banking systems and software, financial accounting, budgeting, contracts management, human resources, legal and related government regulatory compliance.

Key areas of strength include:

FINANCIAL SERVICES INFORMATION MANAGEMENT

IT OPERATIONS MANAGEMENT , VENDOR RELATIONSHIP MANAGEMENT

MERGERS AND ACQUISITIONS , PROCESS ENGINEERING

CAREER HIGHLIGHTS

BANK OF STOCKTON, Stockton, California

1992-Present

CHIEF INFORMATION OFFICER

Direct the development and implementation of strategic planning to modernize information systems and infrastructure at the corporate office and 18 branches in central California for this $850 million bank operation. Provide leadership and framework to actively identify IT needs of all corporate departments and each branch and respond to critical issues. Supervise and direct a 12-member technical staff and 16 other employees. Oversee the management of data processing services, proof and item processing, records research, telecommunications, personal computers and local area networks. Direct major reengineering projects and develop new processes to position institution for advanced growth. Establish support operations for all areas; create Desktop and Telecommunications Technical Support functions. Administer annual budget of over $4 million.

Selected Accomplishments

- Implemented new account-processing software and problem resolution of on-line/batch processing resulting in improved IS Departments.
- Introduced new technologies such as ATM terminals, driving and switching software on the existing legacy mainframe to favorably enhance customers' ability to use the Bank's ATMs and other ATMs.
- Directed the conversion and implementation of UNIX-based banking core account processing, ATM switch processing, general ledger software, and other related software.
- Spearheaded $2.2 million Y2K project resulting in exceeding the federally mandated timeframe.
- Saved 30% annually in maintenance expenses through effective budget analysis, purchasing, and IS problem resolution.
- Led upgrade of AT&T System 75 switch to Lucent Definity G3 and directed installation of Intuity Audix PBX system.
- Structured and negotiated vendor partnerships to facilitate joint systems development projects.
- Implemented LAN/WAN infrastructure improvements and led conversion from Novell to Windows NT environment.

An attractive typestyle and good organization make this an inviting resume. Job titles stand out quite prominently, showing strong career progression.

ANTHONY HIGGINS   Page two

CAREER HIGHLIGHTS (continued)

PRIME CONSULTING SERVICES, Austin, Texas   1989 - 1992

SENIOR CONSULTANT

Consulted with officers and management of Commercial Banks, Savings and Loans, and other financial institutions on strategic management of Information Systems actions and integrations. Directed successful conversions and installations of NCR's Universal Financial System (UFS), including interfaces to other customer platforms. Streamlined use of diverse standardized software applications resulting in consistency of banking systems processing. Trained internal departments in services for UFS to include MIS, tellers, and administrative terminal training with the preparation of appropriate manuals.

AUSTIN SAVINGS AND LOAN, Austin, Texas   1986-1989

VICE PRESIDENT/MANAGER

Managed a team of 9 analysts and programmer/analysts and a documentation librarian in the development, enhancements, maintenance and user support actions for all systems supporting the Deposits and Operations Divisions.

- Administered support and modifications for all Deposit Systems, including check and item processing, ATM Systems and software, telephone voice response, ACH and EFT software and interfaces to the General Ledger, mortgage/consumer loan system and software.
- Directed and managed the project planning, budget management and administration for all projects within this development and support group.
- Led IT in the development of Systems Development Life Cycle plan and assisted in the development of the Disaster Recovery plan.

BRIEF HISTORY OF EMPLOYMENT PRIOR TO 1986:

CHIEF INFORMATION OFFICER /VICE PRESIDENT
The First National Association • Miami, Florida

Reported to President and Chief Executive Officer. Coordinated and directed the design, development, selection, and implementation of company-wide information systems. Partnered with operations department to recruit and hire professional systems staff. Devised user training and support programs.

PROJECT LEADER/SENIOR ANALYST/PROGRAMMER
Ohio Savings & Loan • Cincinnati, Ohio

Designed, coded, and implemented NCR mainframe software systems marketed to the mainframe market. Two of many systems developed were On-line Integrated Deposits and Loans System (Savings and Loan Account Processing Software). Over 400 S&Ls and Service Bureau installations, and Integrated Banking Central Information File System (CIF). Spearheaded 600+ Commercial Banking installations.

TECHNICAL EXPERTISE

Windows NT	IBM Systems	Unisys Mainframe	Windows 9x
LAN/WAN	TCP/IP	Novell Netware	COBOL
SQL Server	UNIX	NCR NEAT/3	NEATVS

EDUCATION

Bachelor of Science, University of Cincinnati, Cincinnati, Ohio

Major: Industrial Management — Minor: Accounting

Denny G. Wong

11650 W. Shepherd ▪ Houston, Texas 77088 ▪ (281) 966-7276
email: denny@flex.net

INTERNATIONAL TELECOMMUNICATIONS & INFORMATION TECHNOLOGY

New Business Development & Advanced Technology Networks / General Management
Voiceover IP / System Design & Integration / E-commerce Solutions
Start-up, Turnaround & High-Growth Operations

Trilingual (Vietnamese/Chinese/English) IT Management Professional with extensive experience building and leading domestic and international business development initiatives within the telecommunications industry. Consistently successful in identifying and capturing market opportunities to accelerate expansion, increase revenues and improve profit contributions. Extensive experience developing partnering alliances throughout Asia and the Pacific Rim. Conversational in Spanish and Thai. Core management qualifications include:

➤ Strategic Sales & Market Planning
➤ Staff Training & Development
➤ Key Account Relationship Management
➤ International Market Development
➤ New Product & Service Launch

➤ Market Research & Analysis
➤ Product & Market Positioning
➤ Sales Forecasting & Reporting
➤ Budget Development & Control
➤ Global Commercialization

Led the startup and development of two international telecommunications companies,
and spearheaded their launch in United States, Thailand, Philippines and Mexico.

Equally strong technical expertise in the design, development and delivery of cost-effective, high-performance technology solutions to meet challenging business demands. Heavy design and programming experience with Windows, Unix, Linux, HTML, ASP, Java, FTP, SAS, Turbo PASCAL, FORTRAN and Visual Basic. Software and database proficiency in MS Office, Access, Lotus SmartSuite, Lotus Notes, SQL and Oracle. Voiceover IP Telephony includes gateways, gatekeepers, billing solutions and unified messaging. Protocols include PSTN networks, ISDN, BRI/PRI, T1/T3, E1/R2, SS7, TCP/IP, H323, SIP, HTTP, MGCP and RTP.

PROFESSIONAL EXPERIENCE

WONG.COM, INC., Houston, Texas   2000 – Present
Cofounder / Vice President of New Business Development / Chief Technology Officer
Partnered with two other entrepreneurs in the development of a telecommunications company designing web-based technologies to support global communication networks. Assumed leadership role in international business development, marketing, sales, systems engineering and operations. Identified and secured seed funding through venture capital and private investor groups. Designed internal and external technology infrastructures to ensure affordability, reliability and durability. **Developed and built strategic partnering alliances with Cisco Systems, Vocaltec, AT&T, UUNet international telco companies, broadband providers, ITSPs and ISPs.**

For a multilingual executive with extensive global experience, the resume leads off with a lengthy summary encompassing both executive and technical skills, then highlights the key accomplishments of each position in bold type at the end.

Denny G. Wong   Page Two

PROFESSIONAL EXPERIENCE
(Continued)

QUESTEL COMMUNICATIONS, INC., Houston, Texas   1999 – 2000
Cofounder / Vice President of Network Engineering
Established and built a global voiceover IP network services company from inception. Full responsibility for strategic business planning, engineering, network architecture, risk management and capacity planning. **Spearheaded voiceover IP expansion and deployment throughout Asia Pacific. Opened and managed operations in the United States, Thailand, Philippines and Mexico.** Designed and implemented Cisco-powered voiceover IP global communication networks.

INFORMATION SCIENCE CORPORATION, Houston, Texas   1998 – 1999
IT Consultant
Assigned exclusively to Dupont/Conoco to expand their global business operations. Created extensive WAN network using T1 and Frame Relay technology to connect all company locations, and developed their Internet e-mail systems.

H.T.I.S. TELECOMMUNICATIONS, INC., Houston, Texas   1996 – 1997
Manager of Systems Engineering
Assumed full responsibility for the design and installation of LAN/WAN technologies, client/server architecture, Windows NT and Novell Networks operating systems and applications software. Proposed integrating voice processing servers and telephony gateway equipment to customer specifications.

RELIANT ENERGY, Houston, Texas   1994 – 1996
Corporate Information Network Specialist
Recruited to assist IT Director in upgrading and enhancing LAN/WAN technologies. Prepared budgets and made appropriate recommendations on hardware and software equipment. Configured Cisco, 3Com, Asanta, WellFleet and SynOptics networking systems.

WILLIAMS COMMUNICATIONS, The Woodlands, Texas   1993 – 1994
Corporate Operations Analyst
Established workstations and file and print servers and installed Windows applications. Configured Northern Telecom (PBX) and Octel telephone systems. **Recipient of Williams Communications Systems Team Service Award.**

EDUCATION

Sam Houston State University, Huntsville, Texas: **BS, Engineering,** 1992
Specialization in Computer Science

CONTINUING PROFESSIONAL DEVELOPMENT

Extensive technical training on Cisco and Lucent Voiceover Internet Protocol and other technologies

PROFESSIONAL AFFILIATIONS

Association of Communications Enterprises
International Engineering Consortium / Cisco Houston User Group

HAROLD WAINWRIGHT

400 Filbert Road
Saratoga CA 95070

408-555-5555
hwain@yahoo.com

EXECUTIVE MANAGEMENT PROFILE

Strategic & Tactical Planning / Project Management / P&L Responsibility
Customer Relationship Management / Team Building & Leadership / Staff Development
IT System Controls & Processes / Applications Development / Database Administration

Results-driven senior executive with proven ability to gain cooperation and build consensus among diverse groups with conflicting business objectives. Nationally recognized as an IT expert within the healthcare industry.

ACCOMPLISHMENT HIGHLIGHTS

- Negotiated a 10-year contract expansion and extension worth $80 million, including desktop support, business recovery, voice and data network, application development, and system operations.

- Secured $4 million project at Premier Health Systems by establishing and maintaining a strong relationship with the head of their executive team during projects at other locations.

- Met or exceeded all revenue and profitability targets set by Top Tier by controlling costs and expanding the scope of project contracts.

- Turned around poor customer satisfaction at two locations, raising the ratings from 4 of 10 to 10 of 10. Established an industry-leading position for that aspect of business operations by resolving technical problems and developing a positive relationship with the executive team.

- Maintain high employee morale and retention in a tight labor market by setting clear standards and providing assistance and encouragement to employees in meeting those standards.

PROFESSIONAL EXPERIENCE

Top Tier Global Services:

Project Executive / Chief Information Officer, Bridgewater Hospital, San Jose, CA, 1997-Present

- Manage a full outsource contract for application development / maintenance, systems integration, and database administration, which includes voice and data network support, telephony, desktop and help desk management, and strategic planning.

- Provide executive leadership to many areas at the hospital, including the committee that prepares for JCAHO audits and the medical information systems committee. Viewed as an extension of the management team and consulted regarding requirements that may impact data flow in the hospital.

- Maintain P&L responsibility, budgeting, forecasting, monitoring, and reporting of finances for the $80 million El Camino project and the new Premier project.

- Address critical strategic and tactical planning issues, interacting with the information management committee and hospital administration to develop effective plans.

- Direct a staff of 40 Top Tier employees and contractors at the hospital. Hired Bridgewater employees and transitioned them to Top Tier by investing in significant retraining and skills upgrading.

- Oversee approximately 12 employees at the service delivery center in Arizona and 6 employees working on the Premier project in Colorado.

- Assist Marketing teams with accounts to be used for corporate references by advising them regarding critical content and structure of proposals.

- Prepare and submit operating reports periodically to senior Top Tier management.

The Accomplishment Highlights technique allows this candidate to present his success stories at the very beginning of his resume; the Professional Experience section that follows gives more details and additional achievements.

HAROLD WAINWRIGHT   PAGE 2

Project Executive, Premier Health Systems, Denver, CO, 2000-Present
- Oversee on-site project manager and assist the organization in developing a strategic plan and building a data center.
- Provide expertise on computer operations, which includes developing processes and procedures.

Project Executive, Health Care Ventures, Santa Clara, CA, 1992-1997
- Managed daily operations for a joint venture between two major healthcare organizations, including finance / budgets, contract expansion, customer satisfaction, and strategy compatibility.
- Directed Top Tier-supplied services that included business applications, network, telephones, help desk, and strategic planning assistance.

Manager, Application Development and Support, Houston, TX, 1989-1992
- Managed the Production Services department, which involved installation, scheduling, and monitoring of all batch production programs to meet service level agreements.
- Led delivery of service to internal Top Tier groups as well as Central Mobile Communications and the World Access airline reservation system.

Advisory Programmer / Project Leader, Houston, TX, 1986-1989
- Led and performed systems analysis for all project phases, including audit readiness, business justification, design, tracking, project controls, and customer satisfaction.

Previously held various technical positions within Top Tier, including application and systems programming, 1973-1986.

AFFILIATIONS, CERTIFICATIONS, & AWARDS
- Information Management Systems Society (20,000 members): Annual Conference Committee, 1998-2001; Annual Conference Committee Chair for Information Systems, 1999-2000; Information Systems Advisory Committee Chair, 1999-2000; frequent presenter at conferences
- Board of Directors, Bridgewater Hospital Foundation: Fundraising Committee Chair—raised approximately $500,000 through charity events over a five-year period
- Information Management Committee Chair, 1998-2000
- College of Healthcare Information Management Executives
- American Medical Informatics Association
- Project Management Institute
- ISSC Leadership Conference, 1994-1996
- Top Tier Project Management Certification, 1993; recertified 1996
- Top Tier Departmental Center of Excellence Award: resulted in assignment to lead a project that rolled out batch processes to five major computer centers throughout the United States

Professional References Available Upon Request.

APPENDIX

Internet Career Resources for Technology Professionals

With the emergence of the Internet has come a huge collection of job search resources for technology professionals. Here are just a few of our favorites.

Dictionaries and Glossaries

Outstanding information on key words and acronyms.

Acronyms	http://acronymfinder.com
Computer Acronyms	cramsession.brainbuzz.com/studytips/acronyms_list.asp
Computing Dictionary	wombat.doc.ic.ac.uk/foldoc/index.html
TechEncyclopedia	www.techweb.com/encyclopedia/
Technology Terms Dictionary	www.currents.net/resources/dictionary
Telecommunications Glossary	www.commworldnca.com/gloss.htm
The Virtual Reference Desk	bigdog.lib.purdue.edu/vlibrary/reference/dict.html
Webopedia (computer industry glossary)	www.webopedia.com
WhatIs?com Technology Terms	www.whatis.com

Job Search Sites

You'll find thousands and thousands of current professional employment opportunities on these sites.

GENERAL SITES

4Work	www.4work.com
6FigureJobs	www.6figurejobs.com
America's Job Bank	www.ajb.dni.us
Best Jobs USA	www.bestjobsusa.com
Brass Ring (high-tech jobs)	www.brassring.com
Career Atlas for the Road	isdn.net/nis
CareerBuilder	www.careerbuilder.com
CareerCity	www.careercity.com
Career.com	www.career.com
CareerEngine	www.careerengine.com
CareerExchange	www.careerexchange.com
Career Exposure	www.careerexposure.com
Career Magazine	www.careermag.com
Career Mosaic	www.careermosaic.com
CareerShop	www.careershop.com
CareerSite	www.careersite.com
CareerWeb	www.careerweb.com
Cruel World	www.cruelworld.com
Digital City (jobs by location)	home.digitalcity.com
Excite	www.excite.com/careers
Futurestep	www.futurestep.com
GETAJOB!	www.getajob.com
Headhunter.net	www.headhunter.net
HotJobs.com	www.hotjobs.com
Internet Job Locator	www.joblocator.com
Internet's Help Wanted	www.helpwanted.com
It's Your Job Now	www.ItsYourJobNow.com
JobBankUSA	www.jobbankusa.com
JOBNET.com	www.jobnet.com
JobOptions	www.joboptions.com
JOBTRAK.COM	www.jobtrak.com
JobWeb	www.jobweb.com

Monster.com	www.monster.com
NationJob Network	www.nationjob.com
Net Temps	www.net-temps.com
Online-Jobs.Com	www.online-jobs.com
Shawn's Internet Resume Center	www.inpursuit.com/sirc
The Job Market Recruiting	www.thejobmarket.com
TopJobs USA	www.topjobsusa.com
WorkTree	www.worktree.com
Yahoo! Careers	www.yahoo.com/Business_and_ Economy/Employment/Jobs

TECHNOLOGY CAREER SITES

America's Talent Bank	www.atb.org
BrainBuzz.com	www.brainbuzz.com
CareerShop IT	www.itcareershop.com
ComputerJobs.com	www.computerjobs.com
ComputerWork.com	www.computerwork.com
Computerworld	www.computerworld.com
Contract Employment Connection	www.ntes.com
dice.com	www.dice.com
EngineeringJobs.com	www.engineeringjobs.com
HowToWeb Jobs	www.howtowebjobs.com
IEEE-USA Job Service	www.ieee.org/jobs.html
Jobserve	www.jobserve.com
PassportAccess	www.passportaccess.com
taps.com (IT jobs in the UK)	http://taps.com
techies.com	www.techies.com

CAREERS FOR MINORITIES AND WOMEN

Blackworld.com	www.blackworld.com
Careers For Women	www.womenconnect.com/info/ career/index.htm
ClassifiedsForWomen	www.classifiedsforwomen.com
IMDiversity.com	www.minorities-jb.com

PROFESSIONAL CAREERS

Contract Employment Weekly	www.ceweekly.com
ProfessionalCareer	www.professionalcareer.com
Vault.com	www.vault.com

GOVERNMENT CAREERS

Federal Jobs Central	www.fedjobs.com
Government Careers	www.getagovjob.com
Jobs in Government	www.jobsingovernment.com

CAREERS FOR SENIORS

MaturityWorks (careers for seniors)	www.maturityworks.org

ENTRY-LEVEL CAREERS

CampusCareerCenter	www.campuscareercenter.com
College Grad Job Hunter	www.collegegrad.com
Jobsource	www.jobsource.com
JOBTRAK	www.jobtrak.com

Company Information

Outstanding resources for researching specific companies.

555-1212.com (directory information)	www.555-1212.com
AllBusiness.com	www.comfind.com
Chambers of Commerce	www.uschamber.com/Chambers/Chamber+Directory/default.htm
Experience Network	www.experiencenetwork.com
Fortune 500 Companies	www.fortune.com/fortune/fortune500
Hoover's Business Profiles	www.hoovers.com
infoUSA (small-business information)	www.infousa.com
SuperPages.com	www.bigbook.com

Interviewing Tips and Techniques

Expert guidance to sharpen and strengthen your interviewing skills.

About.com Interviewing	jobsearch.about.com/business/jobsearch/msubinterv.htm
Bradley CVs Introduction to Job Interviews	www.bradleycvs.demon.co.uk/interview/index.htm
Dress for Success	www.dressforsuccess.org
Job-Interview.net	www.job-interview.net

Salary and Compensation Information

Learn from the experts to strengthen your negotiating skills and increase your salary.

2001 IT Salary Survey	www.psrinc.com/salary.htm
Abbott, Langer & Associates	www.abbott-langer.com
America's Career InfoNet	www.acinet.org/acinet/default.htm?tab=wagesandtrends
Bureau of Labor Statistics Occupational Outlook Handbook	stats.bls.gov/ocohome.htm
CareerJournal (The Wall Street Journal)	www.careerjournal.com/salaries/index.html
Compensation Link	www.compensationlink.com
Crystal Report	www.crystalreport.com
Economic Research Institute	www.erieri.com
ESCAPE Salaries of Engineers	fairway.ecn.purdue.edu/ESCAPE/stats/salaries.html
JobStar	jobsmart.org/tools/salary/index.htm
Management Consultant Salary Survey	www.cob.ohio-state.edu/~fin/jobs/mco/salary.htm
Monster.com: The Negotiation Coach	midcareer.monster.com/experts/negotiation
Salarysurvey.com	www.salarysurvey.com
Wageweb	www.wageweb.com
Working Woman	www.workingwoman.com/salary
WorldatWork (formerly American Compensation Association)	www.acaonline.org

GEOGRAPHIC INDEX OF CONTRIBUTORS

The sample cover letters in chapters 4 through 10 were written by professional resume and cover letter writers. If you need help with your resume and job search correspondence, you can use the list on the following pages to locate the career professional in your area.

A note about credentials: Nearly all of the contributing writers have earned one or more professional credentials. These credentials are highly regarded in the careers and employment industry and are indicative of the writer's expertise and commitment to professional development. Here is an explication of each of these credentials:

Credential	*Awarded by*	*Recognizes*
CCM: Credentialed Career Master	Career Masters Institute	Specific professional expertise, knowledge of current career trends, commitment to continuing education, and dedication through pro-bono work
CPRW: Certified Professional Resume Writer	Professional Association of Résumé Writers	Knowledge of resume strategy development and writing
MA: Master of Arts degree	Accredited university	Graduate-level education
MS: Master of Science degree		
MBA: Master of Business Administration		
M.Ed.: Master of Education		
MFA: Master of Fine Arts		

continues

Credential	Awarded by	Recognizes
NCRW: Nationally Certified Resume Writer	National Résumé Writers' Association	Knowledge of resume strategy development and writing

United States

ALABAMA

Don Orlando, CPRW, CCM
The McLean Group, Montgomery, AL
(334) 264-2020
E-mail: yourcareercoach@aol.com

ALASKA

Ann Flister, CPRW
Best Impression, Anchorage, AK
(907) 561-9311
E-mail: aflister@customcpu.com

ARIZONA

Wanda McLaughlin, CPRW
Execuwrite, Chandler, AZ
(480) 732-7966
E-mail: wanda@execu-write.com
URL: www.execuwrite.com

CALIFORNIA

Georgia Adamson, CPRW, CCM
Adept Business Services, Campbell, CA
(408) 866-6859
E-mail: georgiaa@bignet.net
URL: www.ADynamicResume.com

Leatha Jones, CPRW
Write Connection Career Services, Vallejo, CA
(707) 649-1400
E-mail: Leatha@writeconnection.net
URL: www.writeconnection.net

Nancy Karvonen, CPRW, CCM
A Better Word & Resume, Galt, CA
(209) 744-8203
E-mail: careers@aresumecoach.com
URL: www.aresumecoach.com

Myriam-Rose Kohn, CPRW, CCM
JEDA Enterprises, Valencia, CA
(661) 253-0801
E-mail: myriam-rose@jedaenterprises.com
URL: www.jedaenterprises.com

Anita Radosevich, CPRW
Anita's Business & Career Services, Lodi, CA
(209) 368-4444
E-mail: abcservice@lodinet.com
URL: www.abcresumes.com

Vivian Van Lier, CPRW
Advantage Resume & Career Services, Valley Glen, CA
(818) 994-6655
E-mail: vvanlier@aol.com

CONNECTICUT

Jan Melnik, CPRW
Absolute Advantage, Durham, CT
(860) 349-0256
E-mail: CompSPJan@aol.com
URL: www.janmelnik.com

FLORIDA

Laura A. DeCarlo, CCM, CPRW
A Competitive Edge Career Service, Melbourne, FL
(800) 715-3442
E-mail: getanedge@aol.com
URL: www.acompetitiveedge.com

Art Frank
Resumes "R" Us, Palm Harbor, FL
(727) 787-6885
E-mail: AF1134@aol.com

René Hart, CPRW
Resumes For Success!, Lakeland, FL
(863) 859-2439
E-mail: renehart@resumesforsuccess.com
URL: www.ResumesForSuccess.com

Beverly Harvey, CPRW, CCM
Beverly Harvey Resume & Career Service, Pierson, FL
(904) 749-3111
E-mail: beverly@harveycareers.com
URL: www.harveycareeers.com

Cindy Kraft, CPRW, CCM
Executive Essentials, Valrico, FL
(813) 655-0658
E-mail: careermaster@exec-essentials.com
URL: www.exec-essentials.com

Iowa

Marcy Johnson, CPRW
First Impression Resume & Job Readiness, Story City, IA
(515) 733-4998
E-mail: firstimpression@storycity.net
URL: www.resume-job-readiness.com

Kansas

Kristie Cook, CPRW
Absolutely Write, Olathe, KS
(913) 269-3519
E-mail: kriscook@absolutely-write.com
URL: www.absolutely-write.com

Jacqui Barrett Dodson, CPRW
Career Trend, Overland Park, KS
(913) 451-1313
E-mail: dodson@careertrend.net
URL: www.careertrend.net

KENTUCKY

Debbie Ellis, CPRW
Career Concepts, Danville, KY
(859) 236-4001
E-mail: info@resumeprofessional.com
URL: www.resumeprofessional.com

MARYLAND

Diane Burns, CPRW, CCM
Career Marketing Techniques, Columbia, MD
(410) 884-0213
E-mail: dianecprw@aol.com
URL: www.polishedresumes.com

MASSACHUSETTS

Bernice Antifonario
Antion Associates, Inc., Tewksbury, MA
(978) 858-0637
E-mail: Antion1@aol.com
URL: www.antion-associates.com

Beate Hait, CPRW, NCRW
Word Processing Plus, Holliston, MA
(508) 429-1813
E-mail: beateh1@aol.com
URL: www.ibssn.com/resumes

MICHIGAN

Janet Beckstrom
Word Crafter, Flint, MI
(800) 351-9818
E-mail: wordcrafter@voyager.net

Deborah Schuster, CPRW
The Lettersmith, Newport, MI
(734) 586-3335
E-mail: lettersmith@foxberry.net
URL: www.thelettersmith.com

MINNESOTA

Barb Poole, CPRW
Electronic Ink, St. Cloud, MN
(320) 253-0975
E-mail: eink@astound.net

MISSOURI

Meg Montford, CCM, CPRW
Abilities Enhanced, Kansas City, MO
(816) 767-1196
E-mail: meg@abilitiesenhanced.com
URL: www.abilitiesenhanced.com

MONTANA

Laura West
Agape Career Services, Clinton, MT
(888) 685-3507
E-mail: agape@blackfoot.net
URL: www.AgapeCareerServices.com

NEW HAMPSHIRE

Michelle Dumas, CPRW, NCRW, CCM
Distinctive Documents, Somersworth, NH
(603) 742-3983
E-mail: resumes@distinctiveweb.com
URL: www.distinctiveweb.com

NEW JERSEY

Vivian Belen, NCRW, CPRW
The Job Search Specialist, Fair Lawn, NJ
(201) 797-2883
E-mail: vivian@jobsearchspecialist.com
URL: www.jobsearchspecialist.com

Nina K. Ebert, CPRW
A Word's Worth, Toms River, NJ
(732) 349-2225
E-mail: wrdswrth@gbsias.com
URL: www.a-wordsworth.com

Susan Guarneri, CPRW, CCM
Guarneri Associates/Resumagic, Lawrenceville, NJ
(609) 771-1669
E-mail: Resumagic@aol.com
URL: www.resume-magic.com

Fran Kelley, MA, CPRW
The Resume Works, Waldwick, NJ
(201) 670-9643
E-mail: TwoFreeSpirits@worldnet.att.net
URL: www.careermuse.com

Rhoda Kopy, CPRW
A Hire Image Resume & Writing Service, Toms River, NJ
(732) 505-9515
E-mail: ahi@infi.net
URL: www.jobwinningresumes.com

New York

Ann Baehr, CPRW
Best Resumes, Brentwood, NY
(631) 435-1879
E-mail: resumesbest@earthlink.net

Arnold G. Boldt, CPRW
Arnold-Smith Associates, Rochester, NY
(716) 383-0350
E-mail: arnoldsmth@aol.com

Donna Farrise
Dynamic Resumes of Long Island, Inc., Hauppauge, NY
(631) 951-4120
E-mail: donna@dynamicresumes.com
URL: www.dynamicresumes.com

Judy Friedler, NCRW, CPRW, CCM
CareerPro New York, New York, NY
(212) 647-8726
E-mail: judy@rezcoach.com
URL: www.rezcoach.com

Linsey Levine, MS
CareerCounsel, Chappaqua, NY
(914) 238-1065
E-mail: LinZlev@aol.com

Kim Little
Fast Track Resumes, Victor, NY
(716) 742-2467
E-mail: info@fast-trackresumes.com
URL: www.fast-trackresumes.com

Linda Matias
CareerStrides, Smithtown, NY
(631) 382-2425
E-mail: careerstrides@worldnet.att.net
URL: www.careerstrides.com

NORTH CAROLINA

Alice Braxton, CPRW
Accutype Resume & Secretarial Services, Burlington, NC
(336) 227-9091
E-mail: accutype@netpath.net

John M. O'Connor, CPRW
CareerPro Resumes, Raleigh, NC
(919) 821-2418
E-mail: careerpro2@aol.com
URL: www.careerproresumes.com

OHIO

Deborah S. James
Leading Edge Resume & Career Services, Rossford, OH
(419) 666-4518
E-mail: OhioResGal@aol.com
URL: www.leadingedgeresumes.com

Louise Kursmark, CPRW, CCM
Best Impression Career Services, Inc., Cincinnati, OH
(888) 792-0030
E-mail: LK@yourbestimpression.com
URL: www.yourbestimpression.com

Janice Worthington-Loranca, CPRW
Fortune 500 Communications, Columbus, OH
(614) 890-1645
E-mail: janice@fortune500resumes.com
URL: www.fortune500resumes.com

PENNSYLVANIA

Paula Brandt, CPRW
The Resume Lady, Belle Vernon, PA
(724) 872-9030
E-mail: paula@resumelady.com
URL: www.resumelady.com

Jewel Bracy DeMaio, CPRW
A Perfect Resume.com, Elkins Park, PA
(800) 227-5131
E-mail: mail@aperfectresume.com
URL: www.aperfectresume.com

TENNESSEE

Carolyn Braden, CPRW
Braden Resume Solutions, Hendersonville, TN
(615) 822-3317
E-mail: bradenresume@home.com

Marta L. Driesslein, CPRW
Cambridge Career Services, Inc., Knoxville, TN
(865) 539-9538
E-mail: careerhope@aol.com
URL: www.careerhope.com

TEXAS

Cheryl Ann Harland, CPRW
Resumes By Design, The Woodlands, TX
(888) 213-1650
E-mail: CAH@resumesbydesign.com

Shanna Kemp, CPRW
Kemp Career Services, Round Rock, TX
(512) 246-6434
E-mail: respro@aresumepro.com
URL: www.aresumpro.com

Ann Klint, NCRW, CPRW
Ann's Professional Resume Service, Tyler, TX
(903) 509-8333
E-mail: Resumes-Ann@tyler.net

Kelley Smith, CPRW
Advantage Resume Services, Sugarland, TX
(281) 494-3330
E-mail: info@advantage-resume.com
URL: www.advantage-resume.com

Ann Stewart, CPRW
Advantage Services, Roanoke, TX
(817) 424-1448
E-mail: ASresume@aol.com

UTAH

Lynn P. Andenoro, CPRW, CCM
My Career Resource, Salt Lake City, UT
(801) 883-2011
E-mail: Lynn@MyCareerResource.com
URL: www.MyCareerResource.com

Diana C. LeGere
Executive Final Copy, Salt Lake City, UT
(801) 277-6299
E-mail: execfinalcopy@e-mail.msn.com
URL: www.executivefinalcopy.com

WASHINGTON

Lonnie Swanson, CPRW
A Career Advantage, Poulsbo, WA
(360) 779-2877
E-mail: resumewriter@amouse.net

WISCONSIN

Michele Haffner, CPRW
Advanced Resume Services, Glendale, WI
(877) 247-1677
E-mail: michele@resumeservices.com
URL: www.resumeservices.com

Australia

Gayle Howard, CPRW
Top Margin Resumes Online, Melbourne, Australia
E-mail: getinterviews@topmargin.com
URL: www.topmargin.com

Paul B. Stevens
The Centre for Worklife Counselling, Sydney, Australia
E-mail: worklife@ozemail.com.au
URL: www.worklife.com.au

Canada

Ross Macpherson, CPRW
Career Quest, Pickering, Ontario
(905) 426-8548
E-mail: careerquest@primus.ca

Nicole Miller
Milroy Consultants, Rockcliffe, Ontario
(613) 998-5462
E-mail: af891@issc.debbs.ndhq.dnd.ca

INDEX

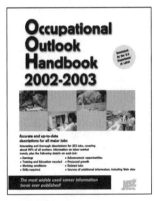
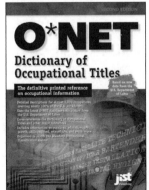

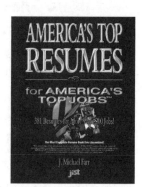
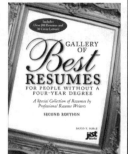

JIST Ordering Information

JIST specializes in publishing the very best results-oriented career and self-directed job search material. Since 1981 we have been a leading publisher in career assessment devices, books, videos, and software. We continue to strive to make our materials the best there are, so that people can stay abreast of what's happening in the labor market, and so they can clarify and articulate their skills and experiences for themselves as well as for prospective employers. **Our products are widely available through your local bookstores, wholesalers, and distributors.**

The World Wide Web

For more occupational or book information, get online and see our Web site at **www.jist.com**. Advance information about new products, services, and training events is continually updated.

Quantity Discounts Available!

Quantity discounts are available for businesses, schools, and other organizations.

The JIST Guarantee

We want you to be happy with everything you buy from JIST. If you aren't satisfied with a product, return it to us within 30 days of purchase along with the reason for the return. Please include a copy of the packing list or invoice to guarantee quick credit to your order.

How to Order

For your convenience, the last page of this book contains an order form.

24-Hour Consumer Order Line:
Call toll free 1-800-648-JIST
Please have your credit card (VISA, MC, or AMEX) information ready!

Mail your order to:

JIST Publishing, Inc.
8902 Otis Avenue
Indianapolis, IN 46216-1033
Fax: Toll free 1-800-JIST-FAX

JIST Order and Catalog Request Form

Purchase Order #: _____ (Required by some organizations)

Billing Information

Organization Name: _____

Accounting Contact: _____

Street Address: _____

_____

City, State, Zip: _____

Phone Number: (___) _____

Shipping Information with Street Address (If Different from Above)

Organization Name: _____

Contact: _____

Street Address: (We *cannot* ship to P.O. boxes) _____

_____

City, State, Zip: _____

Phone Number: (___) _____

> **Please copy this form if you need more lines for your order.**

> **Phone: 1-800-648-JIST**
> **Fax: 1-800-JIST-FAX**
> **World Wide Web Address:**
> **http://www.jist.com**

Credit Card Purchases: VISA_____ MC_____ AMEX_____

Card Number: _____

Exp. Date: _____

Name As on Card: _____

Signature: _____

Quantity	Order Code	Product Title	Unit Price	Total
	———	**Free JIST Catalog**	**Free**	———

jist ®
Publishing

8902 Otis Avenue
Indianapolis, IN 46216

Shipping / Handling / Insurance Fees

In the continental U.S. add 7% of subtotal:
- Minimum amount charged = $4.00
- Maximum amount charged = $100.00
- FREE shipping and handling on any prepaid orders over $40.00

Above pricing is for regular ground shipment only. For rush or special delivery, call JIST Customer Service at 1-800-648-JIST for the correct shipping fee.

Outside the continental U.S. call JIST Customer Service at 1-800-648-JIST for an estimate of these fees.

Payment in U.S. funds only!

Subtotal	
+5% Sales Tax *Indiana Residents*	
+Shipping / Handling / Ins. (See left)	
TOTAL	

JIST thanks you for your order!